"The Other Side and Back is the most grounded and authentic 'entry to the other side' that I have ever read. You know immediately upon reading the first few pages that Sylvia Browne is more than a psychic—she is a master at conveying the truth that exists in the fourth dimension."

—Caroline Myss, Ph.D.,
author of *Anatomy of the Spirit*

In *The Other Side and Back,* world-famous psychic Sylvia Browne goes beyond her own *New York Times* bestseller *Adventures of a Psychic* with an unprecedented and comprehensive "tour" of the afterlife—a world-changing revelation that has helped millions live for today, tomorrow, and forever. . . .

Includes

* how spirit guides and angels "talk" to us daily
* the truth about ghosts and hauntings
* solving "unsolvable" missing persons cases
* how psychic energy can keep people healthy and improve relationships
* why we shouldn't fear aging and death
* must-read predictions for the new millennium and more

✶ THE ✶ OTHER SIDE AND BACK

A Psychic's Guide to Our World and Beyond

SYLVIA BROWNE

WITH LINDSAY HARRISON

A SIGNET BOOK

SIGNET
Published by New American Library, a division of
Penguin Putnam Inc., 375 Hudson Street, New York,
New York 10014, U.S.A.
Penguin Books Ltd, 80 Strand, London WC2R 0RL, England
Penguin Books Australia Ltd, Ringwood, Victoria, Australia
Penguin Books Canada Ltd, 10 Alcorn Avenue,
Toronto, Ontario, Canada M4V 3B2
Penguin Books (N.Z.) Ltd, 182–190 Wairau Road,
Auckland 10, New Zealand

Penguin Books Ltd, Registered Offices:
Harmondsworth, Middlesex, England

Published by Signet, an imprint of New American Library, a division of Penguin Putnam Inc. Previously published in a Dutton edition.

First Signet Printing, July 2000
20 19 18 17 16 15 14 13 12 11

ACKNOWLEDGMENTS
"The Invitation" by Oriah Mountain Dreamer copyright © 1999 by Oriah Mountain Dreamer. Reprinted by permission of HarperCollins Publishers, Inc.

Printed in the United States of America

DEDICATIONS

from Sylvia:

For my family . . .
For Angelia, may I be the wind beneath your wings
that my Grandmother Ada was to me . . .
And always,
for Montel

from Lindsay:

For my mother, Fern Underwood,
who has brought more to my life,
including my introduction to Sylvia,
than I can ever repay

CONTENTS

Acknowledgments

To the talented, vigilant likes of Brian Tart, Bonnie Solow, and Reid Tracy, for giving me the support, freedom, and encouragement to express my passion for writing.

To my beloved staff, my tireless ministers, and my study groups around the country.

To the members of the medical, psychiatric, and law enforcement communities around the country, who continue to embrace this dedicated handmaiden to society with your trust, your confidence, and your friendship.

To my clients, my friends, my audiences around the world, and all the clients, friends, and audiences yet to come. My love for you is an open door you can always enter.

To Dr. Carolyn Doherty of Beverly Hills, California, for her skill, artistry, and rare gentility.

To my son Christopher, whose generosity provided me with a lovely house to write in and whose love made it a home.

To my son Paul, for his friendship and understanding.

To my beautiful daughters-in-law, Gina and Nancy, whom I cherish, and who have given me my greatest gifts of all—Angelia, Willy, and Jeffrey.

To Larry, who makes my life loving and easier.

And last but not least, to my dearest love, Daddy, William L. Shoemaker, who loved everything I ever did.

I give you all my deepest and most eternal thanks.

Foreword

by

MELVIN L. MORSE, M.D.

It is an honor and a pleasure to write the foreword for this book. Sylvia Browne intervened in my life at a time when I had decided I would quit near-death research and devote myself to the full-time practice of pediatrics. She gave me a psychic reading that was so accurate and profoundly moving, it changed my entire outlook on the possibility of life after death. After fifteen years of listening to the stories of children who have survived death, I have learned that it is scientifically respectable to argue that consciousness survives death.

We are all born with a specific biological link to a loving universe. Sylvia Browne has the talent to access this source of universal knowledge, and the wisdom and insight to interpret that knowledge for others. I know my life would have been very different had it not been for a chance meeting with her on a national television show seven years ago.

I studied near-death experiences in children because I thought that the various drugs given to children who are critically ill caused the experiences. I was an arrogant young critical-care physician and cancer researcher at Seattle Children's Hospital. I had heard several near-death experiences myself from children, but had always thought it was the drugs that were talking.

Instead, our study at Seattle Children's Hospital documented that near-death experiences are real, and are linked to a specific function of a certain area in our brains. This area, the right temporal lobe, is our "god module." We all are born with one. We published this study in the American Medical Association's *Pediatric Journal*.

I immediately received criticism of my research and methods. The attacks were often personal. I had a mainstream private practice of pediatrics, and had just finished a research fellowship in children's brain tumors. I regarded my near-death research as a fascinating aside, but not anything that I myself took seriously. I saw my research as a means of publishing, which would look good on my résumé, but nothing more than that. Instead, I seemed to have stumbled into a topic that made everybody angry.

I spoke with the head of my hospital, who said to me: "Melvin, this is what you get for talking to people about death. It is a taboo topic. You should stick to what you do best, practicing real medicine."

Soon afterward I visited Holland, where I was invited to speak by cardiologist Wolfgang von Lummel of Ultrech University. He studied near-death experiences in adults using our same methods and reached similar conclusions. At the end of my talk, a Dutch woman insisted on speaking to me. She had not been invited, but had begged Dr. von Lummel to attend. She said that she had an important message for me.

She told me, through an interpreter, that she was a psychic. She said a child I had interviewed who subsequently died had a message for me. She pulled out a picture she had drawn. She said: "This is the girl. She wanted you to see her picture so you would believe me." In fact, I did recognize the child.

The psychic continued, "You have a picture she drew for you. You didn't show it [in the lecture]. Here, I will draw it for you." She then gave me a specific message from the girl. It was that I was to continue in near-death research, and that two angels would watch over me and assist me. It also contained some personal elements, which had meaning only for me.

I was pretty amused at the entire scene. I fully expected to be asked for a donation later on. I thought that maybe she was an attention seeker who had done some research into my past and made some lucky guesses. She disappeared without leaving her name, and I have never heard from her since.

I flew back to New York and forgot the entire episode. I labeled it one of those quirky things that happen that I couldn't really explain but didn't take seriously either.

My publisher then asked me to appear on a national television show with Sylvia Browne. I groaned, thinking this is the last straw: I will never be able to hold up my head again at the staff meetings at Children's Hospital.

I met Sylvia while waiting to appear on the show. My first impression of her was how down-to-earth and normal she was. I realize what a rude thought that is, but I was expecting some flaky person in New Age garb spouting pseudo-psycho baloney. Instead, as we sat together in the green room, I was completely at ease with her. I had an unbidden impulse to tell her everything that I had been through in the past year, and how I just wanted to be a pediatrician and not think about psychic abilities and death anymore. I couldn't speak, but just wanted to cry. She put me at ease, chatting about my horse ranch and my children.

Suddenly she said to me, "Melvin, I know what a raw deal you got. I want you to know that the children you have helped are on your side." She spoke of the same little girl that the Dutch psychic had told me about. She told me that she had a message for me. Then she told me, word for word, the exact message that the Dutch psychic had given to me. This message contained highly personal elements that would have been difficult to have simply invented or guessed at, and seemingly known only by the little girl and myself.

I had ignored the Dutch psychic but could not ignore Sylvia. She was completely sincere and genuine. I briefly considered that perhaps this was some sort of amazing coincidence, or perhaps a devious plot hatched by the Dutch psychic and Sylvia Browne to fool me. "What possible motive could they have?" I wondered. All that trouble just to convince me to continue in near-death studies?

I remembered what my adviser at Johns Hopkins taught me: "Melvin, if you start believing that a one-in-a-million coincidence can explain what is happening, you have a one-in-a-million chance of being right!" He told me that believing in coincidence is the refuge of the lazy mind; for the scientist there are no coincidences.

I returned home, completely reinvigorated. The obvious explanation was that both psychics had independently received an identical message that had meaning only for me. They were the passive transmitters of information from a child who had died. As a medical scientist, I was determined to learn how such transmissions are possible. Perhaps the fact that I had no spiritual belief system at all, other than that Sunday is for watching football, was why I was meant to continue in this field.

My research has shown that not only are near-death experiences real, but that by studying the mechanism of the experiences, we learn that all human beings are interconnected with the universe and everything in it that ever was and ever shall be. We learn that in fact there is a sound scientific basis for explaining how mediums can talk to the dead and facilitate spiritual and physical healing.

I started with the basic question that a child once asked me about his own near-death experience. He had nearly drowned in a car accident. He told me that the car filled up with water and suddenly everything went "all blank." "Then I was in the huge noodle." I asked him what he meant by the huge noodle. He said, "Well, maybe it was like a spiral noodle. But it couldn't have really been a noodle, because I don't think noodles have rainbows in them. It must have been a tunnel." He traveled down this tunnel and visited both an animal and a human heaven.

"But was it real?" he asked me. This is the question that we all have about these experiences. I took his question to the nation's top theoretical physicists, at Los Alamos, New Mexico. I asked them what is reality and how do we know if something is real or not. I learned from them that the child's description of a near-death experience is much closer to being real than the experiences we perceive through our ordinary senses.

Physicists speak of "non-local" reality as being the basic reality of life. This is a level of reality in which time and space do not exist, and everything happens all at once. This is extremely difficult for us to understand, since we are, at least on one level, biological machines with a ticking internal biological clock. We are so conditioned by our perception of reality through our five senses that we cannot fathom what reality is truly like. It is a pattern of energy that exists in nature, a pattern which contains everything that ever was and ever will be.

Children who have had near-death experiences have no trouble with this concept. One boy wrote this about his near-death experience: "I once saw the Light. It was not like anything you could imagine, for it was like a sound that existed only in the silence of pitch black. . . . The light is a pattern that some call Life. The ups and downs, the happy, the sad, the good, the bad, the only thing that is real and yet not quite in our reach." When I asked another boy how long his near-death experience lasted, he replied: "It could have been a second or it could have been as long as my whole life."

Physicist Paul Davis, in discussing non-local reality, stated: "We have cracked the cosmic code. We, who are animated stardust, have a glimpse of the rules on which the universe runs. How we have become linked into this cosmic dimension is a mystery. Yet the linkage cannot be denied."

When I read this statement, I suddenly knew what the linkage had to be. It must be the same biological structure that allows us to have near-death experiences, that is, the right temporal lobe.

It made perfect sense. On the one hand, we have theoretical physicists who have been trying to explain to us for the past fifty years that our material world is actually based on pulsating, endless patterns of light and energy. On the other hand, we have mystics, psychics, and those who have had near-death experiences telling us that they have had a glimpse of a level of reality in which all knowledge is contained, time and space are meaningless, and is filled with a loving light. Our right temporal lobe is our link to non-local reality or, as a child called it, "the really real" place.

Not only can we glimpse this ultimate non-local reality, but recent scientific evidence suggests that we are constantly interacting with it. Evolutionary biologist Rupert Sheldrake has proposed that we are not biological machines at all, but instead we are based on patterns of energy which code for our bodies and behaviors, patterns that exist in nature or non-local reality. As conscious life evolved, according to Sheldrake, it only reflected changes in the patterns of energy that underlie animal and human forms. This explains the large gaps in evolution and the abrupt developments such as mammals nursing their young, or drastic changes in anatomy such as the evolution of hands and feet. He states that it is the underlying pattern that evolves and changes, and those changes are then reflected in changes in body form or behavior.

In summary, the most recent scientific advances suggest that there is a non-local reality that contains the master program for our bodies, our behaviors, and quite possibly our memories. It is independent of time and space. We can access this reality through a biological structure we are all born with, the right temporal lobe.

At last we arrive at a scientific hypothesis firmly within the current scientific mainstream, which explains how Sylvia Browne can interact with people who have died, or facilitate spiritual healing. She simply has a more developed right temporal lobe than most of us. This could have been a talent she was born with, just as Carl Lewis was born with extraordinary athletic talents, or it could have been triggered and augmented by having a spiritual or near-death experience.

Within non-local reality, the patterns of those who have died continue to exist. Time is meaningless within that reality. So of course they can return to us via the mediation of our right temporal lobe and communicate with us in after-death communications. It is also theoretically possible to contact them.

Now we can understand the scientific basis of spiritual healing. When Sylvia facilitates a spiritual healing, she is most likely directly communicating with the master pattern that programs a given individual.

Through the mediation of the right temporal lobe, it is likely that errors in the patterns of our current bodies can be corrected by accessing the master program. I have documented in my own practice of medicine such a case of a remarkable healing that came about by the spiritual correction of an infant's DNA. Now, at long last, I have come to a scientific hypothesis of exactly how that could occur.

Yet it must be remembered that such healings are extremely rare. As one mother sadly told me about prayer and spiritual healing: "If it was only a matter of willpower and sincere prayers, this cancer ward would be empty tomorrow."

Often grieving parents ask my advice on seeing a psychic. I tell them that I am a neuroscientist and near-death researcher. The only psychic I have had any experience with is Sylvia Browne. I know many grieving parents who have found closure through spiritual readings with her. She definitely helped me at a crucial time in my own life, and I am extremely grateful to her for that.

I do not feel that science can ever prove or disprove the abilities of a Sylvia Browne. My research indicates only that there is no conflict between believing in psychic abilities and the most recent scientific understandings of how the universe works.

In the final analysis, however, my experience with Sylvia was an experience of faith. I could have easily ignored the information she gave me in her psychic reading, or ridiculed and trivialized it. Instead, I trusted the feelings of my heart, not my logical scientific brain. She did not tell me what to do, but rather gave me the courage to do what I knew was right. Read this book and learn how to trust your own intuition and inner voice.

A Note to My Readers

This is a book about you.

It is about your God-given power, how to reconnect with it and how to put it to good use.

It is about the simple things you can do every day to make a real difference in your life, and in the lives of those you love.

It is about meeting your Spirit Guides and Angels, and reuniting with our departed loved ones.

It is about reuniting with your own past lives, and the eternity of your spirit.

It is about your health, your relationships, your family, your children, your purpose for being here, and those other very human concerns that disturb your sleep and your peace of mind.

It is about the magic and miracles and support from The Other Side that are always around you, just waiting for you to learn how to notice them.

It is about never again feeling alone, or helpless, or without value.

It is about never again being afraid to die . . . or afraid to live.

My name is Sylvia Browne. Or, as my treasured friend Montel Williams always says when he introduces me on his TV show, "World Renowned Psychic

Sylvia Browne!" I have spent forty-seven years doing everything from twenty readings a day to lecture series, to radio and television appearances, to investigating hauntings and crimes, to researching the paranormal, to working with more than one hundred medical and psychiatric doctors around the country, to starting my own church, to publishing a best-selling biography, all with a Spirit Guide named Francine constantly chirping away in my ear.

It feels a little odd starting a book about you by talking about myself. It reminds me of the classic line of a narcissist: "But enough about me. What do *you* think of me?" But I guess that's why they call this an "introduction."

I was born in Kansas City, Missouri, in 1936, to my wonderful father, Bill Shoemaker, and my mother, Celeste Shoemaker, whom I'll politely describe as "not exactly a laugh a minute." Still, she was the genetic pipeline to her mother, my spectacular, beloved, brilliantly psychic Grandma Ada Coil, whose own psychic lineage dated back three hundred years. For that reason alone, Mother was very much worth the effort she demanded.

Thanks to God, heredity, and my blueprint—the life's chart we all write for ourselves on The Other Side before we come here—I was born psychic. I even arrived complete with a caul, or fetal membrane, wrapped around my head, which is an ancient sign that a newborn has been given the psychic gift at birth.

Frankly, through the early years of my childhood, being psychic felt more like a burden than a gift. I was five, for example, when one night at a family dinner I "saw" both of my great-grandmothers' faces melting—not a pretty sight, believe me. Within the next two weeks they had both died. Until Grandma Ada patiently explained my vision, and the psychic powers that made it happen, I thought that somehow I had killed them. Later, I would announce my grandfather's death to my family before my father rushed home to break the sad news. I informed my parents when I was three that they would be giving me a baby sister when I was six (no psychic is a hundred percent accurate—Sharon jumped the gun and was born a month before my sixth birthday). I saw visiting spirits as clearly as I saw everyone else in the room, and assumed everyone else saw them too, until Grandma Ada pointed out how and why she and I were "tuned" differently than other people; I would answer the door before anyone knocked, and know who would be standing there before I answered it. One afternoon I frantically pulled my father out of a movie theater screaming, "Sharon can't breathe!" We arrived home to discover she had suddenly collapsed with double pneumonia. . . . I could go on and on. And have, I guess, now that I look back on this paragraph.

I was five when I finally became curious enough to speak up about these "other people" that no one else but me seemed to notice. My family was gathered in the living room talking wistfully about departed relatives when the form of a man began taking shape behind Grandma Ada, becoming more and more distinct until I could see him as clearly as I saw her. I asked her who he was, and she calmly asked me to describe him.

"He's tall, he has reddish-brown hair, he's wearing little wire glasses, and he has a horn around his neck that he uses to listen to people's chests."

She smiled, happy to hear that Uncle Jim had stopped by from The Other Side to say hello. It seems Uncle Jim had died in the tragic flu epidemic of 1917, having caught the virus from one of his patients.

Grandma Ada always reacted to my irrepressible gift with support, love, insight, and the profound compassion of a woman who had been through it herself. Daddy reacted with amused, fascinated pride. Mother took the position that she needed another psychic in the family like she needed a hole in her head, "coincidentally" developed migraines as a hobby, and became addicted to bubble baths.

Probably the most significant event of my childhood—and of the rest of my life as a psychic, for that matter—happened when I was eight. Under strict orders to be sound asleep one night, I was naturally playing with a flashlight. Suddenly the light began to grow until my whole bedroom was glowing. From the middle of the glow stepped a tall, serene-looking, smiling dark-haired woman who quietly said, "I come from God, Sylvia. Don't be afraid." Yeah, right. I set a new land speed record getting out of that room and down the stairs, shrieking at the top of my lungs, throwing my arms around Grandma Ada, who was in the kitchen cleaning vegetables. Barely able to talk through my panic, I told her what had happened. "Oh," she replied, almost stifling a yawn at something so mundane, "that was your Spirit Guide. She's here to help you. Would you pick up the carrots?"

My Spirit Guide turned out to be an Aztec-Incan woman named Iena, who died in her native Colombia in the early 1500s. I made a quick transition from being terrified of her to being downright bossy. I told her I was changing her name to Francine. She was gracious enough not to care, and to this day Francine remains my constant companion, friend, adviser, teacher, confidant and protector . . . to a point. She knows that mistakes and hard times are inevitable and necessary for the progress of the human spirit, and she has let me experience plenty of both. As a Spirit Guide she does a beautiful job. As a shield against life's pain and occasional crushing despair, I'd give her about a D+.

Like all Spirit Guides, Francine had a much clearer overview of my purpose here than I did, right from the beginning. Late one night when I was ten years old, I saw a vision of the classical Greek tragedy and comedy masks, superimposed over each other on my bedroom wall. Before I could even ask what they meant, Francine announced with her usual understated clarity, "Sylvia, this is your life." She also informed me that I would be a well-known psychic someday, helping a lot of people and speaking to large audiences. And sure enough, it has all come true, including the heartbreaking tragedies I confront every day through my work, superimposed over my insistence that a sense of humor is as essential to our lives as spirituality.

I'll repeat two facts more than once throughout the book, because they are very important: No psychic on earth, including me, is a hundred percent accurate, and no genuine psychic, including me, is psychic about themselves. God generously gave us a gift, not to hoard or waste on lottery numbers and Super Bowl winners for ourselves, but to turn around and give to everyone else just as generously. Like a child, this gift is not something we own. It is entrusted to us for safekeeping and nurturing into a productive, compassionate force of its own—and if we abuse it, we deserve to lose it.

Unity in our family being what it was, I was raised Catholic, Jewish, Episcopalian, and Lutheran, with an emphasis on Catholicism. There was a time when I thought I wanted to be a nun. But ultimately I couldn't really maintain a straight face about the idea of being a nun, so I settled for becoming a Catholic schoolteacher for eighteen years instead.

With Francine constantly nagging in my ear and my God-given psychic gift burning a bigger and bigger hole in my pocket, so to speak, I finally caught on that being a psychic and being passionately spiritual were hardly mutually exclusive. I could, and had to, devote my life to both.

I started doing readings. I'm not bragging when I say that it became quickly apparent that I could change and even save people's lives. Yet all my psychic information comes *through* me, not *from* me, so all I can take credit for is having a gift and being willing to say out loud the information I am given.

I started sharing what I knew with groups of friends, then friends of friends. Fifteen or twenty people in someone's living room grew to two or three hundred people in churches and town halls, which eventually evolved into television and radio appearances and standing-room-only engagements to audiences of two or three thousand.

The more I knew about psychic power and spirituality, the more I wanted to know. I became an avid student of theology and comparative religion, and read all twenty-six versions of the Bible as well as every other significant religious book I could get my hands on, from the Koran to the Talmud to the teachings of Buddha to the Egyptian Book of the Dead. In 1974 I created the Nirvana Foundation for Psychic Research (now the Sylvia Browne Corporation), a professional nonprofit organization for study and research into the paranormal. I became a licensed and fully accredited master hypnotist, not for the purpose of seeing how many people I could transform into chickens or ballerinas to embarrass themselves in front of howling audiences, but to tap into the wealth of spirit knowledge that is present and available in every human subconscious mind.

People talk, thank God, so my reputation grew along with my clientele and eventually spread to every continent on the globe. I began to get calls from law enforcement agencies and the medical community, asking for help with everything from unsolved murders and missing persons to physiological and psychological problems that weren't responding to traditional treatment. I was proud and happy to oblige. I've never charged any of them a dime, and I never will. The day I demand a check for helping find a missing child or a murderer, or guide a doctor to a diagnosis or cure for a life-threatening medical or psychiatric problem, is the day I imagine my psychic gift will be taken away, exactly as it should be.

During all this, I always had my personal life to keep me humble and prove beyond the shadow of a doubt that God definitely did not give me this psychic gift to use on myself. I've been married either three times or four, depending on whether you count a one-week marriage of defiance when I was sixteen, which my father promptly and wisely had annulled. But there are no mistakes—thanks to these "learning experiences" I moved to California, where I belong, in 1964, and I've been blessed with two sons and three spectacular grandchildren I adore.

In 1986, motivated by my belief that spirituality without action is just a lot of rhetoric, and my growing awareness that making and keeping the connection between ourselves and the essence of God inside us is the most important connection we can make in this life, I founded the Society of *Novus Spiritus* ("New Spirit"). It is nondenominational, based on my Christian Gnostic theology with shades of many other religions blended in. We now have a ministry of almost sixty and a membership that numbers in the thousands. We worship and celebrate a loving, benevolent God who created us all, and we reject such harsh, cruel concepts as sin, guilt, and retribution. We are an active spiritual community, proud of our daily Prayer Chains that can include hundreds of thousands of people, our work with the homeless and infirm, and as many other humanitarian pursuits as our resources can sustain. Our doors, arms, and hearts are wide open, but at my insistence, we have a strict policy against recruiting. So if you happen to get curious about *Novus Spiritus*, feel free to call my office phone number at the back of this book and ask. We will welcome you happily, but will not hype you, hard-sell you, show up at your door or drag you in off the street to get you there.

All along I have felt that I owe my clients and friends more than I can share in lectures and readings—a book they can take home to help them answer questions when I am not around and, most important, comfort them in times of trouble and despair. I thought it would work best if it was a "how-to" primer that doesn't just explain the basics of life, death, and The Other Side through my spiritual psychic eyes but actually gives simple pointers on how to use them. So one night over dinner I said to my friend Lindsay Harrison, who happens to be an established screenwriter, "Let's write a book together." She said, "I've never written a book before, so I think you should find someone else." I said, "I think it's time you did write a book and I'm psychic, so just shut up and nod." Not being one to argue with logic, she shut up and nodded.

This, then, is the "how-to" book I've been longing to write, based on what I know after sixty-two years of this particular lifetime:

I know that God is alive and well. He created us. He loves us constantly, eternally, and unconditionally, and He is as much a part of us as our parents, grandparents, and everyone else in our ancestry.

I know that The Other Side, and the spirits who live there, are as real as this earth we live on, and that the only thing separating "here" from "there" is a thinly veiled difference in vibrational frequency.

I know that there is no such thing as death, because our spirit has always been alive and always will be. We are as eternal as God who created us.

I know that we leave our Home on The Other Side many times to come to earth, for the purpose of experiencing and overcoming negativity and learning from it in an ongoing process of spiritual perfection. We choose who and what we'll be each time before we come here, and we even write our own blueprint to chart exactly what we want to accomplish on this brief trip away from Home.

I know that we're always surrounded by Spirit Guides, Angels and departed loved ones, and God Himself, and that we can have ready access to all of them by simply learning how.

Finally, I know that if even one thing in this book adds more love, joy, hope, power, and peace to your life, I will consider it an honor and another answered prayer.

From the bottom of my heart, God bless you.

* The *
Other Side
and Back

* 1 *

Help from The Other Side: Our Angels and Spirit Guides

Almost every religion on earth accepts the fact that our spirits survive death. But tell people you can communicate with those spirits and they will think you are nuts. So spirits exist, but we can't communicate with them? I think *that's* nuts. Of course we can! And we do, all the time, whether we are aware of it or not.

The truth is, we are never alone. Every moment of our lives we are surrounded by a support group from The Other Side who knows, loves, and understands us better than we know, love, and understand ourselves.

I'm sure you'd find that easier to believe if you could actually see and hear your spirit support group as clearly as you do the people around you. But look at it this way: When you leave your home and family every day and head off to work, do you immediately stop believing your home and family exist until they are right there in front of you again? Of course not. No matter how difficult, or stimulating, or consuming your day becomes, there is never a doubt in your mind that your home and family will be right where you left them when your day is over.

Since what happens in your daily life is exactly what happens in the life of your soul, your mind and heart can be just as sure that your eternal Home and family are real. You left your Home—The Other Side—and your spirit family to come to this job, this bad camping trip, this hard work called life. Frankly, I'm surprised we're not all born carrying little lunch pails. And when your work/life is over, you'll find that same Home and family waiting right where you left them, so safe and familiar and happy to see you that you'll wonder what gave you the bright idea to leave them in the first place. If, like me, you've gone through life feeling a bit homesick no matter where you were, it is because our souls are remembering and yearning for a place where we have all been before.

Throughout this book, including now, you may find yourself reading along thinking, "How does she know this?" Rather than repeating the answer over and over again, let me pause to offer it here, if only to assure you that I would not waste your time with guesswork: I have spent every day of the past forty-seven years in direct contact with The Other Side, not only through my Spirit Guide Francine but also through the spirits who join my clients during readings. Francine in particular has given me volumes of information, none of which I ever accept at face value. Instead, I have used it to enhance those same forty-seven years of exhaustive research and experience, all of it documented and on file in my office. Not only am I a skeptic, but I am also from Missouri, the "Show Me" state. So nothing appears in this book that I have not questioned, explored, tested, retested, studied and personally validated.

THE OTHER SIDE

The Other Side is where our spirits come from when we enter the womb waiting to be born and where our spirits go when we die. It is heaven, paradise, more stunningly beautiful than our earthly minds can imagine. We usually picture it as being "out there somewhere," above the clouds, past the moon and stars, beyond Oz and Never-Never Land. And that's understandable, since "out there somewhere" is as infinite and mysterious as we imagine The Other Side to be.

But the truth is much more fascinating and comforting than that: The Other Side is right here among us, another dimension superimposed on our own world, some three feet above our version of "ground level." Its vibrational frequency is much higher than ours, which is why we don't perceive it. For an easy analogy, think of a dog whistle—its frequency is so high that it seems silent to the normal human ear, but animals can hear it clearly. (Part of the psychic gift, in fact, is the God-given ability to perceive a wider range of vibrational frequencies, which is why we're able to communicate with the spirit world more easily than "normal.")

People who have seen spirits invariably describe them as "floating above the ground." There is good reason for that—they *are* floating, above *our* ground. On the ground level of The Other Side. We're actually ghosts in *their* world, sharing the same space but unreal by comparison, since it is in the spirit world that all beings are completely and fully "alive."

Typically, Francine gives me information about The Other Side, and I then validate it through meticulous research, including regressive hypnosis, which we will discuss in greater detail in later chapters. On the location of The Other Side, though, that process worked in reverse. Decades ago I was taking a client named Anne through her death in a past life. She described her family, gathered around her bed to say good-bye, and the small, simple, gaslit room in which she was dying. To her amazement, and mine, when the legendary tunnel appeared to take her spirit to The Other Side, it did not lead up from her body to the ceiling or the sky, but across the room and the southern fields beyond instead, only slightly above the earthly plane she was leaving.

When client after client after client, without my leading them in any way, described on tape exactly the same experience, of a tunnel, or sometimes a bridge, that led not *up* to another dimension but *across* to it, I finally remarked to Francine one night as if it would be news to her, "The Other Side is right here!"

She replied, "Of course it's right here."

With some impatience I demanded to know why she had never bothered to mention that. With her typical and occasionally frustrating logic she calmly responded, "You never asked."

You will also read in a later chapter about my own near-death experience. Not that I needed more validation about the location of The Other Side by then, but I am able to confirm that, just like Anne and these countless other clients, I personally saw the tunnel lift up from my body to take me across, not up, to the white light of Home.

We on earth are stuck with our dimension's annoying laws of time and space, laws that contribute concepts like "late" and "crowded" and "traffic jam" and "stressed out" to our vocabulary. The residents of The Other Side joyfully function without those restrictions and instead enjoy the freedom of such universal laws as infinity and eternity. Our lifetimes here last about as long as the blink of an eye on The Other Side, and the entities who reside there have no concept of the word "crowded," since hundreds of them could easily fit into an elevator without even having to inhale.

And how is this for something to look forward to: All spirits on The Other Side are thirty years old. (Yes, that includes us, whether we're age two or ninety-two when we get there.) When my Spirit Guide, Francine, my "resident expert" on the subject of The Other Side, first told me that, I asked, "Why thirty?" She replied,

"Why not?" That ended *that* conversation. But I guess thirty is a good physical age to choose for a general population—we're about as comfortable with our bodies as we're going to get by then. Spirits can assume their earthly appearance when they come to visit us, to help us recognize them, but in their day-to-day lives on The Other Side, not only are they thirty but they also can choose their own physical attributes, from height to weight to hair color.

I need to make something very clear in case it is not already. For the purpose of these descriptions of The Other Side and the differences between life there and life here on earth, I'm using pronouns like *we* and *them*. But please understand that *we* have been *them* many, many times, and *we* will become *them* again when we have completed this lifetime. All of us here and on The Other Side are parts of the same Whole, fibers in the same perfect fabric of God's creation. We are separated by nothing but a natural transition we call "death," a transition that is really the joyful cycle of our eternal spirits going Home again.

Home, contrary to a lot of myths and greeting card artwork, is far more magnificent and complex than just an endless sea of puffy white clouds and blue sky. The Other Side is a breathtaking infinity of mountains, and oceans, and vast gardens, and forests—every wonder of nature that exists here, its beauty magnified hundreds of times. The landscape is punctuated with buildings of brilliant design and variety—classical Greek and Roman architecture for the temples, concert halls, courtyards, sports arenas, and other public gathering places—and homes designed to meet every entity's personal preference, so that a stately Victorian mansion might share a neighborhood with a simple log cabin and a geodesic dome.

Animals, among God's most perfect creations, are alive and well on The Other Side, too. (And to be honest, if they weren't, I don't think I'd have the slightest interest in going there.) All the animals that exist on earth exist on The Other Side, without fear or aggression, and they are appropriately cherished and respected as the pure, innocent, guileless spirits they are.

You will probably be as relieved as I was to learn that entities on The Other Side don't really spend all their time lying around playing harps. That might be pleasant enough for five or ten minutes every once in a while, but for all eternity? In fact, The Other Side's residents are constantly active and stimulated. Frankly, it is ridiculous that *we* refer to *them* as "dead." We should be so "dead." They study, they work, they research—by choice, I must add, and with great joy. They have brilliant social lives, full of parties and music and dancing and sporting events and fashion shows and lectures, literally every possible option for every possible preference. All the arts, crafts, hobbies, and outdoor activities available on earth are available there, taken to their most exhilarating extreme. Words like *boredom, loneliness,* and *tedium* are not part of the local vocabulary.

It is especially fascinating that the entities on The Other Side also create everything from inventions to medical cures to great art, music, philosophy, and scientific breakthroughs. They then transmit those creations through subtle telepathy to those on earth who have the skills, tools, and dedication to make them a reality. If you have ever wondered why significant humanitarian brainstorms seem to occur almost simultaneously to separate people on opposite sides of the globe, now you know—The Other Side likes to make sure its finest contributions get maximum attention here on earth. This does not take a bit of credit away from the brilliant people among us who make these leaps of discovery. The entities on The Other Side need gifted, willing hands and hearts to carry out their work just as surely as we need their divine inspiration.

Telepathy is the most popular form of communication among the spirit entities, but verbal communication is easy, too, since all languages are spoken and understood. The most universal language on The Other Side is the eloquently descriptive Aramaic of ancient Syria, a dialect of which was spoken by Christ and His disciples. However, there's no need to start boning up on our Aramaic before we die. Like all entities on The Other Side, we will have access to all knowledge when we get there, including memories from every one of our past lives, preserved for eternity in the magnificent domed Hall of Records. The Other Side's vast libraries include sacred Askashic records, which Francine defines as the written depiction of God's memory. All the entities have constant, total communion with God, who offers information and answers through "infused knowledge," transmitted directly from the Holy Spirit into the mind.

There is no negativity on The Other Side, no aggression, no ego or jealousy or pride, and no judgment. Those qualities are strictly human-made, not God-made. And those human qualities are exactly why we make the seemingly insane choice of leaving our Home on The Other Side from time to time and trudge through yet another incarnation.

Our purpose in coming here is to learn and to gain knowledge, as the sensing, experiencing extensions of God we all are. I have heard and read different interpretations of this, implying that with each incarnation our spirits "evolve" in an effort to get "closer to God." But that is simply not true. Our spirits were already fully "evolved" when God created them. Because we're part of Him just as He is part of us, there is no such thing as getting "closer" to Him—we're already there.

I once asked a very wise soul, when I was much younger and going through an especially rough time, why life had to be so hard. She answered with a question: "What have you learned from those times when life was easy?" As much as I hate to admit it, she was right. The old adage "If it doesn't kill you, it'll make you stronger" is true. We don't learn from never having hurdles in our path to begin with; we learn from overcoming the hurdles we are confronted with along the way. That is why our spirits sometimes feel the need to leave The Other Side and come here—to experience and overcome negativity in all its forms and learn from it, and then take that knowledge back Home.

Yet if we have access to all knowledge on The Other Side, why even bother putting ourselves through this "negativity" business? Why not just stay in the perfection of Home and read an eternity of wisdom about imperfection?

Brilliant concepts are useful only when they are acted upon. If God had created our spirits to be content with unexperienced knowledge, Neil Armstrong would have never set foot on the moon. Leonardo da Vinci would have been too busy reading art books to create the *Mona Lisa*. Amelia Earhart would have stayed home with a dull ache in her heart every time a plane flew overhead. William Shakespeare would have spent his life going to the theater and never bothered to reach for a pen.

It took the same strength, courage, discipline, curiosity, and faith we admire in those people for us to choose to experience another human lifetime. We owe ourselves and each other profound respect just for having the guts to come here.

Once our spirits make the decision to inhabit a human body, we create a blueprint for this life based on what we're most interested in experiencing and learning to overcome in our eternal pursuit of knowledge. That blueprint includes everything from the kind of parents, families, and childhoods we will have to our career paths, health and financial circumstances, sexual preferences, marriages, children, and the length of our lifetime. We also select an "option line," or area in which we feel we have the most to learn and will therefore be especially challenged by while we're here.

There are seven option lines to choose from: family, social life, love, health, spirituality, finance, and career. If you take a close look at your life, I'll bet there is one item on that list that you just cannot seem to get right no matter how hard you try. At its worst, it spills over into the other six and makes it feel as if you are doing everything wrong. Don't panic. It is not an affliction you have been burdened with against your will; it is actually the area of challenge you have chosen. Think of it as the subject you decided to "major" in this time around so that you can finally master it someday. (That's not always easy, I know. My option line is "family," and trust me, I'm still trying to get a handle on it at age sixty-two.)

In addition to mapping out our blueprints before coming here, we also make sacred contracts with entities on The Other Side to watch over us, protect us, help us and advise us through this earthly journey we have chosen to undertake. The most intimate of these advisers, who, with God's help, conceives and reviews our blueprint with us, and is at our side every step of the way, is our Spirit Guide.

SPIRIT GUIDES

Every one of us has a Spirit Guide, someone we were very close to and literally trusted with our soul on The Other Side, who agreed to be our constant, vigilant companion and helpmate when we made the choice to experience another lifetime on earth. Our Spirit Guides are the best friends we have ever had; they just happen to live in another dimension.

All Spirit Guides have spent at least one life here, so they are able to empathize with the problems, mistakes, temptations, fears, and frailties inevitable in the human world. In fact, most of us either have been or will be someone else's Spirit Guide somewhere along the way. On rare occasions your Spirit Guide is an ancestor or someone you've shared a past life with. But because your relationship with your Guide was formed between your spirit and theirs on The Other Side before you were born, it is impossible for them to be someone you've known in this lifetime.

My Spirit Guide, whom I mentioned earlier, is an Aztec-Incan woman named Iena, although I took it upon myself to change her name to Francine. She was born in northern Colombia in 1500 and was killed in a Spanish attack on her city in 1520. That was her only incarnation on this earth, and we never knew each other until we met and became close friends on The Other Side. The fact that we had never met in a past life has not diminished our intimate connection in the slightest.

The Spirit Guide's job is to urge, nudge, encourage, advise, support, and, as their title suggests, guide us on our life's path. And they have several advantages to help them in their work. First, they have the closest possible bond with our spirits—the very essence of who we are. They have also studied and memorized our blueprints. We, unfortunately, lose conscious awareness of our blueprints during our time on earth and tend to wander off from our intended plans. They can help us get back on track. Their vantage point on The Other Side gives them direct access to God's divine knowledge, and they also enjoy every spirit's enviable ability to be in several places at once, unencumbered by these bodies we make such a big deal out of having. They can be at a lecture or party in the spirit world or visit another loved one on earth while still keeping an eye on us.

Incidentally, in case you are picturing a flock of voyeurs, gaping at our every move and invading our most highly personal, shall we say, "private moments," let me put your mind at ease. They're called "Spirit" Guides, not "Body" Guides. They concern themselves with our spirits and *only* our spirits. Our various bodily functions are not their concern.

Another thing a Spirit Guide won't do—take it from me—is leap in to interfere with the choices we make, or deprive us of our free will. At best, they will offer possible alternatives and warnings. But our agreement with them from the beginning is that we are here to learn and grow, and they know we cannot accomplish that if they are constantly shielding us from the lessons we need to learn.

Spirit Guides communicate with us in a variety of ways, if we'll just shut up and listen to them. You would think that would be especially easy for me, because I have the advantage of being able to actually hear Francine talking to me, and even channel her so that she can talk *through* me, but incredibly, there are still times to this day when I get ornery and don't pay attention and end up with egg dripping down my face. It is a testament to her patience, and to the depth of the bond between us, that she is even speaking to me at all by now.

So don't feel disadvantaged if your Spirit Guide doesn't seem to have an audible voice. They are still sending you plenty of messages, most often through your subconscious mind. What you have always accepted as instincts, or your conscience, or unusually vivid dreams are more likely your Spirit Guide waving flags. These experiences are common. You for no reason drive a different route than usual and find out later you avoided an accident. On impulse you call a friend, only to discover they needed your help at that moment. You go to sleep concerned about a problem and wake up knowing the solution. Anything you've written off to "something told me to . . . " change that to "some*one* told me to." You're receiving your Spirit Guide's signals—and acting on them.

As for your signals to your Spirit Guide, you can and should ask for help, advice, and reassurance as often as you feel the need. But please remember something I learned the hard way—whatever it is you want, be specific.

When my son Paul was five months old, he was stricken with a potentially fatal infection. His fever was soaring past 105 degrees as I raced him to the hospital, where he struggled in intensive care for twenty-six hours before his doctors could assure me he was going to make it. I was terrified and alone for most of those twenty-six hours, and as I paced and prayed and sobbed in that waiting room, I must have pleaded, "Help me, Francine!" a thousand times without any noticeable response.

Once Paul was home again, safe and sound in his own crib, I angrily confronted Francine, feeling betrayed. "How could you abandon me like that when I thought my baby was dying?"

Like all Spirit Guides, who have the divine perspective we lack, Francine is always calm, no matter what I say to her. So with her trademark serenity she simply replied, "Is that what was wrong? I knew you wanted my help, but I had no idea what the problem was. *I can't read your mind, you know!*"

That was news to me. I assumed she knew everything about me. But the more I have thought about it, the more sense it makes. Our Spirit Guides know our blueprints, but those blueprints hardly contain every momentary fear we will ever have. Also, speaking from practical experience, as psychic as I am, I can't read minds, either. When a friend or client says, "Help me!" I'm going to say, "With what?" every time. It was a valuable lesson I'm happy to pass along—your Spirit Guide is available twenty-four hours a day to join God as one of your greatest allies, if you'll just skip the generalities and tell them *exactly* what you need.

I still wasn't ready to let her off the hook, though. She couldn't read my mind, but I had prayed constantly in that hospital room. She didn't have to be a mind reader to hear prayers, did she?

More news to me: When we speak directly to God, a "dome of privacy" instantly surrounds us. The privacy of our conversations with God is so sacred that not even our Spirit Guides can hear them. God is part of us. We are part of Him. No one can trespass or eavesdrop when we are already one with Him to begin with.

One more tip, by the way, is that Spirit Guides seem to be absolutely literal-minded about what you say to them, so when you talk to yours, forget about nuance or unspoken assumptions. Here's a perfect example: If I ask Francine, "Can you describe yourself?" she'll answer, "Yes." Period. Just, "Yes." She's not trying to be coy, she's simply giving the precise answer to your question because she thinks that is what you meant. But if I ask, "Would you describe yourself, please?" she's happy to oblige.

Please don't neglect talking to your Spirit Guide just because you might not know who it is. Don't forget, they have been human at least once before. They are well aware that our memories of them and our lives on The Other Side are virtually nonexistent, so they don't expect us to remember them. If you haven't been introduced to yours, or if a psychic or medium has not identified them for you, make up a name and call them that. It will make your Spirit Guide seem more personal, and your Guide will happily answer to any name you come up with, just for the joy of your finally acknowledging and embracing them. Take it from a woman who changed her Spirit Guide's name from

Iena to Francine for my own childhood convenience—their love for us is as patient, eternal and unconditional as The Other Side itself, where we'll reunite with them someday and, I'm sure, have a good laugh about the long, strange trip they saw us through.

ANGELS

According to a recent Gallup poll, three-quarters of all Americans believe in Angels. Angels adorn everything from T-shirts to coffee mugs to bumper stickers. Entire stores are devoted to Angel paraphernalia. Countless books have been written about them. Successful movies and TV series have been made. One of the most highly rated *Montel Williams* episodes in my more than eighty appearances was called "Are There Angels Among Us?" Montel's office and mine were promptly flooded with letters from people who have had firsthand Angel experiences that changed their lives.

Obviously there is nothing new about Angels—a quick glance at the Bible makes it clear that they have been with us as long as we have been around to witness them and be blessed by their presence. So why this current interest and acceptance of the absolute truth that yes, there *are* Angels among us?

Well, besides the fact that Angels are beautiful enough and powerful enough to warrant all the passion we invest in them, there are two logical reasons we seem to be hearing more and more about them these days. First of all, as the belief in Angels continues to grow, people are less and less reluctant to speak up about their encounters with them. Second, as we become more uncertain and fearful of the world around us in the heightened anxiety of a new millennium, and more aware that our only real security lies in the depth of our own spirituality, more Angels than ever before are gathering to watch over us and protect us.

While all entities on The Other Side interact with each other, Angels are in a league of their own, and they differ from Spirit Guides in several significant ways:

1. Angels never incarnate—they never experience a life in human form. Instead they are direct reports from God, perfect and eternally alive on The Other Side except for brief trips to this dimension for our benefit.
2. Angels do not review our blueprints before we come here or have knowledge of our charts during our lifetime. Depending on the difficulty of the life we've chosen, we recruit a certain number of Angels to oversee our journey from its beginning, but that number can increase during our times of greatest despair and greatest danger, as well as in our greatest humanitarian and spiritual efforts. It is their instinctive mission to help us through our darkest times, and their joy to observe and celebrate our finest hours. If there is such a thing as "normal" on this subject, I used to "normally" see people come into this life with two recruited Angels and increase that number to four or five in the course of their lifetimes. More and more, though, I'm seeing people who arrived on earth with four or five Angels, with as many as ten gathering around them as they meet and overcome the challenges in their lives.
3. Spirit Guides and all other transcended spirits are either male or female. But in their natural form on The Other Side, Angels are androgynous, with identical, exquisitely beautiful features. Their hair color and skin color vary, but they all appear to glisten and glitter from an inner divine light.
4. Because they have never been bogged down with

a human body, they are "lighter" in their molecular structure and more "fluid" than transcended spirits in traveling between their dimension and ours. They can effortlessly appear on earth and disappear again in a heartbeat.

5. A defining description of every human encounter with an Angel is that the Angel came and went without ever saying a word. Angels are completely nonverbal and instead communicate through infused knowledge—the same direct transmission from the Holy Spirit to the mind by which God communicates with all of the entities on The Other Side.

As with everything in God's creation, there is an order to the population of Angels. The higher the order or level, the more powerful the Angel. But also as with everything in God's creation, no Angel—no living entity—is closer or more important to God than any other. Angels can advance from one level to another, earning their advancement by their good deeds and their bodies of experience, not unlike our advancement through school:

Angels—I'd call them "your basic Angels," but there's nothing basic about them—are the freshmen of the group, the ones who descend to our dimension most often to protect and rescue us.

Archangels are the sophomores, in a way the "image makers" of the group because Archangels, unlike Angels, have wings. Their wings, like the headdresses and crowns they sometimes wear, are badges of honor, worn to identify themselves and delineate their progress through the hierarchy. And interestingly, the more they accomplish, the more silver and golden their wings become as they work toward the next level. Archangels are the messengers—it was the Archangel Gabriel, for example, who brought God's announcement to Mary that she had been chosen to carry His son Jesus.

The Cherubim and Seraphim are the juniors, God's witnesses on earth, His onsite reporters. The Cherubim and Seraphim were most notably and magnificently visible when they gathered to joyfully attend the birth of Christ.

The seniors are the Thrones and Principalities, the most powerful of the Angels and, in a way, God's "bodyguards" and "henchmen." The Thrones are static, not active, wisdom keepers who never descend to our dimension. The Principalities do descend, but only in the most dire of circumstances and only when God sends them. Only the Principalities, for example, can intervene at a cataclysmic or potentially fatal moment in our lives and, exclusively at God's direction, actually circumvent our blueprints. And only a gathering of God-sent Principalities and their unparalleled power among the Angels can create a miracle.

Clients, friends, and family have told me more stories of encounters with Angels than I can count, and so many thousands of other similar stories have been published and documented that I'm actually starting to feel sorry for the nonbelievers—it can't be fun being so overwhelmingly outnumbered. My son Chris, who is psychic, spent his childhood talking to his Angels, who were always among his favorite playmates. My granddaughter Angelia, who is six and also psychic, not only talks to and plays with her Angels but was also saved by one when she was a baby. Her mother, Gina, was physically shoved back onto a curb by an Angel's strong hands an instant before an out-of-control car flew past. It missed Angelia's stroller by inches. One client was rescued from the undertow at a beach and delivered safely to shore by a glistening golden Angel who silently disappeared before she could thank him. Another was stopped in midair during a potentially fatal slide down a steep, rocky slope and pulled back up to the mountain overlook he had slipped from without ever seeing his unhumanly powerful savior. Still another watched in helpless awe as the full form of an Angel, bathed in white light, appeared just in time to cushion his child's fall from a second-story window and save the child's life.

Multiply that handful of incidents by several thousand, and you'll have a rough idea of the number of eyewitness accounts I've heard of Angel encounters. Then you have to add the thousands more that were mistaken for something more "ordinary" because the Angels appeared in human form. They can materialize briefly as anything from a little girl to a kindly old man—any form that won't frighten the person they've arrived to help, or that won't attract too much attention to themselves. There's a beautiful Bible verse that reads: "Be not forgetful to entertain strangers, for thereby have some entertained Angels unaware." That doesn't mean next time a stranger shows up at your door, invite them in and trot out the clam dip. But if a stranger suddenly appears, makes some gesture to help and protect you, and then vanishes again without a word before you can thank them, chances are you can direct your thanks to The Other Side.

I don't have to be psychic to know that some of you are feeling left out right about now, wondering where all these Angels were when some disaster or tragedy happened in your life. It's a fair question. I've asked it myself in a few dark times when my Angels seemed to have either dozed off or abandoned me completely.

The answer keeps coming back to Francine—and her constant reminder: "What have you learned from those times when life was easy?" We chose this life and wrote the blueprints, and part of it involved facing negativity and overcoming it for the greater knowledge of our spirit. The Angels know better than we do that sometimes the most loving help they can offer is to stand back and let us learn—and that we'll understand all of it perfectly when we're Home again on The Other Side.

DEPARTED LOVED ONES

With rare exceptions we'll cover in other chapters, everyone you've ever loved and lost through death is alive, well, and happy on The Other Side—and they visit you often. In fact, while Lindsay and I were working on this very chapter one night, her father, who was killed by a drunk driver twenty-five years ago, dropped by completely unannounced. He planted himself behind her and demanded my attention, gripping the last two fingers of his right hand with his left and waving this odd gesture at me until I told her, "Your father's here. What was wrong with the last two fingers of his right hand?" She tried to visualize his hands but couldn't—it had been too long. He told me, and I repeated, "Oh, they were broken, and he couldn't straighten them." The next day she called her mother and, without explaining why, asked, "By the way, do you happen to remember anything strange about the last two fingers of Dad's right hand?" Her mother thought about it and then said, "Not really. I know he broke them and they weren't set properly, so he couldn't straighten them." Since it was the night before Father's Day, we're sure he was reminding Lindsay that he'd be spending the holiday with her.

Even though we weren't expecting him, he did give us a good example of a typical visit by departed loved ones from The Other Side:

1. They're eager to validate their identity beyond any doubt in your mind. They'll indicate anything from a unique physical characteristic to an affectation to their manner of death to a nickname to a specific piece of jewelry—whatever it takes to establish who they are for your benefit. The fewer preconceived ideas you have about how they "should" identify themselves, the better off you will be. For example, if Lindsay had insisted that she'd only recognize her father by something involving either fishing or his favorite team, the New York Yankees, she would have missed a lovely reunion.
2. They're opportunists. When you're thinking about them, or simply in a frame of mind that's receptive to them, they jump at the chance to visit. Lindsay and I were talking about The Other Side when her father appeared. Whenever I speak to an audience, I see virtual crowds of spirits around every person in the room, not just because they know I can see them but also because my audiences are open to all kinds of spiritual possibilities and experiences. As Francine puts it, "When the bell rings, we all run to answer it." I can't count the number of people who've come up to me after a lecture and asked who the tall, dark-haired woman on stage with me was. Francine, like all transcended spirits including our loved ones, adores attention, and it's fine with me, as long as she and I aren't wearing matching outfits, which would look a little too cute for my taste.
3. They all basically come with the same purpose in mind: They want us to know that they're fine, they're with us, and not only are they not dead, they're more alive than ever.

I happen to think that's the most thrilling news we could ever hope to hear, which is why I can never get over a common occurrence during readings. I'll say to a client, "There's a very petite older woman around you, with huge gray eyes and the deepest dimples." They'll respond, yawning, "Oh, that's my mother. So am I going to get that promotion at work or not?" Or, "Oh, that's my mother. Ask her why she left the Studebaker to Bobby when she knew I wanted it." Hello-o-o-o! Someone you loved is here to offer you absolute proof that there's no need to fear death ever again, and you'd rather talk about your job? You're in the actual presence of The Other Side, and your first question is why Bobby got the Studebaker?

Here's another frequent and mystifying exchange during readings: A client asks me to put them in touch with their late Uncle Dick. I see a woman beside them instead, clearly ready and eager to talk. I describe her in detail. The client, a bit impatient, says, "That's not Uncle Dick." No kidding. "That's Aunt Dorothy. I never liked Aunt Dorothy. I want to talk to Uncle Dick."

Please.

A departed relative they recognize has appeared from The Other Side, with divine knowledge we can only begin to imagine here, and they're being fussy about who it is? We're privileged by any visitation from The Other Side. Let's not complain, let's listen!

What if Aunt Dorothy has come because she has something to say? What if she has a message from Uncle Dick, or from another friend or family member who has passed over? What if she wants to apologize for being so mean or irritable or cheap or whatever made them dislike her while she was living? What if she left them a few hundred dollars in an old shoebox and forgot to mention it in her will?

As for Uncle Dick, there are several reasons he might not be available. As we'll see in the "Hauntings" chapter, he might not have transcended to The Other Side yet. He might be *in utero* again, waiting to be born into his next incarnation. He's definitely not going to start chattering away from inside the womb, and God help the woman who's pregnant with him if he does.

Sometimes—although this isn't any cause for concern, I promise—there is a delay before your loved one can begin visiting you. This can occur after a death involving trauma, or when your loved one simply doesn't want to go. My dad, for example, ill as he was at the end, didn't want to leave me. He also had his heart set on watching his great-granddaughter Angelia grow up. He was gone for eight months before he finally showed up, announcing himself by playing the music box he had given me and waking me out of a sound sleep.

Some reluctant or suddenly released spirits make the transition to The Other Side beautifully. Others, after passing safely through the tunnel to the light that signals the crossing to another dimension, have a more difficult time adjusting. The entities on The Other Side are well prepared to help. Some spirits are led through a series of orientation studies and activities, particularly activities the spirit found relaxing and enjoyable on earth, from fishing to gardening to attending the ballet or opera to hiking, swimming, reading, painting, sculpting, et al. Others, like my dad, are simply "cocooned," or put into a deep, cleansing sleep, and watched over until the spirit has essentially slept through withdrawal from the dimension they've just left. According to Francine and countless other spirits with whom I have discussed cocooning, a difficult transition to The Other Side is comparable to a case of the "bends," when a person surfaces too quickly from too great a depth while swimming. Such a transition lasts for several months at most, which, as we know, is less than a heartbeat in the spirit world. When my dad finally appeared, and I asked what took him so long because I missed him so terribly in those eight months of grieving, he said, "What do you mean? I just left!"

I admit, even knowing that there's unsurpassed joy waiting for us when this life ends, I do grieve when someone I love dies—not for them but for me. I'm selfish, and I hate saying good-bye. I believe that whatever helps us through the grieving process is fair and should be respected. If visiting a grave gives you comfort, then by all means do that, but please don't visit a grave on behalf of the loved one you've lost. They aren't there. They'll probably ride to the cemetery with you, and they'll ride back home with you, wishing you hadn't left all those lovely flowers behind, where they'll be enjoyed only by the people who come to leave flowers on *their* loved ones' graves. I've never heard a transcended spirit complain about the size of their headstone, or about someone else's grave up the hill having a better view than theirs. Nothing we do here can compete with the marble sculptures and the view on The Other Side, no matter how much we spend trying, so don't invest a fortune or go into debt in your late loved one's honor. They'll be just as honored if you stay home and put those same flowers beside a photo or memento of theirs so you can both enjoy them together.

A common source of pain among my clients is their regret over unfinished emotional business when a loved one dies. "Our last conversation was an argument" . . . "I never got to tell her I'm sorry" . . . "I'm afraid he didn't know how much I loved him" . . . "I didn't get to say good-bye." The words vary, but the nagging ache of remorse is the same—and needless. Don't forget, there's no such thing as not knowing on The Other Side, no such thing as negativity in that dimension infused with God's unconditional love, and no such thing as unfinished business in the blueprint your loved one composed themselves before they were born. But if it eases your heart and helps you heal, tell them now whatever it is you feel was left incomplete—they will hear you.

While you are talking to the departed loved ones around you, remember to include your pets. The animals on The Other Side include every pet we've had in this and all our past lives, and they watch over us from there with the same pure, steadfast loyalty they gave during their lifetimes. One of my favorite promises from Francine is that when we first arrive on The Other Side, our Spirit Guides and transcended loved ones can hardly get to us through all the animals joyfully waiting to welcome us Home. Abusing the earth's animals is to abuse some of the most divine guardian angels God has given us. It isn't just an outrage, it amounts to shooting ourselves in the foot—we can't spiritually afford to diminish the spiritual perfection that lives among us.

Our departed loved ones can return to visit us more easily than our Spirit Guides can, simply because they've been in our dimension more recently and have readier access to the experience of making the transition between here and The Other Side. Here is a case in point. Several years ago I managed to start a grease fire in my kitchen. (Don't ask.) Like an idiot, I was so busy trying to put out the fire that I didn't notice I was inhaling too much smoke, until the thought hit me that I was suffocating. Panicked and gasping for air, I started running toward the sliding glass doors that led to the balcony. They were about twenty feet from the kitchen, and I remember realizing they were too far away and I wasn't going to make it. I started to pass out. Just then I was tackled from behind with enormous force and thrown down and forward into the fresh air of the balcony. As I lay on my stomach, taking deep, grateful breaths, a shock of golden blonde hair fell into view over my shoulder for just an instant before I felt the weight of the force that had saved me vanish from on top of me. When I sat up again a moment later I was alone on the balcony, staring in at the lingering smoke of the fire, which had burned itself out by that point.

Since Francine's hair is jet black, I knew I couldn't give her credit for rescuing me, so I assumed it was one of my Angels. I was shocked when Francine told me that no, my heroine had actually been my beloved Grandmother Ada Coil, who was my inspiration and closest friend until her death three decades earlier. Being me, I contradicted her. I've tried a thousand times to prove Francine wrong. I'm batting .000 in that effort so far, but this time I thought I had her. "It couldn't have been Grandma Ada, Francine. Grandma Ada's hair was white, remember?" Then I recalled that Grandma Ada's hair had turned white only in her very latest years, from the golden blonde it had always been, including when she was thirty years old—the age we all are on The Other Side, from where my grandmother rushed to save my life.

Please don't let that story confuse you about a loved one's typical appearance in this dimension, by the way. Most of the time they'll appear at the age they were when you last saw them, to help you identify them. This was an emergency, kind of a "come as you are" event. Grandma Ada had no time to change from her thirty-year-old persona on The Other Side to the old woman she was when she left this life—all she had time to do was get here.

It's also important to point out that my grandmother had been "gone" for a very long time when that incident happened. My clients are often surprised to learn that a loved one who died fifty or sixty years ago is still around them. They assume their loved one has either forgotten about them after all these years or that they've come back to this dimension in another incarnation by now.

"Forgetting" is an impossibility on The Other Side. Transcended spirits have immediate access to every memory of every life, every experience, and every person they've loved on this earth. In fact, it is not unusual to be visited by loved ones from past lives we don't even consciously remember. And since time is meaningless there, the decades that might have passed since we said good-bye to them are a few seconds ago as far as they're concerned. So no, they haven't forgotten, and they never will.

As for the possibility that a loved one can't come around any longer because they've already returned for another life, that's unlikely. There are circumstances we'll go into in other chapters in which spirits go right back *in utero* again after death. But for the majority of us, if we do choose to come back for another incarnation—and it is a choice, depending on our need for more experiences here as our souls progress—we typically take an average of a 100-year "break" on The Other Side between lives.

Before you decide that your departed loved ones have stopped visiting you, or never started in the first place, please take a look at the "Hauntings" chapter. Transcended spirits have so many ways of trying to get your attention, just to say, "I'm with you," that it's easy to miss their signals. You don't have to take my word for it. Just keep your eyes, ears, and mind open. Infinite love and affirmation are all around you every minute, waiting to be noticed and share the joyful truth that there really is no such thing as death.

A VISIT WITH THE OTHER SIDE

There's a simple and fascinating exercise that can open the way to some beautiful encounters with The Other Side as often as you like, and it only takes a few quiet moments to accomplish. You can ask to meet your Spirit Guide, or a departed loved one—but again, please welcome whoever shows up. I did this exercise a couple of days ago and was visited by a spirit who identified herself as Lena. I didn't have a clue who Lena was until later, when I checked some genealogy records and discovered she was my great-great-great-great-great-grandmother. Do you want it on your conscience that one of your ancestors introduced themselves and you told them to get lost because you'd never heard of them?

So, with a clear, relaxed, and *open* mind, sit comfortably, as distanced from possible interruptions and distractions as you can manage, and close your eyes.

You're approaching a pair of huge, gleaming brass doors, intricately etched and ornate, the most beautiful you've ever seen. In the center of each door is a large brass ring. The smooth, polished metal feels cool to your hands as you grab the rings and easily swing open the heavy doors.

Inside, you find a perfectly oval room. It's serene and embracing. You feel safe and unburdened, taking deep breaths of fresh clean air as you walk down the three steps into the vast room.

The floors are hardwood, with white rugs as soft as clouds that soothe your bare feet as you walk slowly across them. A fire warms the room from a gray stone fireplace. An arched window reaches to the ceiling, and the ocean breeze it lets in only slightly disturbs the sheer, graceful curtains of loosely spun silk. A white grand piano is set beside the window, reflecting

the pastel light of sunset. Candles glow all around you. You detect a trace of nearby jasmine.

Two chairs wait side by side, identical, of rich white brocade, with legs of curved wood.

You settle into the left chair, so that the chair to your right is empty. Your breath slows. As you look around this oval room from the comfort of your chair, you're quietly filled with the knowledge that you've never felt so peaceful, healthy, alive, and content.

You ask God to surround you with the white light of the Holy Spirit, and you immediately feel the warmth of its all-powerful, unconditional love spread over you and through you, until the light is part of you. You know the joy of being adored.

From the stillness to your right you notice movement, and you turn toward it.

A figure steps forward and takes a seat in the empty chair beside you. You're not afraid, knowing no harm or darkness will approach the divine light that protects you.

The figure waits, patient, still and open. You're blessed by its presence.

Finally, softly, you speak . . .

Sometimes the figure will be someone you recognize, a dear departed friend or family member. Talk to them. Share your heart with them. But don't forget to listen, too. Even if all they have to say is, "I'm here and I love you," what a wonderful thing to hear from someone you were so afraid you'd never see again.

If it's not someone you recognize, ask their name. If

they don't tell you right away, that's okay. Just keep talking, keep asking questions, and keep listening. In the process of telling you why they've come and what they have to say, they may reveal their name sooner or later. It may be an ancestor, it may be your Spirit Guide, it may be someone with a message from a loved one. But whoever it is, welcome them!

If you want to build on this exercise, have a friend sit with you during it. Afterward, write down a detailed description of the figure who came to visit, fold your description in half so your friend can't see it, and ask them to describe the figure to you. You'll be amazed at how often their description matches the one you've written, whether they're psychic or not.

You might be tempted to dismiss the results of this exercise as "imagination." For the record, my Spirit Guide says *imagination* is one of the worst words in our vocabulary, because it's such a convenient and lame excuse for so many real experiences we should pay attention to.

What if it is "just your imagination," though? The feelings of peace and well-being you'll come away with will still be very real.

On the other hand, what if it's not . . . ?

Again, we really are never alone. There's proof of help from The Other Side all around us, and proof of the eternal lives of our spirits. All we have to do is learn to recognize it when we see it, and if there's any one purpose for this book, it's nothing more and nothing less than that.

* 2 *

Everyday Magic and Miracles: Discovering and Creating Joy in Your Life

We live among magic and miracles every day, and we all have the power to create them. If it has been awhile since you thought about magic and miracles, or if you have given up believing in them, take heart. They are not gone, we have just temporarily lost track of them. Since magic and miracles bring joy and hope and a sense of excitement to our lives, we owe it to ourselves to start recapturing them.

Part of what has separated us from magic and miracles is merely a process of human nature—when we see things too often, we forget how special they are. If a unicorn appeared in the yard one morning in the early light, we'd feel blessed. If a herd of unicorns appeared in the yard every morning like clockwork, we'd probably call Animal Control to retrieve them so they wouldn't damage the lawn. To witness live footage of the parting of the Red Sea once would leave us speechless with awe. After two or three weeks in a row of the same thing, I can almost hear us yawning and reaching for the remote control to see what else is on. So it is not that magic and miracles have disappeared from our lives. They haven't. We are surrounded by them. We just need to reconnect with them and stop taking them for granted.

We also get blocked from life's magic and miracles by the destructive emotion of guilt. I'd guess that eighteen of the twenty clients I talk to are consumed with guilt, and it becomes a more powerful force than magic and miracles could ever hope to be. So we need to address guilt and get it out of the way. If you've said or done something you knew would hurt someone, step up, take responsibility, apologize, and make an active effort to undo it. (Saying "I'm sorry" with no behavior to prove it is meaningless.) If you've said or done something that hurt someone and you can honestly say that wasn't your intention, apologize and then *let it go*! Don't tell me it's not that simple. It is if you are willing to stop embracing guilt as if it plays some kind of positive role in your life and recognize it as the waste of energy and the enemy of the spirit it is.

Of course, in this flawed life I have led, I had to learn this lesson the hard way. A perfect example is the death of my father. We adored each other, and I virtually camped out at his bedside in his final days. On the last day, I left his hospital room only for a brief minute, to stretch my legs and get a drink of water. And while I was gone, he died. My grief at losing him was compounded by my agonizing guilt over not being with him as he took his last breath. I should have stayed with him rather than go for a stupid drink of water. Shouldn't I, of all people, have been right there holding his hand when he started his journey Home? But, finally, I was able to stand back far enough to ask myself the *real* question: Was it my intention, for even one second, not to be with him when he died? Absolutely not. And that is when I learned once and for all to confront my guilt as I confront my other bad habits. Every time that negative voice in my head starts down the "I could have/I should have" road, I check myself and make the positive voice in my head interrupt with a loud "Stop!"

This method is simple, but it works. Make a promise to yourself that for the next week you're going to declare war on guilt. Any intentional pain you've caused, make it right. Any unintentional pain you're blaming yourself for, silently yell "Stop!" the instant it enters your mind, until you're so tired of being yelled at you won't even let those guilty thoughts creep in to begin with.

Then you can channel all that energy you've wasted on guilt into an essential element of maximizing the chances of everyday magic and miracles—learning to love yourself. Not to love yourself is to disrespect one of God's creations. It is to doubt your own power before you have tried using it, and to believe you are not worthy of the magic and miracles God has in store for us.

You were probably taught from an early age that there is something wrong with loving yourself, that it is egotistical and unattractive and you should be ashamed of yourself for even thinking such a thing. It is true that self-love doesn't mean considering yourself superior to anyone else. That *is* egotistical and unattractive. I'm not promoting a world full of people swaggering around with swelled heads. Self-love, put simply, means that you treat yourself well and with respect. You surround yourself with people who treat you well and respect you. You live your life according to the advice you would give your child or your closest friend.

The quickest way I've found to rediscover my love for myself in those dark times when I lose track of it is to make a list of the things I know I'm not. It seems to flow more easily and naturally than paying myself a list of compliments, but it has the same overall self-assuring effect. I'm *not* dishonest, for example, I'm *not* mean, I'm *not* judgmental, I'm *not* a coward, I'm *not* an irresponsible parent and grandparent, I'm *not* petty, etc., etc. What you are not helps define what you are, and it also gives you an idea of qualities you'd like to work on so your "not" list can grow and, in turn, add to your list of "I am."

Also check yourself regularly for something I call determinism. This is that ridiculous barrage of supposed "facts" we are told about ourselves, usually when we are young, that limit us and, if we are not careful, unfairly predetermine who we are. Let me share a few of my favorites, to show you what I mean:

- "You're hopeless with mechanical things."
- "Of course you're fat—it runs in our family."
- "You never were any good at managing money."
- "So your marriage is unhappy. Don't complain. You're lucky you found someone."
- "I'm not surprised you're sick so often. You were a sickly child."
- One of my mother's mantras: "Face it, Sylvia, your sister Sharon is the pretty one, you're the one with the personality."
- A friend of mine was told she could give up on her dream of having long hair, since her hair would simply never grow.
- A man I've known all my life struggled with a low self-image well into adulthood after his father refused to let him try out for Little League because "you don't have an athletic bone in your body."
- A woman I worked with wore red every single day, despite the fact that, frankly, she looked terrible in it. I finally found a discreet way to ask her about it. She said she actually hated red and had been sick of it for years, but she'd been told as a child it was flattering on her.

Make a list. Write down every word of determinism you've been given by the people around you. Then tear up the list and throw it in the garbage where it belongs.

You determine who you are. *You* decide what you

can and can't do, what you do and don't look good wearing, where you want or don't want to live, what your priorities are and aren't, what you believe and don't believe, and what your limits really are. We all have limits, and you'll defeat yourself if you're not realistic about them. But again, they're for *you*, not anyone else, to define. I'm five feet ten, for example, so it would be idiotic for me to insist on trying to be a jockey. I can't carry a tune in a wheelbarrow—that's not determinism, that's just a fact—so why set myself up for constant rejection by auditioning for the opera? The point is, *I* say I'm not going to be an opera singer, I'm not letting anyone else decide that for me. Nor would I be willing to go through life feeling like a failure if my parents had had their hearts set on my being an opera singer. Arbitrary expectations are another form of determinism, and they're just as unacceptable.

AFFIRMATIONS

One of the most important keys for eliminating insecurities and establishing a habit of self-love is the use of affirmations. These are simply expressing in words what we honestly want and who we honestly want to be as a treasured child of God, and then repeating those words over and over until the subconscious mind accepts them as fact so that our behavior will follow accordingly. Through affirmations we can think ourselves healthier, stronger, more positive, prettier, more handsome, kinder, more patient, more confident, more courageous—whatever will help us love ourselves more.

Religion and literature provide many beautiful affirmations, and you'll find some of my favorites in an appendix at the end of this book. But please don't hesitate to make up your own. If you're like me, when you memorize something, no matter how gorgeously and truthfully written, it can become so automatic that it loses its meaning when you recite it often enough. I hate to admit this, but I can't honestly say I've never bowed my head and recited the Lord's Prayer without wondering during it where the woman next to me bought her shoes. So by all means learn and use every affirmation you find that resonates in your soul. But your own affirmations, spoken out loud or silently from the depth of your heart, will work as well as anything ever written.

If you're wondering how to make up your own affirmations, think about the determinism and "negative affirmations" you've accepted as truth. You've learned to believe them because you've heard them so often, right? Well, you can learn to believe their exact opposites if you hear them every bit as often, and that's where affirmations come in. Just as you can find out what you are by discovering what you're not, your first affirmations can be a counterattack to anything and everything negative about your self-image, no matter where it comes from.

Starting with *you*. *Never* put yourself down, even jokingly. Declare it strictly forbidden. No more "I'm stupid." No more "I'm fat." No more "I'm clumsy," or "I'm ugly," or "I'm too short," or "I'm too tall," or any form of "I can't." You're replacing those a hundred times a day with, "I'm very smart about many things," and "I have the power to have any body I want," and "I'm graceful," and "I'm attractive," and especially—*"I can!"*

As for the people around you, if they put you down or undermine loving yourself in any way, they are off limits too, unless they learn to shape up. Insulting words and behavior are unacceptable, it is that simple. Being around anyone who doesn't make you feel good about yourself does more psychic damage than you might realize. Don't forget, we're all here to learn to overcome negativity—not to accept it, embrace it, invite it into our homes and cook dinner for it.

Remember that harsh "Stop!" I yell at myself when I start to fall into the guilt trap? That's the "Stop!" I want you to yell silently every time someone insults you. And whatever you do, don't stand there defending yourself, arguing about the insult. There's no sillier argument than yelling back and forth with someone about whether or not you are stupid or fat or ugly. You're none of those things, so why on earth would you let yourself get pulled into an argument about something you're not? Take this as an example. If someone marched up and said, "You're a giraffe!" would you spend one second trying to convince them you're not? No, you'd reply, "That's ridiculous," and walk away. (And then, I hope, you'd give some serious thought to why you'd want to hang around with someone who thinks you are a giraffe.) So in addition to the silent "Stop!" you're going to yell at every insult, I want you to add, "That's ridiculous," either silently or out loud, and walk away.

Most of all, for every insult anyone aims at you, by their words or by their actions, make it a habit to instantly neutralize it with an affirmation, over and over again, until you believe your affirmation more surely than you could ever believe anything negative about yourself. Try replacing insults and negativity with affirmations for three short months, and you'll be amazed at the openness to magic and miracles you'll create.

There is a logical but often overlooked reason why affirmations work: They are direct communication with the soul mind, and the soul mind, with its eternal knowledge and wisdom, *always recognizes and resonates with the truth*. How do we know that affirmations are the truth? Because no matter what details we include and what exact words we use, affirmations are positive acknowledgments of our sacred value as God's children. They are vital nourishment for the soul mind, and an immediate, magical, and miraculous way to smile at the God inside us and feel Him smile back.

LETTERS TO THE UNIVERSE

An effective way to reinforce your affirmations, and your deepest wishes, is to write them down, in the form of Letters to the Universe. Address them to God, to the universe, to your Spirit Guide, to your Angels—whoever makes you feel most intimately connected to your own divine power. Include plenty of affirmations in your letters to remind yourself how worthy you are to receive the greatest blessings life has to offer. There's no need to remind God, who already knows how worthy you are, He's just waiting for *you* to figure it out. Then write down, very specifically, everything you really want (whoever said, "Be careful what you want, because you just might get it!" knew what they were talking about). Make sure your letters include physical, emotional, and spiritual wishes, since the most rewarding life is a balance of all three. Make a commitment as you write them that you'll invest your fair share of effort toward going after those wishes. God does help those who help themselves, and none of us get to just lie around on the couch and have everything we want brought to us on a tray. Once you've finished, put a copy of the letter in a safe, out-of-the-way place, and burn the original. No, not so that the ashes can float upward for God to read, but to enhance the energy of your Letter to the Universe with the powerful energy of fire. As for the copy, keep it hidden away for six months and then reread it. At the very least, you'll find a few surprises, including the probability that your next letter will contain several changes. But you might also find that in those past several months, you and God's perfect universe have teamed up to create some magic and miracles.

The energy of fire, by the way, is one of the reasons I love candles. I recommend that you keep plenty of them around and use them often, especially during affirmations and Letters to the Universe. There's not a candle in the world that has any power of its own. But the ritual of lighting candles has power in its agelessness, and the energy of lit candles will help you focus your power and energy as well. And there's an added bonus you might not be aware of—the spirit world can't see artificial lights, but they *can* see lit candles and are attracted to them like, if you'll pardon the expression, a moth to a flame.

One of my favorite candle rituals, and one of the most powerful, is to sit on the floor in the middle of a circle or cross of candles—one at my feet, one behind me, one to my right, and one to my left—and go into a completely relaxed or meditative state. I picture the white light of the Holy Spirit igniting my solar plexus (the core of the stomach, just below the breastbone) and glowing through me to the Circle of Light around me, letting the Holy Spirit burn through my body to cleanse and heal and destroy any negativity and doubt in the path of its divine white fire. Make a habit of this simple Circle of Light exercise, maybe at the start of every new week, and I promise that, with practice, you'll actually feel a power surge from it that will leave you renewed, energized, and sometimes quite literally healed.

CREATING MIRACLES

We all really do have the power to heal.

A few words of caution first. Please don't ever believe that illness or death is in any way a punishment from God, or that if you're unable to heal yourself or a loved one, you've somehow failed. God doesn't punish, ever. Illness and death are included in life's blueprint. As you'll discover in the further discussions of blueprints, not only can we choose whether or not to modify the illness and death we charted as we go along, but we also have our choice of five "exit points," or times to leave this earth. There is a higher purpose to the decisions we make when writing our blueprints, and when acting on them, that we may not understand now, but we understood once and we'll understand again when we're back Home on The Other Side.

A combination of three elements can make a miracle—prayer, belief, and affirmation—together with the will of the intended recipient of that miracle. Here's a case in point:

I was forty-three when I arrived at my third exit point following major surgery. I refer to it as a "near-death" experience, but physiologically I did die—my heart stopped, my body temperature started plunging, and I completely flat-lined. Yet prayers were being said all around me, and I've never been short on belief, nor have any of the people who were praying for me. I distinctly remember being in a tunnel, headed straight for God's beautiful white light and frankly delighted to be going there, when the voice of a woman beside my hospital bed filled my spirit: "Sylvia, please, you can't leave, you're so needed."

An affirmation. As much as I wanted to keep right on going toward that light of Perfect Love, I knew that voice was right. I had too much left to do, and the higher good wouldn't be served if I took the opportunity to bail out. The instant I made that decision, even though I wasn't thrilled about it, I came back. My physician, Dr. Jonathan Kelly, confirmed later that my physiological response to "you're so needed" was immediate. My heart started again, the monitors began blipping again, and my body temperature rose slowly but surely back up to normal.

Prayer, belief, and affirmation. There's no doubt about it, it was a miracle. I sulked about it for weeks, but it was definitely a miracle—and an utterly personal decision between God and me, triggered by my willingness to really hear and respond to that voice reminding me that I wasn't through here yet.

You might have seen a *Montel Williams* segment a few years ago in which a woman who'd been declared terminally ill by two of her doctors asked me how much longer she had to live. I still remember looking into her eyes and *knowing* what I said to her was true: "You're not dying." I never pull punches or just tell someone what they want to hear to make them feel better for a minute or two, and it was obvious from her look back at me that in that moment she believed me. She let my energy force overtake hers long enough for that affirmation to penetrate and engulf her spirit. She still writes to me now, healed and healthy.

Prayer, belief, and affirmation. Another miracle. Not a miracle I created, but a decision she, open to God, made that she wasn't finished here yet.

The opposite works just as reliably, believe me. I've worked with more than one client who had an illness I knew didn't have to be terminal, and told them so, but they weren't about to let me talk them out of dying. There's not an affirmation in the world that can stop a major illness or death in someone who's already made a decision with God and refuses for their own reasons to change their mind.

Invest your energy in the prayer, belief, and affirmation that can create miracles for your loved ones. Just remember that, again, there's no such thing as failing. You have the power to intervene—as the woman at my hospital bedside did with me, and as I did in that example from Montel's show—but your loved one and God have their own agenda, too. Either way, there's no such thing as wasted prayers, belief, and affirmations. What more powerful send-off could we give someone, or hope for ourselves? We welcome the birth of a "new" spirit with a celebration of blessings and good wishes. Why not offer the same celebration when that spirit goes Home again?

DÉJÀ VU

Yet what about more ordinary miracles? Once we've stopped cluttering our minds with guilt and determinism and replaced them with self-love and the power of affirmations and belief, our eyes and hearts will be more open than ever to the magic in the world all around us. Like "daily unicorns" and "weekly Red Sea partings," unexplained phenomena are so common we lose sight of how special they are, or perhaps we've never understood what they were in the first place. Déjà vu, for example, is an experience most of us have from time to time. If we think of déjà vu as nothing more than a pleasant momentary diversion, it doesn't seem all that magical. But if we recognize it for what it actually is—a glimpse into The Other Side—it takes on a whole new significance.

There are two kinds of déjà vu. The first occurs when you visit a certain house, city, road, foreign country, or some other specific location you've never been before and suddenly realize it seems familiar. Sometimes you find you even know your way around. It happened to me most dramatically on my first trip to Kenya in 1980. I was actually telling my guide where the geographical highlights were before he could tell me, and I knew it had nothing to do with my being psychic. What it was, and what all of us experience when we feel familiarity with an unfamiliar place, is our spirits' memory of a past life. We *have* been there before; it was just in another body, in another time. The spirit memory is usually deeply buried in the subconscious, so those moments when it emerges into our conscious minds are not just magical, they are powerful, miraculous glimpses into the eternity of our souls.

That same kind of déjà vu applies to people as well. We all know people who seem familiar to us the moment we meet them, strangers we feel we have known all our lives. To be honest, we probably haven't really known them all our lives—only a few of our lives. But I'll bet if you take a long look at each person who has somehow touched your life and ask yourself the simple question, "Have I known this person before?" you will be surprised at how easily you can answer yes or no. Don't assume, by the way, that a past-life connection with someone should obligate you to a connection this time around. They may have been the bane of your previous existence. Or they may have been nice enough last time, but they've chosen to come back this time as a complete jerk. You don't have to act on past-life familiarity at all, just notice it when it happens and recognize it as another window into your eternity.

Some past-life connections even slip into our lives through a side entrance when we least expect or even want them. Margaret, a client, arrived in my office terribly upset late one rainy afternoon, unable to shake the feeling that her mean, overbearing, and recently deceased mother-in-law was still hovering around, trying to nag her from beyond the grave. As it happened, the mother-in-law was very much with her, not trying to nag but trying to apologize for all the trouble and pain she had caused Margaret over the years. Not until the mother-in-law reached The Other Side did she realize, and communicate to Margaret through me, that the two of them had been sisters in a previous life and had never resolved the constant, competitive jealousy they had felt toward each other during that lifetime. Between the apology and the understanding of that past-life relationship, Margaret was finally able to forgive and find peace of mind about her mother-in-law once and for all.

The second kind of déjà vu is so common, subtle, and seemingly trivial that we rarely give it more than a passing thought. It consists of a moment in which every detail, from what you are doing to whom you are doing it with to your surroundings to what you are wearing and thinking and feeling, is so familiar that you are absolutely sure you are reliving an exact duplicate of a moment from your past. It never lasts more than a few seconds, and it is never a significant event. It is more like "Once before I was sitting right here, watching TV just like this, reaching for a glass of water that was at this same place on the nightstand . . ." Invariably it is gone again by the time we've noticed it. Not surprisingly, then, we fail to realize how amazing those déjà vu moments really are. To understand them clearly, we need to understand more about blueprints.

As we have discussed, before our spirit enters the womb for another lifetime, we compose a chart or blueprint, with God's help, for the life we are about to live. That blueprint contains all the broad strokes of this new life, although we can modify our charts throughout our lives. If your chart reads that at age thirty-two you'll be involved in a car accident, for example, you can modify it to be a fender bender as opposed to a fatal collision. If at age fifteen your chart clearly states "illness," you have the power to control whether that illness is a cold or pneumonia. Or let's say your chart says you'll be a "healer," and that's where your passion lies, but you hated medical school and flunked out. That doesn't mean you've failed at pursuing your passion. There are all kinds of "healers" in this world, from social workers to grief counselors to masseurs to priests and ministers and rabbis to firefighters and other emergency personnel to just good friends and family members who are compassionate listeners with a talent for healing difficult emotional situations. There is plenty of room for lateral movement in our blueprints, so please don't picture your charted life as a narrow path with very few choices along the way. Instead it is a road as wide and as full of possibilities as you, with God's help, can dream it to be.

We also write into our chart a few signposts to let us know we're on the right track according to our blueprint. From time to time those little signposts appear to us in the form of déjà vu. Because they hit us with such a sudden flood of total familiarity, we logically assume we must somehow be duplicating a moment we've lived before in this life. We're not. What we're experiencing is a tiny signpost from the blueprint we created on The Other Side before we were born. In this type of déjà vu, our spirit is resonating so profoundly with the realization "I remember the chart I wrote" that it echoes from our subconscious, where the spirit mind exists, to our conscious mind. For that instant both our subconscious and conscious minds are receiving an affirmation that we're in perfect synch with our blueprint. Even more than that, we're getting a quick glimpse at the eternity of our lives on The Other Side, as our spirit remembers, acknowledges, and yearns for Home. Déjà vu, in other words, isn't just magical; it can be a momentary state of bliss.

COINCIDENCE

Those same magical, miraculous, blissful glimpses at the signposts in our charts appear in another very common form as well, with the added bonus that we don't just remember them, we see them coming. Because we don't understand their significance, we rarely give them much thought—after all, they're "only a coincidence."

You've been thinking about someone for no apparent reason, and suddenly you run into them for the first time in a long time. You hear about a book or a movie, and suddenly it seems to be all anyone around you is talking about. You're planning a trip to England, and suddenly you're almost tripping over news about England, casual mentions of England, people who've just returned from England, and store clerks and bank tellers and telephone operators with British accents. I saw a fabulous dog I'd never seen or heard of before at the Westminster Dog Show, found out it was a breed called bichon frise, and decided I can't live without one, and suddenly I couldn't walk three blocks without meeting two or three bichon frises out for walks with their owners.

At any rate, you've experienced enough coincidences to know how they go. The point is, you have the thought, and sooner rather than later it becomes real before your very eyes. Or, to put it more accurately, you are foreseeing a little signpost in your blueprint shortly before that signpost appears—more cause for celebration that you are following the path you charted for this life, and yet another tangible link between you and the divine eternity God's given all of us.

SYNCHRONICITY

There's also a fascinating close relative of coincidence called synchronicity, a word popularized by the brilliant Swiss psychiatrist Carl Jung. Jung was in his office with a patient one day discussing Egypt when a beetle known as an Egyptian scarab walked across his desk. "Coincidence" was too much of an understatement for the appearance of an Egyptian beetle thousands of miles from where it belonged at the exact moment Jung was talking about Egypt. It was a clear sign to him of the truth that the universe God created isn't random and chaotic, but ordered, and perfect, and patterned—or, in a word, synchronized, from which Jung coined "synchronicity." Basically, synchronicity is an especially meaningful coincidence. Like Jung's Egyptian scarab, it always involves some unmistakable physical sign of some kind, not only to call your attention to the magical harmony of the universe but also to give you tangible proof that you are *exactly* where you charted yourself to be, *exactly* when, *exactly* with whom. God, who co-wrote your blueprint with you, is giving you a visible "thumbs-up," a nod to say, "Yes, I am with you, and I am watching, and at this moment you are in perfect synch with your blueprint. Good work." True synchronicity isn't likely to happen as often in our lives as coincidences are. But watching for it, and recognizing it when it occurs, means not missing a private smile between you and God.

DREAMS

When the day ends, we sleep. In fact, we spend fully one-third of our lives sleeping, which is a brilliant part of God's plan, since sleep opens up a whole other world to nourish, inform and expand our souls. During sleep, obviously, our conscious minds take a break—and isn't it a relief to shut *them* up for a while?—and allow our subconscious minds, where our spirit minds live, to take over. Of course, one of the primary ways the subconscious expresses itself is in dreams.

There are hundreds of theories on dream interpretation, and thousands of studies have been done, but no one has yet solved even a fraction of the mysteries hidden in dreams. I've read, studied, researched, and taught dream interpretation. For the most part, I believe that the Gestalt theory (Gestalt is an approach to psychology developed in Germany) comes closest to the truth. According to this theory, all the elements of your dreams are parts of you, separated into symbolic pieces for you to examine and work on.

Dreams fall into three categories: release, wish and precognition.

Release dreams are your subconscious mind letting go of all the emotions your conscious mind has not dealt with and expressed. When you have a dream that seems to be about one very strong emotion in particular—anger, grief, passion, fear, confusion, embarrassment, etc.—it is almost certainly a signal from your subconscious that it is time to confront and resolve that emotion during your waking hours. Release dreams are a great safety valve, and they can also be a helpful guide to some important unfinished emotional business that needs attention.

Wish dreams are exactly what they sound like—sometimes, as the lovely song says, a dream really is a wish your heart makes when you are fast asleep. Years ago an unhappily married client told me about a dream in which she'd been alone with Robert Redford. They were in a beautifully appointed drawing room, he in a tux, she in a flowing ballgown, both in the style of *The Great Gatsby*, and they were waltzing. She was still a little breathless just telling me about it, and I'm sure she was harboring some tiny glimmer of hope that I was going to confirm that what do you know, it really did mean that she and Robert Redford were destined to be together. No such luck. Its real meaning came out when I asked her how she'd felt in that dream while waltzing with him. She answered, "Pretty. Graceful. Loved. Wanted. Safe." All the feelings her soul was wishing to feel that her marriage couldn't offer. If we don't make the mistake of taking wish dreams too literally, they can throw a valuable spotlight on wishes you may not have even put into words for yourself yet. Sexual dreams, for example, aren't necessarily about sexual desire at all, or about some deeply buried attraction to the partner in your dream. They're usually a wish for more intimacy in your life, which doesn't have to be physical at all. A dream about a new house doesn't mean you should leap up the next morning and put your house on the market. It can mean there's something about yourself (*you* are where you live, after all, regardless of what house you're in) that you're longing to change. A dream about giving birth definitely isn't a cue to get pregnant. That "new life" you're giving birth to could be yours, some good idea you are about to bring to fruition, or some new spiritual depth in yourself you are starting to unearth. In other words, always look at the overview rather than the specifics of wish dreams. You'll be surprised how much you can learn about yourself and what you're *really* wishing for.

The third type, "precognition dreams," simply means dreams that predict some future moment, conversation, or event. I've lost count of the number of clients who have said, "I can't predict the future in my dreams—I'm not psychic." But you don't have to be consciously psychic for the spirit mind in your subconscious to reveal its amazing power and its ever-present awareness of your past—including your past lives, your present, and your future. Don't forget, your spirit mind doesn't just know your life's blueprint, it *created* that blueprint. So never underestimate what you're capable of while you are sleeping. In fact, before you dismiss precognitive dreams as something you cannot do, try this, just for one month: Every time you have and remember a dream you think might have been a prediction of some kind, write it down, put it away, and don't look at it until that month has passed. If you make a habit of it, and if you are patient, you have some magical surprises in store.

ASTRAL TRAVEL

Have you ever had a dream about a departed loved one that seemed to be very real, very much in the present, and, unlike most dreams, proceeded in a logical order from beginning to end? There's a very good chance that it wasn't a dream at all. It was your spirit making an actual visit to that loved one via astral travel.

Astral travel occurs when the spirit leaves the body during sleep or very deep meditation and takes excursions on its own. You can actually ask God before you go to sleep to help you travel astrally. It's useful for any number of purposes, from visiting departed loved ones to dropping in on people and places you miss right here on earth, even to quick trips to The Other Side if you're practiced and focused enough. The people you visit here on earth may not see you, but it isn't unusual for them to hear you. I have many clients and friends who've been awakened out of a sound sleep by a loved one repeating their name over and over again. If that happens to you, call that loved one and ask about it. Chances are you'll find that at the time you were awakened, they were either meditating about you or asleep themselves and "dreaming" about you. But one way or the other, their spirit made contact with yours, all through the quiet magic of astral travel.

If you want to visit a departed loved one via astral travel, you might want to ask your Spirit Guide for their help. Remember, if you drop in on that loved one unexpectedly, they're likely to appear as they did (or would) at the age of thirty, since everyone is thirty years old when they're at Home on The Other Side. If you didn't know them when they were thirty, you might not recognize them. With a little warning from your Spirit Guide, your departed loved one can assume the form you are familiar with, as they do when they make the trip from The Other Side to visit you. Also, give your Spirit Guide a specific location where you want your loved one to meet you—on a park bench, beside a lake, in a cherished church or temple.

You might want the experience of meeting them on The Other Side. If that idea appeals to you, I strongly recommend you get together with them in a huge, breathtaking, classically domed building called the Hall of Records. Trust me, it actually exists. I've been there, I've seen it, and I've even had the good-news/bad-news experience of holding my blueprint in my own two hands. The good news is, this blueprint concept is not just a rumor or a pretty fantasy; like all the other writings in that massive building, my blueprint was recorded on a scroll in graceful gilt script. The bad news is, beyond that moment at which I was reading it, I couldn't read a word of it. I'm not sure if it's because I'm not allowed to be psychic about myself and would therefore be blocked from reading my own future, or if none of us is allowed to read our actual blueprints of what is to come. But whether you ask to meet a departed loved one in the Hall of Records or ask God to help you astral-travel there on your own for a tour, make one more request of Him before you fall asleep—ask for the added blessing of remembering it! As with dreams, we sometimes wake up from astral travel with no memory of it, or with just quick flashes of confusing images we promptly dismiss. It is such a magical experience that I promise you will not want to forget it.

It was an unexpected trip to the Hall of Records that inspired me to suggest keeping a tape recorder running while you sleep, especially after a prayer for astral travel or a reunion with someone in the spirit world. That particular trip actually occurred during a hypnosis session. I've been a licensed hypnotist for twenty-five years and have found it to be an invaluable tool not only for my research into past-life regressions but also for access into the subconscious mind where my clients might be holding and blocking information that could help them. Sleep and hypnosis are very closely related, of course, because the subconscious is so available during both; so the tape-recorder idea applies beautifully during both conditions.

I was doing a hypnosis session with a client I'll call Susan, letting her subconscious mind take her wherever it wanted. The more she talked, the more aware I was that her spirit was on a journey far, far away from the room we were sitting in. It is hard to describe how and why this particular session was so intense for me, since I've learned to maintain my objectivity during hypnosis. But I remember an odd sense that something significant was happening. I finally asked, "Where are you, Susan?"

She began to describe a vast domed building, with aisle after aisle after aisle as far as the eye could see, containing an infinite number of shelves lined with scrolls. As her description became more detailed, I recognized it as a place I had traveled to myself—she was walking through the Hall of Records on The Other Side.

And, to my shock, for the first time during a hypnosis session, I realized that I was walking with her in those stunning, endless aisles of scrolls.

I started to say something but immediately stopped myself—a question or comment of any kind about my being there would have amounted to leading her. It turned out I didn't need to say a word. "You're here with me," she said.

She talked and walked us through that amazing place beneath that magnificent dome until I spotted a beautiful dark-haired woman in blue gossamer, two aisles over, approaching us. I knew it was Susan's Spirit Guide, and I knew her name was Rachel. Still I kept my mouth shut. Again Susan spoke up. "Someone's with us."

I asked her who it was. I was straining to keep the excitement out of my voice by now. Like I said, I'd never accompanied a hypnosis subject on a journey before, let alone heard such immediate validation that our spirits really were on this trip together. She answered, "It's a woman. She has dark hair. I don't know why, but I think she's my Spirit Guide."

At that instant Rachel saw us and called out, "Susan . . . !" I bit my tongue, determined to let Susan keep taking the lead. Sure enough, she breathlessly said, "Did you hear that?"

I asked what she'd heard.

She replied, "She said my name."

What an exhilarating moment. Yet it was not quite as exhilarating as the discovery we made when we played back the audiotape of that session. At that crucial point my voice clearly said, "Who's with us?" Susan's voice clearly said, "It's a woman. She has dark hair. I don't know why, but I think she's my Spirit Guide."

And then a third voice, clear as a bell on the tape, said, "Susan . . . !"

That was the first time I'd heard a spirit voice imprinting itself on an audiotape. But it would not be the last.

BLEED-THROUGHS

I was conducting a trance session one night, in which my Spirit Guide, Francine, was speaking through me to a large group, telling the story of Christ's crucifixion at Golgotha in Jerusalem. There were fifty or so tape recorders running; but except for Francine, using my voice, the room was absolutely silent—the slightest noise can break my trance. Francine and I can't both inhabit my body at the same time, so I never have any awareness or memory of what she says. But from what I was told, and from hearing the tape later myself, it was a wrenching, emotional evening. Francine made the crucifixion of Christ so real and so intensely personal that everyone there felt as if they were there themselves, weeping at the foot of the cross.

My phone started ringing off the hook early the next morning. Six of the people who'd taped the session the night before, none of whom had talked to each other, were anxious for me to hear exactly what they were hearing on those tapes.

It was impossible to miss. On six of the fifty tapes made that night was the heartbreaking sound of people wailing, sobbing in grief and sorrow as the story of Christ's crucifixion progressed.

Francine told me later it was a phenomenon called a "bleed-through." The past and present are brought together in one place with such force that there is no difference between them. Not only were the people in that room transported to Golgotha two thousand years ago, but the throngs who mourned Christ at His crucifixion were among us that night, their agony unmistakably captured on tape for all of us to hear, despite the fact that at the time, except for Francine's narrative, no one heard a single sound.

Shortly after that unforgettable evening I was investigating a haunting at an odd old house in the North-east. As usual, my research team and I examined the entire house when we first arrived. I then settled into one of the rooms where most of the alleged paranormal activity had been reported—just me and my trusty tape recorder, alone behind a closed door for several hours of total silence.

When I played back the tape later, every few minutes I heard the relentless, piercing and frankly annoying barking of what sounded like a very large dog.

We asked the owners of the house, and the neighbors, and the local police about that barking dog, even though I hadn't heard it myself that night. They had no idea what we were talking about. There was no dog, barking or otherwise, within a mile of the room I'd spent those hours in, and the owners, who'd lived in the house for many years, assured me they'd never heard a dog bark anywhere near their home.

I often picture Francine watching me from The Other Side, drumming her fingers, wondering when I'm going to stop running around like an idiot asking everyone else what's going on and simply find out from her. But as anyone close to me will confirm, I always look for the logical, earthly explanation first. In some ways, I'm the most skeptical person you'll ever meet. Finally, with nowhere else to turn, I asked her about the dog on the tape.

"That was your white bull mastiff," she calmly informed me.

Aha! At long last Francine was wrong about something! I'm sure I sounded downright smug when I pointed out, "I don't *have* a white bull mastiff."

"Of course you don't. In this life. But you did in a past life, and it still goes with you sometimes to protect you."

Not for one moment do I doubt that we've lived many, many times. I'm as capable as the next person of forgetting it every once in a while, however.

I could go on and on about my personal experiences with spirit voices making use of the magnetic nature of audiotape to imprint themselves, which is why I can't encourage you enough to leave a tape recorder running while you sleep. That is the time when spirits are especially likely to pay a visit to the spirit mind of your subconscious and your spirit mind is especially likely to visit them.

You might have a more restful night if you set up your tape recorder in a room separate from the one you're sleeping in, so you won't be lying there listening for odd noises until sunrise; the physical location of your body is beside the point for this exercise. To increase the odds of something miraculous being captured on tape, ask God for exactly what you want, with your Spirit Guide's help. Whether you want to astral-travel to someplace or someone here or on The Other Side, or you want a departed loved one to visit and leave a trace of themselves for you to hear, ask God and be patient. If nothing happens the first night or the thirtieth night, that doesn't mean nothing ever will. This exercise used to be much more thorough in the good old days of reel-to-reel tape recorders, when eight-hour tapes were available. If you need to narrow your taping down to just a couple of hours instead, the most likely time for spirit activity is between 3:00 A.M. and sunrise, for reasons we'll explore in the "Hauntings" chapter. As for playing back the tapes, you obviously have too much to do to simply sit and listen to what could be hours of silence. I play mine when I'm driving, doing housework, reading and/or soaking in a hot bath. It is fascinating how, when your mind is "tuned" to expect silence on that tape, no matter how you occupy yourself with something else while it's playing back, you really will notice the slightest taped sound that doesn't seem to belong there.

Like the other suggestions in this chapter, the simple

process of hitting a button on your tape recorder helps to illustrate the real point. Being open and available to magic and miracles, creating as many opportunities as possible for them to occur, and then knowing in your heart what your spirit already knows—that magic and miracles are as real as we are if we'll just take the trouble to notice—really will make your days and your nights richer and ultimately transform your life.

DEVELOPING YOUR PSYCHIC ABILITY

All of these exercises can be enhanced by some regular practice at developing your psychic ability, which is less mysterious and out of reach than you might think. Not everyone can be a psychic, but everyone has psychic instincts. It's the difference between being a concert pianist and simply being able to play the piano. Just because you may not end up giving recitals at Carnegie Hall doesn't mean you can't thoroughly enjoy the ability.

I've been asked a thousand times why I don't teach a course in how to be more psychic. The answer is, it would be the world's shortest course. But if you are interested in taking it, it goes like this:

1. Ask a question, silently or out loud.
2. Say, from your heart, in your own words, to your own Higher Power, any version you like of: "Hit it, God!" That's your cue to step aside to receive a far greater Wisdom than yours.
3. Be willing to accept the first response you get.

Using the piano analogy, that is the "Chopsticks" of developing your psychic intuition. Even after forty-seven years of readings, I admit I'm still amazed at how hard Step 3 can be, so don't be discouraged if you find yourself having trouble with it, too.

I once gave a reading for a perfectly lovely, well-groomed woman I guessed was a corporate executive, or maybe the manager of an upscale boutique. She wanted to discuss her career and asked what I saw. Imagine how hard it was for me to accept, let alone repeat out loud, the first response I was given: "You have a worm farm." My life revolves around my credibility, and I was supposed to look this woman in the eye and say, "You have a worm farm"? But who am I to second-guess God, so that's exactly what I told her. To my surprise, she casually replied, "Yes, I do," as if she assumed I have dozens of worm farmers in my clientele—and on we went to talk about her upcoming career change.

Mastering Step 2 is obviously the key to being confident about Step 3. But once you've practiced making sure that the information you're getting is coming from God, not from you, it's really none of your business to try to make sense of it. Just take a breath, summon your courage, and say it.

Once you've said it, stand by it as you continue to practice. "Fishing" is strictly forbidden for this exercise. Fishing is nothing but desperate guess work that has nothing to do with God whatsoever. I have had the embarrassing experience of seeing psychics fishing themselves into a frenzy, trying to turn a wrong answer into a right one. Suddenly the worm farm becomes "or maybe a snake farm, or an alligator farm, or maybe it's just a regular farm, but you have a problem with worms." Or, to really cover themselves, "Maybe you owned a worm farm in a past life." No! If you got "a worm farm," say "a worm farm" and commit to it!

You can practice these three steps by yourself or with friends, whether you have a spare two minutes or a spare two hours. Just make sure to ask questions you couldn't possibly know the answers to, and record and date your answers on paper or on tape so you can start to track and calculate your accuracy. To give you a yardstick on your percentages, remember, there is no such thing as a psychic with a hundred percent accuracy. A seventy-percent accuracy rate is above average for most legitimate professional psychics. Mine is significantly higher, for which I again thank God. So again, just as you can enjoy playing the piano without devoting your life to it, you can have a wonderful time discovering and developing your own power and, in the process, open your mind to all its enormous God-given potential.

SYNERGISM

When your power joins forces with the power of others for the highest good, you can create a phenomenon called synergism, which with God's blessing is one of the greatest sources of magic and miracles on earth. *Webster's Dictionary* defines *synergism* as "the simultaneous action of separate agencies which, together, have greater total effect than the sum of their individual effects." How they managed to make something so exciting sound so dull I'm not quite sure. But if you replace the word *agencies* with *people*, and the word *effects* with *power*, the definition fits our purposes much better. Synergism, or synergy, is the simultaneous action of separate people which, together, have a greater total effect than the sum of their individual power.

Let's say 100 of us have gathered in a room for some common purpose, and on a scale of 1–10 each of us has a belief in that purpose of 10. Simple math would indicate that the "total belief" in that room equals 1,000. But thanks to the force of synergy—the power of all that combined belief—the total is actually 100,000 or 1,000,000 instead. Synergy feeds upon itself, with results that can be nothing short of awesome.

It was through synergy that I started my church, *Novus Spiritus*, which continues to grow because we never lose sight that our ultimate purpose is for the highest good. Our common purpose is far more important than any one of us, including me. It's not a membership of thousands facing me but a membership of thousands *and* me all facing God. Together our power far exceeds the sum of our individual power added together. *Novus Spiritus* has grown from 50 to more than 5,000 while always following one strict rule: We never attempt to recruit or convert anyone. We're quietly, tirelessly powerful, helping everyone from the homeless to the homebound, making far more of a difference as a whole than 5,000 plus people possibly could, all due to synergy, fueled by God's active presence among us. And the magic and miracles we've been able to create have exceeded all of our prayers.

Of course, the beliefs of *Novus Spiritus* are a combination of the power of other synergisms from a very long time ago, including a most notable one in which Christ and twelve disciples—thirteen men—formed a synergy that will last an eternity.

Then there are prayer chains, to be discussed at length in the "To Your Health" chapter but which have to be acknowledged in a conversation about synergy. While writing this chapter I received a letter from a man named Ken, who had a terminal heart disease. His only hope, he was told, was a transplant, but he was far, far down the list of potential recipients. Through my office, he asked to be included in our prayer chain. He wrote me days later to announce that, to his doctors' absolute amazement, he no longer needs a transplant. His heart is healthy again. That's a perfect example of synergy in action, making a miracle no one of us could have made happen on our own.

Please don't get the idea that synergism counts only if it has a specifically religious purpose. The highest good has any number of forms of expression—from John Walsh, who has created a nationwide synergy called *America's Most Wanted*, to the founders of charities, and victims', children's, and animal rights organizations, to such groups as Alcoholics and Narcotics Anonymous and Al-Anon. All of these are far greater than the sum of their parts, and all of them make miracles happen every day.

Remember the "coincidence" example about planning a trip to England and suddenly finding yourself surrounded by references to and reminders of England and everything British no matter where you turn?

The same thing is true of magic and miracles. The more you think about them, talk about them, and participate in making them happen, the more you'll find they happen to you.

I wish nothing less for you, and I hope this chapter helps bring them your way, while God lovingly guides you toward them.

* 3 *

Your Personal Life: A Spiritual Psychic's View of Relationships and Families

No subject comes up more often in my readings, lectures, salons, and TV appearances than relationships—with family members, with lovers, with spouses, with friends. Nothing affects us more deeply, confuses us more, frustrates us more, brings us more joy or shatters us more completely than our connections to the people we share our lifetimes with. Just when we get irritated enough to kid ourselves into thinking that relationships are more trouble than they are worth, we go to a funeral and realize that how we loved is really all anyone talks about when we are gone.

Frankly, relationships are also the most glaring proof I have that I'm not even a little psychic about myself. I haven't exactly been turning cartwheels at the thought of writing this chapter, because I know I have to own up to a lot of mistakes in the way I've handled my personal life as a woman, a daughter, and a parent. At least I can offer insights about relationships as both a deeply spiritual psychic and someone who's had her share of what we'll politely call "good learning experiences." There is virtually no relationship blunder a client can confide in me that I haven't made some version of myself.

I should make it clear right up front that I absolutely believe in and try my best to live by the Golden Rule of doing unto others as we would have them do unto us. All relationship problems would be solved forever if everyone just followed that one simple, perfect piece of wisdom, as we do on The Other Side. If life on earth were that simple and perfect, though, none of us would bother to leave The Other Side and come here in the first place. We all have blueprints to follow and mistakes to make and knowledge to gain, and the toughest part is leaving the people in our lives better for having known us, without sacrificing ourselves in the process.

I just want to make one deal with you before we get started, to make sure you get the most out of this chapter: I'll tell the truth if you will. It's tempting to blame other people for relationship problems, and let's face it, sometimes they deserve it. Then again, sometimes they don't. We're the authors of our own blueprints, after all, and the only ones in charge of our own behavior. So the more responsibility we are willing to take, the better our chances of making our relationships work.

SOUL MATES AND KINDRED SPIRITS

If you've seen me in lectures or on *Montel*, you might already know that this "soul mate" thing is a subject that really gets on my nerves. In fact, I'd like to track down and kick right in the shins the person who started the rumor that one of our main purposes in life is to find our soul mate.

It's not.

The odds against it are astronomical.

And even if they weren't, the soul mate we find in the course of this lifetime wouldn't necessarily be a lover or spouse at all. The closest thing I have to a soul mate on this earth is my granddaughter Angelia.

Many people look so disillusioned when I announce that the soul mate search is a myth, like I'm taking their favorite fairy tale away. I'm not, believe me. Giving up the idea that there is a soul mate for us somewhere and it's our job to find them can be downright liberating. Few things bring tears to my eyes more quickly than clients who stay in abusive relationships because they have confused the constant emotional intensity with their concept of what having a soul mate must be like. Even clients with perfectly nice marriages sadly tell me that their greatest failure was in never having found their soul mate. The term *soul mate* gets mistaken for everything from infatuation to lust to an excuse for stalking, obsession, and domestic violence.

Maybe it will help if we get straight what a true soul mate is.

We are created with spirits that have both male and female aspects. We live lifetimes as both genders, as a matter of fact. I have never met anyone who's always been male or always been female every time around.

We are also created with an "identical twin" spirit whose male and female aspects are essentially mirror images of our own. That twin spirit is our soul mate. Our soul mate is not the other half of us, any more than we are the other half of our soul mate. I don't consider myself half a person. Do you, really? I certainly don't think there's anything romantic about thinking we are all a bunch of halves walking around. If I'm not half a person, and you're not half a person, why on earth would any of us spend one minute, let alone a lifetime, looking for "another half" that doesn't exist and that none of us *whole people* would have any use for anyway?

On The Other Side we're probably closer to our soul mates than we are to any other spirit, but we're hardly joined at the hip. We and our soul mates happily pursue separate friendships, separate interests, separate work and studies, and above all, our own separate identities. With our soul mates we enjoy the most intimate love there is—free, unconditional, liberated and liberating, with a mutual knowledge only true identical twin spirits can share.

Like all spirits on The Other Side, each of the soul mates can choose to be born on earth for another lifetime. They might only come here once or twice, like my Spirit Guide, Francine. They might feel the need to come again and again—I'm on my fifty-fourth time around, and my last, I'm delighted to announce. But compared to eternity, even fifty-four lifetimes amount to about a minute and a half.

Which brings up an obvious question: What are the chances that you and your soul mate are ever going to show up on earth at the same time? Why would you feel the need to, since you are always together on The Other Side anyway, and this experience we call "life" is really nothing more than just a quick trip away from Home?

Not to mention the odds against the two of you being on earth in the same general age range, enough geographical proximity for you to run into each other somewhere along the way, and the right gender for the two of you to become a couple, which seems to be the top priority of the whole soul mate myth?

So please, give yourselves (and me) a break and stop looking for a soul mate who in all probability is having a great time on The Other Side right now, waiting for you to come Home. Don't set yourself up for all that pressure and disappointment. Don't cling to a bad relationship in the misguided belief that your soul mate and you belong together, even if you're miserable. Don't devalue a perfectly good relationship because you're missing that "soul mate feeling." Don't believe for one second that there's only one person on this whole planet you're "destined" to be with—what a depressing thought *that* is! And I definitely don't want you to reach the later years of your life thinking you failed because you never found someone who wasn't even here but whom you'll be having a wonderful, effortless reunion with if you'll just be patient for a few more "minutes" until you're Home again.

What you *will* find as you move through this lifetime are any number of *kindred souls*—spirits you have known in one or more past lives. I'm sure you have experienced the instant feeling of familiarity, either good or bad, that happens on meeting a kindred soul. Sometimes that instant familiarity is the springboard for yet another earthly experience together, as friends, as lovers and spouses, or family members.

But sometimes it should make you run as fast and as far away as your legs will carry you. I have a client who married a man she was sure she'd known in a past life. She was right—in a past life he was the man who sentenced her to death during the Salem witch trials. In this current life she's still trying to convince him she's a good person, which she is, and he's still assuring her that no, she's not, and he finds a way to disapprove of every single thing she does.

That brings up the subject of karma, another pet peeve of mine because it gets misinterpreted and ends up making people go through a lot of misery since it is, after all, "their karma." In the example I just mentioned, there are those who would say that it is my client's karma to keep at it lifetime after lifetime until she is finally "acquitted" by her former executioner. And I say, that's ridiculous. Why should she waste several lifetimes being miserable, all for the sake of getting this one person to eventually declare her acceptable? That's not how it works!

All karma means is "a balance of experience." When you write your blueprint on The Other Side, you know what you have worked on and learned in past lives, so your new blueprint will be composed according to what you decide you still need to experience. It is not inflicted on you. You choose it, based on your own goals for the lifetime you are about to tackle.

So while some would claim my client's karma is to win this man's approval, I can make just as good an argument that her karma is to learn to look him right in the eye and say, "Who cares what you think?"

I believe that any concept that gets too complicated and convoluted to spiritually nourish and inspire us and make our lives richer has outlived its usefulness. If you want a simple, genuinely productive way to use the word karma, here's one that I wholeheartedly recommend. I came to the grocery store checkout line with three items. The woman in line in front of me had a full cart. She noticed my paltry little armload and was sweet enough to invite me to go ahead of her. I assured her I was in no hurry, and after all, she was there first.

To which she replied, "Please go ahead of me. I need the karma."

Fair enough. I thanked her and took her up on it.

Now, *that's* a healthy approach to this whole idea of karma, and one we can all actually make use of. I can't tell you how much I appreciated that, not because it saved me some time in the grocery store, but because she'd found such a simple, practical, humanitarian purpose for a word so frequently misunderstood that it sometimes does more harm than good.

So when it comes to relationships, don't get too bogged down by the karma issue, or by the soul mate issue. I know how romantic it can seem at first glance to reunite with someone you knew in another place, time, and life. But remember the "Salem witch" client who stays in a miserable marriage. Go further than that. Really think how many people you know in this life—not just the people you're close to, but acquaintances as well. Multiply that by the number of lifetimes you've had here. If you aren't sure, feel free to use mine—fifty-four. Add the spirits you know on The Other Side whom you've never happened to run into here on earth (probably thousands, to be conservative about it). Before long you'll realize that it is not especially amazing to run into familiar spirits during this lifetime. It would be much more amazing if you didn't.

I'm very close to several people whom I have known through several lifetimes. I'm also close to some I've never known before. So when that feeling of familiarity comes over you, it's fine to acknowledge it to yourself. Keeping your psychic instincts alert is always a good idea. But don't base your entire "you're in"/"you're out" decision on a feeling of shared past lives. Some people from past lives cross your path precisely to see if you have learned to stay away from them yet. Besides, no matter how many people you have already known, I promise there are new ones out there who are fascinating and worthwhile despite the lack of a shared past.

There's an exercise in the "Life After Life" chapter that will help you discover and explore your own past lives. Basically, it starts with remembering some vivid day or detail from five years ago, then ten, then slowly moving right on back through time past your birth in this life to the life that preceded this one, and the life before that, and the life before that, if you like. Here's another fascinating approach to that exercise: Before you begin, declare to yourself and to God and your Spirit Guide that the purpose of this particular exploration is to search your past lives for a specific person who inspires that feeling of familiarity. Keep going back and back and back and see if you can find them. They may look nothing like they look now. They may be a different race, a different gender, a different nationality, a whole different relationship to you—it won't matter. Your spirit will recognize theirs immediately.

If you don't find them, that's okay, it doesn't mean

you're wrong about having known them before. It just means you didn't connect this time. If you do find them, stay long enough to see what's going on between the two of you. Who are you to each other—friends, lovers, spouses, parent and child, siblings, enemies? How do you feel in their presence—safe, loved, frightened, threatened, angry, stimulated, happy, sad, weak? Are they someone you look forward to seeing again, or can't wait to get away from? Should you be paying attention to any dynamics in that past-life relationship, good or bad, that resemble the relationship you have with them now?

Recognizing relationship patterns—in this lifetime and over a series of lifetimes—is one of the most difficult, enlightening and liberating tasks we can set for ourselves. It takes a lot of self-honesty and objectivity, and frankly, it can be painful, and embarrassing. But there's a great payoff. Once we figure out that relationships aren't random luck-of-the-draw events that happen to us but that they're the result of our own patterns, we can reclaim our power and sense of control, remind ourselves that we really are the authors of our own blueprints, and finally take the first steps toward breaking those patterns that aren't serving us well.

Here are two sayings about patterns that I really love. One is, "It's a sign of insanity to repeat the same behavior over and over again and expect different results." The other is simpler but equally true. "When you do what you did, you get what you got."

Now, seriously, doesn't that make a whole lot more sense than "I'm staying in an unhappy relationship because it is my karma"?

We've all known (and usually envied) a handful of people whose patterns lead them to happiness, success, peace of mind, and great relationships. The easy thing to say is that they're just luckier than we are. But what's more accurate is to say that they have accepted the connection between what you do and what you get and taken full responsibility for whatever improvements need to be made. For them, "When you do what you did, you get what you got" is good news, because they've insisted on it and refused to settle for anything less.

If you don't happen to be one of those people who loves the way their relationships are going—and I'm talking about friendships as well as lovers and spouses—it's time to take a long, hard look at the people around you, and an even harder look at yourself. Because no matter how much we hate to admit it, no one is in our lives that we haven't chosen to let in.

Do you surround yourself with people who:

- make you feel better about yourself, or worse about yourself?
- tend to be stronger than you, or weaker than you?
- are in better, or worse, financial shape than you?
- are more educated than you, or less?
- are more likely to dominate you, or to let you dominate them?
- have had more success with relationships, or less?
- have a better employment track record than you, or a worse one?
- have more real friends than you, or fewer?
- place a higher value or a lower value than you on honesty, integrity, and commitment?
- are closer to their family members, or more estranged than you are?
- are more active than you, or less, in exploring their spirituality?

The honest answers to those questions and others like them can help you recognize any patterns you may be repeating, within this lifetime or a series of lifetimes. Taking responsibility for them ("I can't help it" is the exact opposite of taking responsibility, by the way) is the first giant step toward getting rid of those patterns once and for all and starting to replace them with healthy ones.

From my readings for thousands of clients and my own past mistakes, I've come to realize that most of us are more thorough, thoughtful, and cautious about shopping for a car than we are about who we allow into our lives. In a million years we wouldn't just point at a car we like the looks of and say, "I'll take it!" without little details like cost, mileage, or, for that matter, whether or not it even runs. But we've all seen and/or had relationships in which we essentially did exactly that—bought it on impulse and then spent an emotional fortune trying to repair something that will never be worth as much as we've put into it.

That is why I'm a big believer in The Interview. Especially when you're thinking about getting intimately emotionally involved, but before you've fallen into the "temporary insanity" of infatuation (usually about a three-month siege), while you still have your wits about you.

The Interview is simply the process of asking enough direct questions to find out the *character* of this person you're inviting into your life. The questions a couple of paragraphs ago will give you a good start, and you can add your own on top of those depending on your priorities. Pay close attention to the answers, and then pay even closer attention to whether or not the answers match the person's behavior. When there's any difference between what they say and how they behave, ignore the words and *believe the behavior*!

I know how obvious that sounds. I also know how easy it is to ignore and/or make excuses for the inconsistencies thanks to hormones, a natural impulse to trust, and an eagerness to love and be loved. But someone who claims to have a $100,000-a-year job wouldn't have to borrow money from you, or even find some casual way to ask how much money you have when you're just getting to know each other. Someone who claims to believe in the importance of honesty wouldn't lie to you or be evasive. Someone who claims to believe in commitment wouldn't cheat. Someone who claims to have a shred of interest in spirituality would never mistreat a child or an animal, both of whom are God's true perfect innocents.

And someone who claims to love you would never deliberately demean, abuse, or try to control you.

Take it from me.

DOMESTIC ABUSE

This may not seem like a relevant section in a book about how The Other Side affects this life and how this life affects the eternal lives of our spirits. Yet I have good reason to believe that many of the spiritual and psychic concepts, techniques, and exercises in this book can help someone who is on the devastating receiving end of an abusive relationship.

That's because I was in a physically and emotionally abusive relationship myself in the early years of my adulthood. Psychologists could have a great time piecing together how I got myself into it—abusive mother, father I adored whose approval offered me the only security I knew as a child. Plus there was a pattern of my own I've struggled to overcome, of confusing love with gratitude toward someone who was offering to save me from a bad situation.

Belaboring how I got into an abusive relationship isn't nearly as valuable as sharing how I got out of it and what I've learned about domestic abuse as both a spiritual psychic and a survivor. (You'll never hear me refer to myself as a "victim" of anything.) If even one of these points helps one person who feels trapped in an abusive relationship move one step closer to the door, a lot of my prayers for this book will be answered.

And in case this needs to be said out loud, I'm talking to everyone who's on the receiving end of abuse. Males and females. Abuse is an outrage no matter which gender is dishing it out and which gender is being expected to take it.

To provide a frame of reference, the domestic violence in my life happened decades before the legal system considered it any of their business. I was a schoolteacher then, with two little sons. There were no hotlines, no battered women's shelters, and dialing 911 meant nothing more than you'd misdialed 411 for information. That's not to say "poor me." That's just to tell you that I do know exactly how hard it is to escape an abusive situation—and I'm sure escaping mine was the most important thing I have ever done in my life. One night after yet another violent outburst, this man stormed out of the house. The instant he left, I bundled up my children and nothing else, and we never went back. My sons and I ended up in a rundown tenement in a housing project for a while. They still remember it as a fun, happy place to live, because the three of us were safe and free and together.

Several spiritual insights and tools helped me summon the emotional strength and courage to get away from abuse, and stay away. First of all, this book has a later discussion on cults that might help make clearer what's really happening. Cults and abusive relationships have a lot in common. They thrive in isolation and secrecy, which promote control and dependency and systematically eliminate alternative places for the cult member/abused to turn. Both cults and abusive relationships require absolute obedience to a self-proclaimed god who makes all the rules, regardless of fairness or logic or the overall welfare of the group. They are not and never will be a democracy, because if equality exists the whole structure of the cult/abusive relationship falls apart. In order to maintain the illusion of superiority, the cult leader/abuser has to constantly reinforce the inferiority of the cult member/abused and the perpetual threat of dire punishment for questioning the self-proclaimed god's authority. The initial approach is always flattering, seductive, and deceptive. The cult leader makes the prospective member feel "chosen" and "privileged" to be part of something that "outsiders" are too stupid or shallow or unholy to understand; the abuser slowly but surely sells the message that they're the only person who loves the abused enough to want them all to themselves, while "outsiders" who worry and criticize are just jealous of a relationship that's really none of their business. All turmoil, unhappiness, or frustration in the cult/relationship is the fault of the cult member/abused. Everything would be fine if they'd just stay quietly and obediently submissive. The point comes when the cult member/abused has been programmed to associate submission with survival. And "programmed" is exactly the right word. It can be as hard to convince the abused that staying could be fatal to them and their children as it would have been to convince the members of Heaven's Gate that there was no UFO behind the Hale-Bopp comet waiting to welcome them after their mass suicide. Make no mistake, in both cults and abusive relationships, everything from the first flattering hype that seduces you into isolation, to the eventual insults, fear tactics, and whatever else it takes to keep you "in your place," not one moment of it is for your benefit or the benefit of your children. Recognizing that sooner rather than later can save you years of misery and possibly even save your life.

At the end of "The Dark Side" chapter is a list of

Tools of Protection. I use them every day. I recommend that everyone use them every day, especially anyone who is being emotionally or physically abused. They really will help protect you, but they'll also accomplish something else. They are a constant reminder that at your core you are a sacred, eternal spirit, created by God, His genetic heir. When you truly *know* your own holiness as a child of God, there's not a chance you will tolerate even a moment of disrespect, let alone abuse. Demeaning you is demeaning your God soul, and that's not just unacceptable, it's sacrilege.

Even though it rarely looks that way, there are usually two false egos at work on either end of an abusive relationship. Don't forget, the word ego means "I am." Anyone whose ego, or "I am," is whole and healthy has no need at all to control or manipulate or bully or diminish someone else's power to feed their own. An abuser's ego is so weak and undernourished that they have to steal from whoever's vulnerable enough to let theirs be taken. On the flip side, the abused often fall into a false ego trap, too, in which they get so determined to *win* at the expense of their dignity, their self-respect, their sanity, their safety, and even their own children that they lose sight of everything else. "Winning" in their minds means, "You will change, you will respect me, you will love me, you will repay me for everything I've gone through to stay with you!" But the problem is, actions really do speak louder than words. So telling someone they have to change while you stay with them really says, "I don't mean it, you obviously don't have to change at all, since I'm still here." Telling someone you demand respect while you're tolerating constant disrespect really says, "You can disrespect me all you want, I don't mind enough to do anything about it." Telling someone you insist on being loved when their behavior toward you is the exact opposite of love gives them the message that it's okay, you don't really expect them to love you at all if they don't want to. As for repaying you for putting up with it—why should they, when there haven't been any meaningful consequences that prove what you've put up with has been unacceptable? Remember, whatever you "accept," you're declaring "acceptable." In my situation, once I caught on to my own false-ego urge to *win* and reconnected with my own "I am" and my own divine God center—and, even more, the God centers of my two beautiful children, who deserved as safe and happy a home as I could offer them—I realized that there was actually a way to win once and for all: I forfeited. I basically said to my abuser, "Congratulations. You win. It's all yours—Boardwalk, Park Place, this big pile of pretend money, all of it. I'm not going to play anymore." I took my sons and never went back, and sure enough, when I refused to play, there was no game, so in the most gratifying way possible, I did win. In addition to my sons and the clothes on our backs, of course, I also walked out with my "I am" and my power, that left him ego-less and powerless since he had none of his own. He begged me to come back. But by then I understood that it wasn't *me* he wanted back. It was the false identity he'd found in abusing and overpowering me that he missed so much. He'd also given me the perfect defense against coming back, too. All I had to do was remind him that he'd made it very clear how worthless, stupid, inept, inadequate and crazy I was, so I wouldn't dream of expecting him to tolerate one more moment of a partner who was so clearly unworthy of him. Well, guess what—he hadn't really meant any of those things, he'd just said them because he was upset. Translation: On top of everything else, he was a liar. No, thanks. Not good enough for me, and *certainly* not good enough for my two little boys. How could I possibly raise them to value dignity, respect, and honesty in a home where none of those things existed?

God didn't create any of us to be miserable. What misery we wrote into our blueprints is there for us to overcome, not to put up with and even encourage. There is no awards ceremony on The Other Side where they hand out medals for being a martyr. We're responsible for our own blueprints, and for giving our children a safe place to act on *their* blueprints. And abusers are responsible for their own blueprints as well. Trying to change them or "save them" means taking on their blueprints and their life themes, which means you're neglecting your own. In fact, by accepting their abuse, you're actually postponing their progress. If they wrote it into their blueprints to be an abuser, it's there for *them* to overcome. So if you really want to help them, make them start working on overcoming it. In other words, for your sake *and* theirs, say "no" and get out of there! A friend, a family member, a church, a synagogue, a clinic, the police station—there *is* an escape route for you. There are wonderful, caring shelters where both women and men who are being abused can find a safe place for themselves and their children. Just one of many excellent sources of help is the National Domestic Violence Hotline, at (800) 799-7233. You can call them twenty-four hours a day, seven days a week. Please, whatever you do, if you or your children are in emotional or physical danger, dial that number. Staying in an abusive situation means you've given up on yourself, and that means you've given up on God—even though He never has given up on you and never will.

LOOKING FOR MR. OR MS. RIGHT

Now that I've made relationships sound like so much fun . . . But as I said at the beginning of all this, they can bring exactly as much joy as sorrow, and as much healing as pain.

You may have heard the saying: If you really want to find a new love interest, stop looking. This is true for a couple of very good reasons.

We are all psychic sponges, picking up impulses and energy and messages from the people around us. Whether we call them instincts or a sixth sense or just funny feelings, they are the psychic impressions people make on us before they've ever spoken a word or even looked our way.

What we tend to forget sometimes is that we're also psychic transmitters, sending out just as many impulses and energy and messages to all the other psychic sponges we meet. And you certainly don't need a psychic to tell you how prey naturally reacts when they sense a hunter in the area. Any elk, rabbit, or goose will back me up on this—they race to escape.

This isn't to suggest that you just sit there drumming your fingers, waiting for Mr. or Ms. Right to drop through the ceiling into your lap. What you should do is go about your business, celebrating and investing in the love you have in your life now—your friends, your family, even your pets—and learn to trust the blueprints you wrote before you came here, and God's constant readiness to help it happen without your trying to force it along out of the unfortunate worldly emotion of impatience, not to mention the silly belief that we know better than God does what we need.

At the end of this book you'll find a list of affirmations. They are for your daily use, as many times a day as you can. They are not something to do while you wait. They're something to do while you *don't wait* but instead actively live your life, with these constant reminders of your divine, eternal, worthy spirit, and its direct lineage to God. The more you learn to appreciate, respect, and love the God soul inside you, the more quickly you'll master the biggest secret of all to finding and keeping healthy, happy relationships throughout your life:

No other relationship on this earth
will ever offer as much potential security, comfort,
and peace of mind
as your relationship with yourself.
Learn to love your own company,
and other people are bound to follow.
After all, no one wants to miss out on a good time.

FAMILIES

In the first chapter we discussed "option lines," or the one area of life we chose to be most challenged by while we were composing our blueprints. There are seven option lines—family, social life, love, health, spirituality, finance, and career.

I chose family as my option line. What that basically means is that I could whip your family problems into shape in a single reading, but I've spent most of my sixty-two years trying to figure out my own. I was so busy trying to wedge this odd, fascinating, complicated group I'm related to into my own imaginary cookie-cutter version of "normal" that I conveniently tried to ignore everything I know—about life and about the fact that, for better or worse, "families" are still made up of *people*. I'm gaining on it, though. At least I'm learning that yes, what I know really does apply to the people in my family as well, no matter how ridiculous we might look in little matching outfits, all lined up together waving out from behind a white picket fence.

What I know is that every member of every family, including mine, wrote a separate blueprint before we came here. We all chose to be related to each other. Since our blueprints are the detailed road maps of what we came here to learn, there must be a wealth of lessons and challenges to master in each family relationship or we wouldn't have chosen them. So if nothing else, we may not always appreciate the lessons or the people we chose to teach them to us, but we can make the most of the opportunity and be grateful for the education, if only because getting it right this time means we won't have to come back and do it all over again.

Family members have a right to expect common courtesy from each other, but just as with all our other relationships in life, trust and respect have to be earned, nourished, and maintained. "Genetic bond" does not mean "special dispensation" and/or "anything goes." It doesn't even mean you have to like each other or relate to each other. In fact, that's one of those areas in which what I know went right out the window. Ignoring completely the fact that each of my sons arrived with his own blueprint and his own lessons to learn, I dreamed up a lovely image of what a brothers' relationship should be—inseparable buddies, arms perpetually slung around each other's shoulders, there for each other through thick and thin, and each other's greatest source of comfort.

Well, somewhere along the line it became obvious to both of them—in fact, to everyone but me—that they don't happen to like each other very much. About all they have in common is me and their other relatives, the same physical locations throughout their childhoods, and their height. Other than that, they have different goals, different interests, different temperaments, different personalities, and because of my own needs and expectations and fantasies, I kept trying to huddle them together anyway, determined to make them crazy about each other if it killed me. And it could have, assuming you can die from wringing your hands too much, if they hadn't each taken me aside in separate conversations and gently pointed out that if they met each other at a party, and didn't know each other from Adam, there wouldn't be enough common interest between them to spend five minutes together. What's more, they were both perfectly comfortable with that fact. *I* was the one who was losing sleep over it.

When I had my near-death experience and flat-lined after major surgery, I knew while I was in the tunnel, headed for God's light, that both of my sons would survive their grief and be just fine. I couldn't have cared less whether they would do it separately or together. Our eternal spirits really do understand everything beautifully. It's our flawed, vain, stubborn, selfish conscious minds that keep getting in the way.

Life is much more peaceful in my family since I finally learned that my sons are two distinct individuals who have a right to their own relationship preferences. My relationships with each of them are as different as the two men themselves, and I cherish them both. As their mother, I expect them to mind their manners, be polite and peacefully coexist, or stay away from each other if they can't manage that. But also as their mother, my spirit promised theirs at birth as much respect, patience, understanding, and support for the blueprints they composed as I expect from them for mine. It's not as if I composed mine with any fewer mistakes than theirs, after all.

Adding to the complications within families, as with everyone else we meet, is that we don't just arrive with our own blueprints, mixed in with several genetic characteristics from ancestors on both sides of the family, but we also arrive as composites of our own unique past-life experiences and relationships. If you've ever looked at someone you're closely related to—including your own children or parents—and wondered how two people with the same blood could have so little in common, there's your answer. Your spirits have each been here many times before, with their own blueprints, struggles, and lessons each of those lifetimes. When you look at it that way, what are the odds that you *would* have something in common with every person you happen to be related to in this life?

Genetics play an important role in our identities, not by some haphazard series of quirks in the gene pool but because of our blueprints. By choosing our parents as we compose our blueprints, we're choosing the genetic factors that will lay the groundwork for the goals we set for ourselves before we came here. However you feel about what physical, mental, emotional, and physiological qualities you inherited from both sides of your family, you actually have yourself to thank, or to blame. Either way, though, always remember that you chose them for a reason.

It's very possible that there are some kindred souls in your family—spirits you've known in other lives and had relationships with, both good and bad. You and other family members are undoubtedly meeting for the first time. That doesn't make any of the present relationships among you either more or less significant. It just explains some of the dynamics you might have struggled for years to understand—an easier closeness or telepathy with two of you than with others; a discomfort or mistrust or outright anger you can't trace or seem to solve; a refreshing mutual breath of fresh air and a lack of "baggage"; an especially deep sense of safety, comfort, and familiarity with one relative in particular; an odd lack of connection between two of you no matter how hard you try, as if you're being expected to assume a deep bond with a stranger whom you might even look like. The variations go on and on, but the reasons for them are simple logic—past-life relationships, and the lack of them, exist in every family.

You will find countless examples throughout this

book of clients' past-life relationships with family members, and of my own, for that matter. But here is a well-known one that makes more and more sense the more you think about it: I was given the psychic information, and confirmed it through Francine, that Bill and Hillary Clinton shared a past life as brother and sister. No, that does not make their current relationship incestuous. My son Christopher and I were husband and wife in a past life. This hardly means that in a way I gave birth to my own ex-husband. It is the connections that continue to evolve from one lifetime to the next, not the specific relationships.

Even when the specific relationships do repeat themselves, it signals an opportunity to learn, grow, and progress. A client named Joel felt hopelessly trapped in a marriage that by his own admission he was staying with not out of love but out of guilt. He was unhappy and imagined she was too, but on the frequent occasions when he thought of leaving, he was so overwhelmed with inexplicable waves of guilt that he could not imagine living with himself if he actually went through with it. It hardly took my psychic gift to point out that no relationship based solely on guilt is healthy or worth preserving. But it did take my psychic gift to discover that he and his wife had been married in a past life, and he had left her for another woman when she was diagnosed with a terminal illness rather than stay by her side until the end. Unearthing the real source of his guilt liberated him from it. When I saw him again two years later, he ecstatically informed me that he was about to marry a woman with whom he was very much in love, and that his now-ex-wife was happily remarried as well.

It is perfectly natural to have emotional reactions to those previous connections and/or non-connections. Whichever the case, it is also worth your while to use this information toward understanding your family's dynamics and making peace with them, instead of using it as a new series of excuses for feuds and grudges.

Do I believe that when the chips are down, families need to stick together? Absolutely. I wanted nothing to do with my mother, with good reason, but I would never have let her go without whatever she needed to be comfortable and well cared for. Likewise, my sons would be there for each other in a heartbeat if a major crisis came up. Ultimately honoring a family connection is part of our essence and part of the challenge that inspired us to choose to be born into this particular group of people in the first place.

That is as true in cases of adoption as it is in biologically connected families. If you wrote it into your blueprint to be born to someone who would then give you up to someone else, you did it for a reason that is important to the progress of your spirit. We've got to stop using the term "*real* family" to describe a genetic connection. It implies that an adoptive family is "*un*-real," and in most cases that's not accurate and not fair.

I do want to make a distinction, though, between honoring a family connection and this confusing concept of "owing." The idea of "We're family, so you owe me" gets used much too often as another way of saying, "I can treat you worse than I'd treat a total stranger if I want to, and you have to forgive me because we're related." Isn't that stupid? And yet we've all been there—had a nasty argument with a parent, spouse, or sibling in the grocery store parking lot, calling each other every name in the book, and then being adorably polite to the checkout woman while she weighs your produce because we wouldn't dream of offending someone we've never seen before in our lives. I'm sorry, but that's completely backward. No, I don't mean let's all be adorably polite to each other and rip into the grocery store checkout woman. I mean, doesn't it make sense to reserve your best behavior, not your worst, for the people you personally chose to play the significant role of "family" this time around?

CHILDREN

Every time you look at a newborn baby or a toddler, try to make a point of remembering that inside that tiny body still piecing together vocabulary words lives a wise, whole, experienced spirit and one of the most psychic beings on earth. Having just arrived from The Other Side, they often have vivid memories of their blueprints, their Spirit Guides and Angels, and their past lives. If they're lucky, no one's had a chance yet to make them feel weird or naughty or self-conscious when they want to talk about it.

I've heard so many people say, on hearing that, "I can't buy it. It's too bizarre." You know what I think is bizarre? Believing babies are all blank slates when they come here. If that's the case, how are children born with passionate interests in things like trains, or the Revolutionary War, or marine biology, or tall ships, or medicine, or archaeology, or anything else they've not had even a moment's exposure to? Children can be born with fears of things like heights, or water, or confined spaces, or spiders, or thunder, even though no one else around them is afraid of those same things. How? Child prodigies emerge from "ordinary" parents to make stunning achievements in the worlds of art, sports, education, and music. How? Honestly, compared to the perfectly logical past-life explanation, isn't the random-whim-of-fate concept the harder to buy of the two?

There are a couple of stories in the "Life After Life" chapter about my granddaughter Angelia's clear memories of her previous life as my Grandmother Ada. Please don't assume that it's one of those flukes that just figures in a family as spooky as mine. Client after client after client share comments all the time that their young children have made in casual passing:

- A five-year-old beamed up at his mother after she'd fixed his favorite meal and said, "You're the best of all fifteen moms I've ever had."
- A six-year-old couldn't keep a straight face during a well-deserved scolding from her father. Her father asked what on earth she thought was so funny. She told him: "Remember when I was the dad and you were my son and I used to yell at you like that?"
- A couple took their four-year-old on his first hike. They arrived at a footbridge crossing a stream, and the four-year-old came to a stop and announced, "Oh, no. I'm not going on any bridges this time." To the best of their knowledge, not only had he never seen a bridge before, let alone been on one, he didn't even know what a bridge was.

I've heard literally thousands of similar stories in my office, and more often than not, whichever parent I'm hearing it from has tried every explanation, from dreams to TV to precocious playmates to the dreaded "overactive imagination," to make sense of these unprovoked remarks. They list everything except the one explanation that makes the most sense, i.e., past-life memories, even though every one of those parents also believes that the spirit transcends death. Your children are only confirming what you already believe. Why the frantic effort to come up with any other explanation than that? The parent then invariably wants to know how they should respond when and if their child makes another "strange" comment like that. I ask how they did respond. Now, granted, they were caught off guard, but responses generally range from

"Stop it!" to "Shut up, you're creeping me out!" to "People will think you're crazy if you keep talking like that!" Only about two out of ten parents recognize it as a fascinating invitation to tour their child's spirit and past-life memories, not to mention chat with a recent arrival from The Other Side.

"Encourage your children to share whatever's on their minds, and learn to be their best, most open-minded listener" is obviously a good idea for every phase of parenting. But also urge them at a very early age to explain references you don't understand. Ask them questions like, "Who were you before this?" and "Who around here have you known before?" without judging or sounding skeptical about the answers. That is a great way to build their trust in you, to validate the notion that whatever they have to say is important, and to create an openness between you that will last a lifetime if you'll keep nurturing it.

I'm also willing to bet that you'll learn more from those conversations than you ever imagined about how fascinating your children are and how much they remember that you probably knew at their age too, until you were told there was something wrong with you if you tried to talk about it.

Young children are also more likely than adults to see spirits, ghosts, Spirit Guides, Angels, and any other entities from the dimension of The Other Side. Again, it makes sense—after all, they just came from there. If they mention seeing people you don't see, or hearing voices you don't hear, don't just ask them to tell you about it—pull up a chair and settle in for a mesmerizing conversation. Ask them to describe their "imaginary playmates" while you're at it. Chances are, they're not imaginary at all, and you're blessed to have an eager little pipeline to the spirit world.

In fact, one of the smartest things you can do for your own education and your child's self-confidence is to eliminate the phrase "you're imagining things" from your vocabulary. For one thing, you're probably wrong. For another thing, I don't know about you, but I don't appreciate it one bit when someone tells me I'm imagining something that seems very real to me. Why should a child appreciate being dismissed like that any more than we do? It's worth repeating: Children are among the most psychic beings on earth. Please remember that the next time you try to kid yourself into thinking that "we never argue or fight in front of the child" means your child doesn't know exactly what's going on. Yes, that means even when they're sleeping—in fact, *especially* when they're sleeping, and the spirit mind of the subconscious is wide awake. It doesn't matter whether or not they can consciously hear you. Their little subconscious minds never miss a thing.

That is why I'm such a big believer in talking to your children while they sleep. Don't worry about their not understanding what you say to them. Their conscious vocabulary may be limited by age, but the spirit you're talking to through the subconscious is ageless and as fluent as you are.

The peace, security, and healing you can give your child during sleep really will make a difference, not only to them but also to the bond between your divine spirit and theirs. I realize it sounds a little far-fetched. But try it anyway, every night for two weeks, when you stop by their crib or bed to check on them. It certainly can't hurt, it only takes a few moments, and if I'm right about how much it will help them, how can it possibly not be worth doing?

All you do is move close enough to your sleeping child that he or she can hear your quiet voice without being awakened by it, and then say some version of the following, in whatever words come easily from your heart:

> "My dear child, I feel blessed that you chose me as the caretaker and nurturer of your sacred spirit as it starts its new life on earth. I promise you the best effort of my soul to keep you safe, healthy, happy, and connected to the God who created you and lives inside you with every breath you take. May you keep all the joy and wisdom your past lives have given you, and may all sorrow, fear, illness, and negativity from those past lives be released and dissolved for all time into the white light of the Holy Spirit."

It really does take a village to raise a child. May we include the world's children in all our prayers, and work every day at making a better, kinder, safer village than we've had.

I read something recently that struck me as a beautiful way to end a chapter on relationships. It applies to couples, to friends, to family members, to anyone else we let into our lives, and mostly to the all-important relationship between ourselves and the divine light of God inside us. It's called "The Invitation."

> It doesn't interest me what you do for a living. I want to know what you ache for, and if you dare to dream of meeting your heart's longing.
>
> It doesn't interest me how old you are. I want to know if you will risk looking a fool for love, for your dreams, for the adventure of being alive.
>
> It doesn't interest me what planets are squaring your moon. I want to know if you have touched the center of your own sorrow, if you have been opened by life's betrayals or have become shriveled and closed from fear of further pain. I want to know if you can sit with pain, mine or your own, without moving to hide it or fade it or fix it.
>
> I want to know if you can be with joy, mine or your own, if you can dance with wildness and let the

ecstasy fill you to the tips of your fingers and toes without cautioning us to be careful, to be realistic, to remember the limitations of being human.

It doesn't interest me if the story you are telling me is true. I want to know if you can disappoint another to be true to yourself; if you can bear the accusation of betrayal and not betray your own soul, if you can be faithless and therefore be trustworthy.

I want to know if you can see beauty, even when it's not pretty, every day, and if you can source your own life from its presence.

I want to know if you can live with failure, yours and mine, and still stand on the edge of a lake and shout to the silver of the full moon, "Yes!"

It doesn't interest me to know where you live or how much money you have. I want to know if you can get up, after the night of grief and despair, weary and bruised to the bone, and do what needs to be done to feed the children.

It doesn't interest me who you know or how you came to be here. I want to know if you will stand in the center of the fire with me and not shrink back.

It doesn't interest me where or what or with whom you have studied. I want to know what sustains you, from the inside, when all else falls away.

I want to know if you can be alone with yourself and if you truly like the company you keep in the empty moments.

—Oriah Mountain Dreamer, Indian Elder

* 4 *

To Your Health: Psychic Prescriptions for the Mind and Body

Twenty years ago, lying on a hospital gurney in Mountain View, California, I was going in for minor surgery when I looked up at the anesthetist and casually announced, "Your wife's going to crash your car into a phone booth. She'll be fine, your car won't."

He had obviously learned to tolerate all sorts of incoherent blather from anesthetized patients, and he did everything but pat me on the head as he steered me through the swinging double doors of the operating room. "That's nice," he said. "Now, just relax."

I remember wondering what was "nice" about it just before I went under.

When I opened my eyes in recovery, he was sitting by my bed, staring at me, pale and shaken—not the reaction you are hoping to wake up to fresh out of surgery. I managed to mumble, "What's wrong?" I braced myself for the news that while operating they'd discovered I was riddled with some remarkably devastating disease.

He finally found his voice. "I just got a call. My wife hit a phone booth and totaled my car."

A little abruptly I said, "Of course she did!" but I was too relieved to sympathize.

Fortunately, the anesthetist was more amazed than

offended. He ended up sharing that story with his co-workers, who shared it with other colleagues, and so on. As a result, twenty years later I'm blessed with pro bono consulting and reciprocal referral relationships with ninety-six medical and psychiatric doctors throughout the country. If I ever had doubts that psychic answers come *through* me and not *from* me, this work in particular would erase them once and for all. I've never had formal medical training of any kind, so I'm invariably as surprised as my clients by the information God gives me to pass along. It's the "Hit it, God!" process we discussed earlier, often in physiological language in which I'm only now starting to become fluent.

Not long after that encounter with the anesthetist, a client walked into my office for a reading. She looked lovely and perfectly normal; but before she even got to her chair I said something I've never said to a client before or since: "Don't sit down! We've got to get you to a urologist right away!"

A doctor friend of mine was able to see her immediately, and he called me two hours later. "Thank God you brought her in. This woman has a very advanced bladder infection. If she'd waited any longer to get help, she would have been in serious trouble."

"Thank God" is right.

My sensitivity to clients' medical problems grew quickly, almost as if floodgates had opened; and I began doing "psychic scans" of every client the instant they entered the room, tuning in to every area of the body and sharing whatever information came through.

One woman had been diagnosed with a rare, incurable blood disease. Her doctor referred her to me in the hope that I could give her some spiritual comfort as she struggled with her illness. But during the reading it came through loud and clear to me that the diagnosis was wrong. All she needed was to have her thyroid checked by a good endocrinologist. She did. Its hormone-producing level was startlingly low, but easily treatable and certainly not fatal.

A man arrived wanting to straighten out his love life. And it was a mess, believe me. But I immediately knew he had a more pressing problem that could be fixed far more easily. I cut him off in mid-sentence to say, "You are going to get that bad knee operated on, aren't you?" After a long, startled silence he told me he was scheduled for arthroscopic surgery later that week. He was already sitting when I walked into the room to start the reading. Since I hadn't seen him limping, he couldn't imagine how I'd picked up on a problem with his knee. I gave all the credit to God, where it belongs—in that case and thousands of others. He often "hits it" before I've even had a chance to cue Him, on subjects I hadn't necessarily planned to ask about.

A girl in her early twenties, with acute acne and frequent painful rashes all over her body, came to me for a general reading, not expecting a psychic to address her skin problems. I didn't have to be psychic to notice them, and I asked what she'd done about them. She told me she had tried every dermatologist and prescription skin product she could find. Nothing seemed to make any lasting difference, and she'd given up hope that anything ever would. The cure "hit" me loud and clear, and I passed it along exactly as I received it: "You're allergic to dairy products." She promised with some skepticism that she would try swearing off milk and cheese temporarily and let me know what happened. She called two weeks later, ecstatically reporting that her skin problems had vanished completely.

Another young woman had been trying unsuccessfully for months to get pregnant, and doctor after doctor had failed to figure out why she couldn't. I referred her to a specialist who confirmed my belief that ovarian cysts were the real culprit and began treating her for them. She sent baby pictures of her newborn daughter a year later; and I've always wondered if she was thanking me or cursing me in those first weeks of no sleep, stretch marks, and four a.m. feedings.

It was exhilarating to discover that I could also be helpful "by remote." Answers come just as clearly during phone readings and browsing through the morning mail. Even if a client has no medical problems, I'm able to alert them if a friend or family member does, which occasionally puts the client in an odd position. I was doing a reading one day for a very beautiful, very healthy actress who was grieving the recent death of her mother, the topic at hand, when I suddenly blurted out, "Is your husband urinating a lot?" She was working eighteen hours a day at the time and hadn't noticed. I assured her he was, and that it was due to an enlarged prostate he should have checked. Three months later he casually mentioned at breakfast one morning that he had a doctor's appointment that day. He had been urinating a lot and wanted to find out why. The words "enlarged prostate" came out of her mouth before she could stop them. He asked when she'd found time to get a medical degree and laughed it off until his doctor examined him and echoed those same two words. That night at dinner he demanded she tell him where on earth this "enlarged prostate" business came from. She had never told him until then that she'd been to see me. He thought all psychics were frauds and a complete waste of time and money. They argued about it until she played him the tape of her reading, after which he and his enlarged prostate sheepishly apologized.

Throughout these many years, and after thousands of letters from clients and doctors reporting successful outcomes to my medical suggestions, the subject of health has become a source of profound satisfaction for me. Yet though I cherish my *pro bono* relationship with the medical community, I can't stress this caution enough: Neither I nor any other psychic should ever be used as a substitute for the health care of a trained, responsible professional, but only as supplements who can often guide you and your doctor in a productive direction.

MIND AND BODY

Everyone who has a car knows the drill: For repairs and regular tune-ups, nothing can beat a skilled mechanic. But we're asking for trouble if we don't take responsibility for day-to-day maintenance. The same holds true for these bodies we're traveling around in. For serious problems and checkups, nothing can beat a skilled physician. But day-to-day maintenance is our job. We can take a much more active role in our own health and well-being than simply throwing down a few vitamins every morning and saying, "There!" We need to understand and use the facts of how the body works and heals, and the fascinating, intimate relationship between our bodies and our minds.

There's nothing more literal in this world than the way the body responds to exactly what the mind tells it. If you think the body can outsmart the mind, or that it somehow goes off by itself and creates its own reality no matter what the mind has to say, remember this: Under hypnosis—when the subconscious mind is in charge—if you're told that the hypnotist's finger is a white-hot poker, and the hypnotist touches you with that finger, a blister will form where you were touched. The body doesn't intervene and say, "Hold it, you can't fool me, I can't be burned by a finger." It hears "white-hot poker" and responds appropriately. With the mind having that much power over the body, how can we possibly doubt its control over every aspect of the body's health, or lack of it?

For a country that prides itself on being health-conscious, we're reminded everywhere we turn that we are actually supposed to be sick. I'll bet more Americans can name six over-the-counter cold remedies than can name the first six presidents. Flu season is announced with so much media fanfare I'm surprised we haven't all started exchanging gifts to celebrate it. Word that a virus is going around spreads more quickly than gossip. Not an hour of television goes by without HMO stories, news that some unusual strain of bacteria is popping up all over the country, and a barrage of commercials showing people Just Like You and Me in the throes of everything from heartburn to headaches, to constipation, to diarrhea, to PMS, to sinus infections that apparently make little triangles appear between your eyebrows. I'm a big believer in staying well informed on health issues, but I also believe we're programmed every day to think that if there is not something wrong with us, there should be.

Here's how powerful such programming can be. When a close friend of mine was a child, her mother could often be heard barking, "Get into that bed! You're very sick!" She was so harsh and relentless about it that at a very early age my friend came to think that getting into bed means you're very sick. As a result, even now, at sixty years old, there's not enough money to make my friend get between the sheets of a bed. Even on the rare occasions when she's in the hospital, she insists on lying on top of the bedding. Lying on the bed rather than in it isn't just a phobia; she's become literally allergic to sheets. No matter what kind, if she lies between double sheets, she wakes up covered with a rash of what looks like bedsores. Mind you, thanks to this lifelong "allergy," she's accumulated a stunning wardrobe of comforters and duvets, since she changes them as often as most people change their linens. But just like the white-hot poker illustration, her mind is so convinced that "in that bed = very sick" that her body reacts every time.

On the flip side of that coin, two days after a hysterectomy I was up and back to business as usual—not because I'm Wonder Woman, but because no one told me that a hysterectomy is supposed to be a big deal with a long, slow recovery process.

One of the most amazing examples I've ever seen of a lack of programming happened on a trip to Kenya a few years ago when I witnessed a native Kenyan woman giving birth. She dug a small hole in the ground, gripped a metal bar she was holding and squatted over the hole, pushed the baby out of her body into the hole, severed the umbilical cord with her teeth, placed the baby in a cloth pouch tied around her neck, and went back to work in a nearby field. Does this mean Kenyan women are uniquely hardy? Of course not. But it does strongly suggest that word hasn't reached them about what a painful, complicated process childbirth is supposed to be.

Not for a moment am I advocating that all women give birth in dirt holes. I'm no martyr—not only were both my sons born in the hospital, but I also welcomed all the comfort, help, hygiene, and medical attention the staff had to offer. And to you men who are reading this, don't even think about demanding that the mothers of your children leap up right after childbirth and scrub the floors because "if a Kenyan woman can do it, so can you." Until you're the ones getting pregnant and giving birth (which, let's face it, would probably drop population growth to a fast zero), I'm afraid you'll have to bow to our expertise on this subject.

Witnessing that extraordinary birth reinforced for me the fact that our bodies follow the literal orders our minds give them. In that case, the woman's mind obviously wasn't programmed to associate childbirth with debilitating pain and bed rest. We don't have to accept the programming we're given, either. My Grandmother Ada broke her hip when she was eighty-six years old. After surgery her doctors told her she would never walk again. A month later I walked in to find her on her feet cleaning her house, pushing a chair in front of her for support. Horrified, I asked her what on earth she thought she was doing. She was supposed to be flat on her back in bed. What was her reply? I've adopted it as my own when I feel any kind of illness trying to sneak up on me: "I don't have time for that foolishness."

I think we've all had this experience. You're trotting along through the day, feeling perfectly fine, when someone says, "Are you okay? You don't look well." Sure enough, as the day wears on, you start to notice that you're really not feeling so great after all. Ten times out of ten, the person who said you don't look well isn't blessed with the amazing power to judge your health better than you can. The only power they have is the power of suggestion. Before you know it, you're thinking, "If I don't look well, maybe I'm *not* well." Your body, always eager to please, hears "not well" and dutifully conjures up some kind of discomfort. Next time, instead of "Maybe I'm *not* well," try thinking, "I don't have time for that foolishness." Keep right on thinking it until you mean it. It's a safe bet you'll get through the rest of the day feeling just as fine as you did to begin with.

That leads to my *strong* belief that we should eliminate a whole other definition of "body language" from our vocabularies—i.e., the stream of careless clichés that can cue the body to develop health problems. An extreme illustration was a friend of mine whose boyfriend had left her. She kept repeating over and over, "He broke my heart." I kept asking her to please stop saying that, but clichés are hard habits to break. Two months later she was in surgery for a double by-pass.

Make a deal with your spouse or a friend to notice how often you use this form of negative "body language" and work together to break the habit. Here are just a few examples:

- "He/she makes me sick."
- "He/she is a pain in the neck (or other body part)."
- "I'm worried sick (or worried to death) about . . ."
- "He/she wears me out."
- "You're giving me a headache."
- "You're going to give me an ulcer."
- "Something is weighing heavy on my heart."
- "You're going to be the death of me."
- "I'd rather die than . . ."
- "He/she/this is nauseating . . ."

If you listen closely, you'll be shocked at the frequency with which you're subtly sabotaging your body and almost ordering it to break down.

Similarly, your body is absolutely literal in the way it responds to the environment around it. I first started noticing this many years ago when I visited a dear friend, Dr. James Cochran, who was in the hospital dying of bleeding ulcers. I held his hand and asked him what was going on, and he looked back with the saddest brown eyes and said, "I don't know, Sylvia, I guess I just can't stomach life anymore." Not long after that I was at a doctor's appointment of my own, trying to get rid of a recurring bladder infection. Another friend, Dr. Jim Fadiman, who'd known me forever, listened patiently to my list of symptoms and then said, "You know better than this. Talk to me, what's going on with you?" Without a moment's thought I blurted out, "It's my family. They just really piss me off." And I wondered why my bladder was acting up? We had a good laugh over that.

I've run across countless variations on that theme with clients in all these years since. Very often, if there are issues in our lives that our minds refuse to address, our bodies will speak up loud and clear:

- Your neck chronically hurts? Who or what is the pain in your neck?
- You have chronic backaches? Who or what are you carrying on your back?
- Eyesight failing? What in your life don't you want to see?
- Chronic laryngitis? What don't you want to say . . . or what did you say that you shouldn't have?
- Hearing starting to fail? What are you trying not to hear? By the way, have you ever noticed that it's always only one person in a couple, never both of them, whose hearing goes? The words "take a hint!" leap to mind.
- Chronic breathing or bronchial trouble? What do you need to get off your chest?
- Dizzy spells? Who or what is keeping you off balance?

The list goes on and on. But the point is, remembering how literally the body reacts to information, many recurring health problems can be healed when the mind identifies the *real* source of the problem and starts taking steps to address it.

There's another important lesson to be learned: We owe it to our bodies to be as attentive and responsive to their signals as they are to ours. I went through a phase when my two sons were young in which I guess I decided to prove once and for all that I was, in fact, Wonder Woman. I was going to be the world's most attentive, perfect full-time mom, wife, homemaker, and daughter, while maintaining an overbooked schedule of readings, speaking engagements and media appearances. Looking back, I'm sure I was also trying to keep running so fast that I wouldn't have time to notice how unhappy I was. At any rate, the fact that I didn't pay attention to little things like eating, sleeping, and time for myself seemed beside the point at those rare times when I thought about it at all. Late one afternoon, after several weeks of this "Hear Me Roar" kick, I was flying up a flight of stairs, arms loaded with children and laundry, when I nicked my foot on one of the steps. It hurt, but it was just a tiny nick, and after a brief annoyed glance at it, I sprinted right on with my day.

The next morning my foot was swollen to four times its normal size, thanks to the onset of a serious case of cellulitis. It was weeks before I was fully recovered and pain-free again. The message from my body was loud and clear. "Okay, hotshot, if you refuse to slow down, I'll *make* you slow down!" I'm sure it had been sending me all kinds of signals for weeks, but my mind was too busy and cluttered to notice.

I see clients every day who haven't made the connection yet that they're physically unhealthy because they're living and/or working in a mentally unhealthy environment. I've learned the hard way that prolonged tension, unhappiness, and depression are guaranteed to show up in some form in the body sooner or later if they're not expressed or resolved. Many doctors are well aware of that fact, too. Cancer patients, for example, are very often urged to supplement their medical treatments with a change in lifestyle to something more peaceful and positive; and many times the results are successful. Not every time, sadly, but often enough to be well worth considering.

We've all heard that stress causes ulcers. That's true, but it's also just the beginning of the story, as almost all of the medical community recognizes. If stress and other strong unpleasant emotions are powerful enough to cause internal bleeding, they are powerful enough to cause any number of other disruptions in the body. We're not unlike walking pressure cookers. As you know if you've ever used one, you have three choices with a pressure cooker—make sure it can vent its steam, move it off the stove, or end up with a lid and your dinner on the ceiling. We have the same three choices with our bodies—vent our steam, change to an environment or situation that won't create steam in the first place, or blow up one way or another.

No, that is not an invitation for all of us to run around yelling and screaming and slugging each other and calling it "venting steam." For one thing, it's unattractive. For another thing, there are laws against it. For still another thing, it's just a fact that any pain we cause someone else will eventually do more damage to us than to them. And frankly, we've all got enough problems without piling that on ourselves on top of everything else.

But there are all sorts of ways to vent without causing harm, and it's essential to your mental and physical health that you find as many as possible that work for you. Talk to a therapist, a discreet friend or family member, a minister, a rabbi, a support group, a crisis hotline—anyone you can trust to listen without judging you. Cry. Yell. Write a long, detailed letter to whomever you are angry with and then burn it. Tell your Spirit Guide you need help and exactly why. Pray. Do what a friend of mine does. Write on a plain old brown potato the name of the person or job or whatever is frustrating you, then bury the potato, not in the ridiculous hope of putting a curse on them (sorry, but there is no such thing as a curse), but for the satisfying gesture of burying them right out of your life. Invest in a punching bag, or wear yourself out beating up on every pillow in the house. Walk. Run. Work out. Hit golf balls, or go to a batting cage and hit baseballs. Go to an amusement park—I defy you to be preoccupied with your problems when you're upside down on a loop coaster. Do what I once did when I was so angry at my first husband I really believed I might explode. I jumped on a bicycle and rode as hard and as fast as I could, telling myself I was actually riding away from him.

Also, talk to your doctor. I don't know anyone whose life has ever been improved by becoming dependent on recreational or unauthorized prescription drugs or alcohol, but there's no weakness in asking for supervised help from a safe medication that can make it easier to cope with stress, a crisis or trauma. A lot of people have gone to a lot of trouble to develop everything from effective antidepressants and antibiotics to echinacea, acupuncture, and non-addictive herbal sleep aids. If your doctor can't offer you well-informed alternatives, find one who can.

Trauma, of course, can have an equally dramatic impact on the body. Since making the mental connection between illness and its source can greatly assist healing, here are three guidelines I've found very useful in health readings with my clients:

1. Sudden trauma—death of a loved one, loss of a job, a divorce or breakup, devastation from a natural disaster, etc.—tends to strike the body from the chest up. If you're suffering from a head cold, bronchitis, ear and sinus infections, heart problems, or any upper respiratory inflammations,

look back six months to a year and see if you can trace it to any major upheaval in your life. If you find it, deal with it immediately. Never try to use your body as a burial ground for emotional pain.

2. Deep-seated trauma—ongoing unhappiness at home or at work, ongoing family problems you haven't addressed, unresolved conflicts with friends, overdue apologies and unacknowledged guilt, etc.—usually strikes between the chest and the waist. Ulcers, chronic indigestion, an "acid" stomach or stomach cramps, *et al.*, often mean there's something you're continuing to "push down" rather than address and get rid of once and for all.
3. Childhood and past-life trauma—obviously the most difficult to uncover, but a qualified psychic or hypnotherapist can help—typcially attacks from the waist down. Chronic constipation or diarrhea, colitis, problems with the reproductive organs, etc., are frequently a signal that your subconscious is holding on to something your conscious mind isn't aware of, and it needs to be released.

Sometimes, precisely because our bodies aren't capable of repressing or rationalizing anything, I think they're actually smarter than we are. Abuse them, neglect them, feed them poorly, push them too hard, or stop paying attention to them, and they definitely speak up.

CELL MEMORY AND PAST-LIFE TRAUMA

We owe it to ourselves to become actively conscious of other aspects of health that have a powerful impact on our minds and bodies, aspects so deeply rooted that only a handful of the medical community is just now beginning to explore them.

As we've discussed, before our spirits on The Other Side enter the womb, we each make a blueprint. Health issues and illnesses are included in that blueprint, although we can modify it while we're here—a cold, for example, doesn't have to progress into pneumonia if we take care to prevent it. On The Other Side we have access to conscious memories of all our past lives and write our blueprints accordingly. But those conscious memories fade into subconscious ones as we head into the lives we've undertaken.

The cells we're made of, each one of them alive, retain those past-life memories and respond to them, just as our spirit responds to the familiar experience of inhabiting a body again. It is much like those special places we all have in our lives that we associate with happiness, or sadness, or fear, or trauma. The emotion hits again every time we return there, no matter how many years have passed since the events that created the association. The spirit experiences that same familiarity when it returns to another body, while the cells of that body absorb the spirit's memories and react as they've been programmed, unable on their own to discern the difference between the past and the present, or this life from past ones.

As I said in chapter 3, young children often have memories of their past lives, since their time on The Other Side is still so recent.

When my son Christopher was about to turn three, I casually asked him one day, "Who were you before this?" He informed me without a beat of hesitation that he had been a cowboy and had a horse named Cinder. He'd been shot in the stomach outside "a place with swinging doors." Though fascinated, I was wondering if he had been watching too many TV cowboy shows when he added, "And then my daughter ran out and held my head while I died." That's not the imagery a three-year-old would come up with. I remembered that conversation a thousand times when, in the years that followed, Chris developed sharp, chronic stomach pains. His doctors could not find any physiological reason for them. One night while he slept, I decided to start working on him myself, to see if I could use the information he'd given me to get to the real root of those pains. I sat on the edge of his bed and quietly spoke to his subconscious mind. "Chris, I know you were shot in the stomach before, and I know it was very, very painful. But that was in another time, in a past life. You're safe now, and your stomach is fine and healthy, and you'll never have to go through that again." The next morning his stomach pains were gone, and they never came back.

Soon after that a client asked me to spend an hour with her two-year-old son. He was becoming increasingly hysterical every time his mother stepped into the shower. He would scream, "Mama, no! No, Mama, don't!" and try desperately to pull her out of the bathroom. Between my Spirit Guide Francine and the child's Spirit Guide, I found the source of the problem, and I told the woman I wanted to talk to her child while he slept. She was afraid that with his very limited vocabulary he wouldn't understand me. But I assured her that his spirit, ageless as it is in all of us, would have no trouble. That night when he was sound asleep, I gently stroked his forehead and whispered, "In 1942 you and your family were taken to a terrible place called Dachau . . ." I gave him all the tragic details of how he'd watched as his mother and father and two brothers were led away to the awful, lethal gas showers, and how he'd died in that same hideous shower himself four months later. "It was as cruel and unspeakable as anything that's ever happened on this earth, but it has passed, it is over, thank God. In this life you and your mother are safe and well, showers can't hurt her, and no one will ever come and take you or her away like that again." I kept talking to him for more than an hour, until I could actually feel a deep peace come over him. A few weeks later his mother wrote to tell me that his terror of her taking a shower was gone.

Over the years doctors have referred a number of children to me whose persistent illnesses weren't responding to traditional medicine, and I've found that 98 times out of 100 these children respond to the reassurance that the trauma or death in the past life they're still remembering is over now. For example, one child who was born with what appeared to be acute asthma had actually been wrongly accused of stealing a horse in his most recent life and hanged for a crime he didn't commit. A beautiful little girl with the biggest amber eyes I've ever seen had died of blood poisoning from an untreated cut in the late 1800s, and when I met her, she had been unresponsive to leukemia therapy. Another child who suffered from night terrors was, it turned out, reliving through his subconscious the horror of the Spanish-American War battle in which he and his brother had lost their lives. In every one of those cases, consistent affirmations to the spirit mind in the child's subconscious during sleep to release these past-life traumas resulted in the child being healed.

If you have a young child with a chronic illness or phobia, *in addition to seeking qualified medical help*, try quietly reassuring your sleeping child, "You can let go of your past life now. It's over, and everything that hurt you in that life is gone forever. You were born into this new life safe and healthy and whole, and you don't ever have to suffer from that other life again."

Amplify that exercise with a prayer, for the child, for a loved one, or for yourself if you are suffering something similar that you want to get rid of once and for all:

> Dear God,
>
> Whatever my spirit mind and my cell memory might be holding from a past life that is harmful to me in any way, please help me release it into the cleansing white light of the Holy Spirit. Amen.

If you're skeptical, or just plain don't believe a word of this, try it anyway, just for one week. It certainly won't do you any harm, and it just might make the same dramatic difference for you that it has made for so many of my clients, friends, and referrals from medical and psychiatric doctors.

Cell memory can be just as powerful a force in adults as it is in children, both physically and emotionally. Remember, the familiarity of inhabiting a body again creates a kind of déjà vu in the spirit that then triggers a physiological reaction as the body responds to cues from the spirit mind.

Let's say, for example, that at the age of thirty-four you suddenly develop a serious bronchial/upper-respiratory problem, with no apparent source and no satisfying response to treatment. Perhaps in your last life you died of pneumonia at the age of thirty-four, at a time when it was invariably fatal. Your spirit mind, in the familiar environment of a body, may be saying, "Oh, look. I'm in a body again, and it's thirty-four years old. That means a breathing-related illness—I always have a breathing-related illness at thirty-four."

Or, as happened to a recent client, you are fifty years old and for the first time in your life you have become absolutely terrified of water. But if you drowned in your past life at the age of fifty, and your spirit mind and cell memory are holding that information without making the distinction between then and now, why wouldn't you suddenly fear water when you turn fifty?

It's been demonstrated through Kirlian photography, which captures on film an image of the energy or "aura" that emanates from every living thing, that an amputated limb continues to appear in energy form as a part of the body long after it is gone. Fascinating studies have been documented, particularly by Dr. Thelma Moss, of people whose amputated limbs continue to cause pain as if they're still very real and attached to the body—as the spirit mind and cell memory perceive them to be. Past-life trauma and death can cause the same reaction, and exactly the same kind of "phantom pain."

But once the spirit mind really gets the message, "Different time, different place, different life, different body," it can release the pain or fear or trauma or illness it is holding. That is an easier process than you might think. You don't even have to know the specifics of the past life your spirit mind and cell memory are still reacting to—you just have to acknowledge that a past life could be the source of the problem.

MENTAL HEALTH

My pro bono work with the psychiatric community has been a source of enormous gratification. The first referral I had from a psychiatrist friend was a teenage girl he thought might have a problem in "my territory." She was convinced she was haunted by a dark, shadowy figure that had attached itself to her and followed her everywhere she went, twenty-four hours a day. She'd become so terrified of this figure that she was unable to function, leaving her house only for therapy, unable to sleep, anxious and deeply depressed by her belief that the shadowy figure wanted to harm her.

I admit, when my friend first asked me to see her, I assumed she *was* being haunted, by some poor confused ghost I'd know how to deal with. But the instant she walked in my door, I knew there was no ghost with her or anywhere near her. I happily shared that news, foolishly expecting her to be relieved. She wasn't. She lumped me in the same category as everyone else who'd told her the shadowy figure didn't exist.

There was no way I was going to let her leave my office as troubled as she was when she got there. I wasn't about to disappoint my psychiatrist friend on the first patient he sent me, and besides, I am not a gracious loser, especially to an imaginary monster. The problem was, I couldn't seem to make any headway with her no matter what I tried. I prayed with her, I took her through a healing meditation, I even resorted to performing an exorcism on her. Hours later, I was exhausted, and as far as she was concerned, I was entertaining but useless, because she was still haunted.

In my success anxiety I'd neglected to do what I should have done in the first place. I sat back, closed my eyes, and silently said, "I give up, God. She's all Yours. Please help her, and just tell me what to do."

The answer came in an instant, clear as a bell. Purely following instructions, I opened my eyes, studied her for a long beat, and then announced with feigned surprise, "You know what? You're absolutely right, there *is* someone with you! I can't imagine why it took me this long to see him! But what's amazing is, he's not some huge, dark figure at all—he's just a little boy!"

She stared at me. "A little boy?" I could tell she wasn't arguing with me, she was just confirming what she'd heard, so I continued.

"He's beautiful, only nine years old. He's very

frightened because he's lost, and he's staying close to you because he hopes you'll take care of him."

After a bout of silence she smiled, for what I could tell was the first time in a long time. Her voice was full of compassion when she said, more to herself than to me, "I can handle a little boy!"

Sure enough, she could. Slowly but surely she started resuming her life again, finding it easier and easier to ask the little boy to please play by himself for a while when she was busy, and stay home and wait for her when she went out, until finally he disappeared completely. The last time I heard from her she'd graduated from college and was trying to choose from a long list of impressive job offers.

I was taught a valuable lesson about fear that day. Instead of wasting your time telling someone that what they're afraid of is ridiculous or imaginary, try finding a way to reduce it to something they can manage, dismiss, or defeat entirely. Very often their initial relief will pave the way for long-term healing.

I still chuckle—not at the patient but at myself—about a woman who was referred to me by a clinical psychologist in the Midwest. I was told that this woman believed with all her heart that she had a snake wrapped around her waist. Since she was terrified of snakes, this was having exactly the effect you'd imagine it would.

For this session, I prayed for God's help before the woman arrived, and the moment I laid eyes on her I shrieked, "Oh, my God, you've got a snake around your waist!" I leaped out of my chair, grabbed this imaginary snake from its imaginary grip on her, and proceeded to wrestle it all over the office. For an imaginary snake, it put up quite a fight, too; and if you want to know the truth, by the time I managed to get the upper hand enough to beat its imaginary head to death against the wall, I was actually kind of into the whole thing. That accomplished, I summoned what was by then my purely imaginary dignity and introduced myself. An hour later, a very happy, snake-free woman left, undoubtedly thinking I was far crazier than I could ever have thought she was.

Then there was the woman who was in misery because her eyeglasses were constantly talking to her. Thanks to prior help from God and her psychiatrist, I was ready for her, too. As soon as she told me what the problem was, I took her (completely silent) glasses from her, put them to my ear for a couple of minutes, and then handed them back with an impatient, "You're right, they are talking. But they're *boring*!"

She put them on, listened, and then said, more than a little surprised, "They really are, aren't they?" So much for the talking glasses—from then on, she just couldn't be bothered.

I can't say this often enough: There are many mental and emotional illnesses I'm not qualified to address or cure, and no psychic, including me, should *ever* be used as a substitute for a psychiatrist. I refer as many clients to my excellent network of psychologists as they refer to me, and I strongly believe that if we were all as diligent about emotional health as we are about our physical aches and pains, we'd see a vast and lasting improvement in our overall well-being. A psychiatrist friend of mine once told me something I've never forgotten, and the more I learn about the complexity of the mind/body connection the more true it becomes: "The mind can kill, and the mind can heal."

PRAYER CHAINS

Of course, the greatest healer of all is God, and a choir of voices asking in unison for His healing power and compassion can be an awesome force. So if you've never been part of or on the receiving end of a Prayer Chain—as the saying goes, don't knock it till you've tried it.

Many churches, temples, and spiritual centers throughout the country have organized Prayer Chains. I've had one in place for many years that has a reach of about 250,000 people through my office phone number and website, which you'll find in the back of this book. You are more than welcome to participate in ours, or simply use it as a framework for starting a Prayer Chain of your own:

Every day at 6:00 A.M. Pacific time a member of my staff collects messages from the office answering machine that's available twenty-four hours a day, which invariably include the names of people around the world who want to be included in that morning's prayers. We don't need to know the person's specific problem, and it would breach confidentiality to ask anyone to leave such personal information on the machine. Just the name of anyone who needs special help is enough.

The list of names is immediately passed along to the fifty ministers of my nondenominational church, *Novus Spiritus*. Each of those fifty ministers passes the names to fifty members of the Prayer Chain, who pass them along to fifty more, and so on, while that same list is also distributed through the *Novus Spiritus* cyber ministry on my website. At the triple Trinity (three times Three) hour of 9:00 Pacific time, wherever we are throughout the world, we offer a prayer for every name on the list:

Dear God,
in the mind, body, or soul, wherever their pain resides,
may it be released with Thy help
into the healing white light of the Holy Spirit. Amen.

My files are overflowing with letters from people who've been healed by our Prayer Chain and others like them. Again, if you're skeptical, let me repeat—it can't hurt to try it. You have got nothing to lose but the price of a phone call, and the awesome force of a quarter of a million people raising their voices to God on your behalf to gain.

"THE LAB"

For a private calming and healing experience, my Spirit Guide, Francine, passed along a lovely meditation—or mental exercise, if meditation is something you've always thought of as too time-consuming or simply beyond you. She calls it "The Lab." As she explains, The Lab is a special place you can take yourself to, any time, anywhere, when you have a few quiet moments. "When you create your own Lab in your mind," she told me, "we on The Other Side can see it and join you there to help you with whatever problems are troubling you."

The Lab has been a great source of comfort and replenishment through the years, for me, my family and friends and staff, and the clients I've shared it with. I pray it will do the same for you.

In your mind, create a rectangular room, of whatever size feels ideal and comfortable to you. Leave the far wall open, but color the three remaining walls a soft, calming green. To the walls add large windows that allow you a beautiful view of water, clear blue and serene, to lend power to your healing. In the center of your room, create a table, large enough for you to lie

on, with the most exquisite carvings and designs you can imagine.

Piece by piece, decorate your room with your own vision of the furniture, artwork, plants, candles, flowers, and other decor you love most. The more details and personal touches you give your room, the more real it will seem to you, so take your time and make it perfect.

In the open wall, suspend a breathtaking stained-glass window. Study every inch of its magnificent design as you create it, and in its center place the symbol that has the deepest spiritual meaning to you. Make the window's colors the most brilliant blue, gold, green, and purple you've ever seen.

Now slowly walk through the beautiful Lab you've created, appreciating every perfect detail you've blessed it with, until you've arrived in front of the stained-glass window, which is illuminated from behind so that you can feel the warmth of its soft rainbow glow.

As you stand there, the brilliant colors of the window beam out one by one to penetrate your mind and your body, entering deep inside you so that you can feel each ray cleansing your soul.

Blue—tranquility and heightened awareness fill your body . . . your heart . . . your spirit . . .

Gold—you embrace your divine dignity . . . your intellect sharpens . . .

Green—a laser of healing reaches to your core, empowering, exhilarating . . .

Purple—the color of royalty, your birthright as a child of God . . . your spirituality grows deeper, more sacred, nourishing, and nurturing . . . your spirit soars . . .

Now ask the white light of the Holy Spirit to surround and heal you. Feel its pure white, loving glow bathe you in peace, stability, power, control—the top of your head . . . each contour of your face . . . your neck and shoulders, releasing the tightness and the tension . . . working its way down your chest, your spine, each bone, each muscle letting go of every pain, every burden . . . your waist, your abdomen, calming, cleansing . . . slowly down your legs, the strain leaves them, so relaxed they're barely able to support you . . . your feet, cooling, soothing, refreshing . . .

Move slowly to the beautiful table you created. The white light of God's love moves with you, wrapped around you, a magnificent glowing cloak flowing soft as the finest silk as you lie down on the table. Its surface is smooth and firm, perfect support. You're safe and protected. All fear leaves you, released and resolved in the cloak of God's light.

Silently you ask The Other Side to come to you. They've been waiting to join you in your beautiful room, and they arrive in an instant and gather around the table—your Spirit Guide, your Angels, your departed loved ones, bringing with them the great teachers and doctors from The Other Side to comfort and heal you. Surrounded by perfect health, perfect wisdom, perfect acceptance, your mind clears, relieved of its stress and burdens as your Spirit Helpers lift them from you one by one and absorb them forever. All sadness, all grief, all depression, all emotional chaos unravel—an angry, churning sea of unspoken pain calmed to clear, tranquil water by the Hands of God's Healers, who move closer now, reaching out. You feel their peace.

Their Hands wait above your body, and you ask them in silence for their healing power on the source of your greatest physical discomfort. You close your eyes and feel the cool, sure, skillful touch of those Hands, hard at work with divine grace and certainty, quietly soothing, quietly calming, quietly taking away your pain and making you whole again. You surrender, one with God, one with these Healers, all doubt gone, every cell releasing its memories of illness and trauma and restored to its healthiest, most vital moment.

Soon, healed and at peace while the Hands continue working, you fall deeply asleep. A minute, an hour, a day . . . time doesn't matter, time doesn't exist. You're content, knowing you'll awake refreshed, with a renewed sense of well-being, life more manageable, nothing to fear because there's nothing you can't handle with God's help.

You are His child. You are blessed.

It's a new day.

Thank God.

* 5 *

Life After Life: How to Discover Your Own Past Lives

I know with absolute certainty that we live many lifetimes on this earth. The more we understand about our past lives, the more sense our current lives make. Understanding our past lives is a valuable key to recognizing death not as an ending but as simply another transition in the ongoing, eternal journey of our spirits.

My Catholic-Judaic-Lutheran-Episcopalian upbringing inadvertently laid the groundwork for my belief in reincarnation. Frankly, the idea of getting only one shot at this very complicated business of life never made sense to me. How could a loving God judge our success in one brief lifetime and then decide whether we should spend the rest of eternity in either heaven or hell? I have also had this talkative Spirit Guide named Francine who'd been with me since I was eight years old, telling me about my past lives and what The Other Side was like. She further explained that our spirits are nothing more or less than pure energy, and energy can't be destroyed, so obviously our spirits can't be destroyed either. That did make sense to me, as the truth always does sooner or later.

The reality of reincarnation and past lives came into full focus for me on a cold, rainy afternoon almost forty years ago. I was a master hypnotist by then, and

I was in my office during a session with a client who wanted help with his weight problem when suddenly, with no warning, he appeared to flip out on me. He started talking about Egypt and the building of the pyramids in the present tense, as if he was just visiting me during his lunch hour on the pyramid construction site. Then he lapsed into a long, impassioned dissertation in some unintelligible blather I could not understand. My extensive training in hypnotherapy had taught me that if a patient seems to be experiencing any kind of psychotic episode, it can be very harmful to interfere or stop them abruptly. So I let him carry on and kept calmly talking to him, making sure not to lead his thoughts in any way. After about a half hour, as suddenly as he had "flipped out," he "came back," returning to the shy, pleasant man who'd arrived in my office in the first place.

Like every other hypnotist at the time, I'd read about the Bridey Murphy case. In 1952, a woman named Virginia Tighe, under hypnosis, began speaking in an Irish brogue and stating her identity as Bridey Murphy, a nineteenth-century woman from Ireland. In the course of several recorded sessions with hypnotist Morey Bernstein, Virginia Tighe, in the persona of Bridey Murphy, sang Irish songs, told Irish stories, and gave intricate details about her life in Cork a hundred years earlier. The recordings were eventually sold and translated into more than a dozen languages, and Bernstein's book *The Search for Bridey Murphy* became a best-seller.

I'm not sure how strongly the Bridey Murphy case was on my mind when that session ended. I'm only sure that at no time did I even slightly lead or make suggestions to my client that could have induced him to speak in tongues or take on the identity of an Egyptian pyramid builder. I'm also sure that when, with my client's permission, I sent a tape of our session to a professor friend of mine at Stanford, I didn't say a word about what the tape was, I simply asked him to listen to it and tell me what he thought.

The professor called me back three days later, and I could hear the excitement in his voice the instant I picked up the phone. He didn't even bother with "hello" but jumped right to, "Where did you get this tape?!"

Still not wanting to influence his reaction, I said, "Why do you ask?"

It turned out he'd spent those three days listening to the tape, researching it, and playing it for his colleagues, who confirmed his amazed conclusion. What sounded to me like my client's "unintelligible blather" was actually the very fluent speaking of an ancient (seventh century B.C.), obscure Assyrian dialect consisting of word pictures, almost like spoken cuneiform.

Needless to say, I put in a quick call to my client. And needless to say, he reacted exactly as you or I would if someone asked out of nowhere, "Do you by any chance speak ancient Assyrian?" He had no clue what I was talking about.

Spiritually, I was already convinced that reincarnation existed. That hypnosis session whetted my appetite to transform belief into action. I talked to my fellow hypnotists at the Nirvana Foundation for Psychic Research that I founded in 1974, and to my doctor friends in the psychiatric community, and suggested that we study and use clinically approved past-life regression techniques in future hypnosis sessions, with our clients' full knowledge and permission, and meticulously record whatever evidence of past lives—if any—revealed itself.

I've personally done thousands of past-life regressions through hypnosis since then, as have my colleagues. Never have I even casually implanted suggestions or asked leading questions but always let clients provide a hundred percent of the information in those sessions. To say the results were overwhelmingly conclusive is an understatement. Memories of our past lives are stored in rich, stunning detail in the spirit mind of the subconscious, just waiting to be unlocked and expressed. I have enough proof of authenticated past-life regressions in my files to fill another book—and I do mean authenticated. We never assumed the past-life information a client gave us under hypnosis was factual until we verified it. If someone claimed, for example, to have been a dry-goods salesman named Clifford Underwood, living in Peoria, Illinois, in 1897, it was discounted unless we could prove that there was a dry-goods salesman named Clifford Underwood in Peoria in 1897.

By the way, in those thousands of regressions, I have run across only one reincarnated "celebrity"—an eighteenth-century British economist I'd never heard of but a few historians had. I don't even remember his name. To those of you who have had past-life readings and been told you're the reincarnation of Napoleon, or the Virgin Mary, or William Shakespeare, or Cleopatra, I'd strongly suggest you get a second opinion before you alert the media.

One day during a regression, while a client under hypnosis was describing a former incarnation in pre–Civil War Richmond, I happened to ask, in passing, "What was your life's purpose?" Without a moment's hesitation he answered, "I was here to learn to be a builder." His response came so quickly and with such certainty that I jotted it down. That night I suggested to the other hypnotists that they ask that same question of their clients, without elaborating on it or leading them, and see what happened.

They did, and the responses they got came as quickly and certainly as the one I'd received. We all started making a practice of asking the question and keeping both written and taped records of the answers. We found remarkable similarities among those answers as we proceeded with thousands more past-life regressions. The same forty-four "life purposes" came up over and over again. After years of further questions, study, research, and conversations with my Spirit Guide, our work resulted in the development of what I call *life themes*.

LIFE THEMES

The realization that clients were instantly able to identify the purposes, or life themes, of their past lives led to the obvious conclusion that the life themes of our current lives must be just as important, and very much worth trying to identify. When we compose our blueprint on The Other Side before we're born, we choose two of those forty-four life themes for our upcoming existence on earth—a primary theme, which is who we are, and a secondary theme, which is what we're here to work on. For a simple analogy, think of it as a process of planning a trip. Our primary theme is the basic goal of traveling from point A to point B. Our secondary theme is the biggest obstacle we will have to overcome along the way. Our blueprint is the highly detailed road map of the route we intend to take.

All of us arrive here with both a primary and secondary life theme. Figuring out what they are, and which is which, is a valuable exercise for clarifying and simplifying our lives—and I'm in favor of leaping at every opportunity to do that. Having a frame of reference for the basic "itinerary" of this life can help keep us on track, and recognizing that one recurring hazard that is bound to continually try to pull us off course will keep us from being blind-sided and overwhelmed by it. It's the difference between seemingly random confusion and a well-informed "Oh, *this* again. I know what this is, and I'm prepared for it."

As we discussed in chapter 1, the whole reason we leave The Other Side to come here from time to time is to learn, and to experience and overcome negativity. So not only do we not always choose easy life themes for ourselves, but many times we choose a primary theme and a secondary theme that conflict with each other, to really challenge ourselves. A case in point: My primary theme is "humanitarian." That's who I am. My secondary theme, what I'm here to struggle with and beat, is "loner." Talk about a conflict! I have to be a humanitarian. It's my joy and my passion and as essential to me as breathing. But throughout my life I have ached to disappear to Kenya, sit by myself under a baobab tree and do nothing but write from sunrise until sunset. That's never going to happen. There have been times when I've resented having to sacrifice the "loner" part of me and fought hard against giving it up. The challenge of the secondary theme, though, is to regard it not as a burden but as a force in my life that I chose, and find ways to make peace with it.

As you read these forty-four life themes and brief descriptions of each of them, pay close attention to your responses to them. I have no doubt that your spirit will resonate with a resounding "Yes, that's who I am!" when you recognize your primary theme. You may have a more subtle response as you search for your secondary theme, but as a guideline, look for something that has pulled strongly at you in your quiet moments for as long as you can remember but that even the people closest to you might be surprised to hear. If it's something that, despite your yearning for it, would complicate your primary theme or even make it impossible, like mine, chances are that is indeed your secondary theme, and exactly the challenge you chose to do battle with this time around, for the life-after-life progress of your soul.

Activator. Activators are here to pick up the slack that others leave behind. They get the job done and done right. They're troubleshooters, and they're gratified by accomplishing the task in front of them, no matter how large or small it is. Activators have to be careful not to spread themselves too thin.

Aesthetic Pursuits. A person with an aesthetic theme is driven by an innate need to create some form of artistic beauty—music, drama, writing, sculpture, painting, choreography, crafts, etc. That drive can lead to fame and privilege, which is enjoyable if the secondary theme is compatible, but tragic if the secondary theme is in conflict. Judy Garland, Vincent van Gogh, and Marilyn Monroe are examples of a primary "aesthetic pursuit" theme in unresolved conflict with a secondary theme.

Analyzer. Analyzers need to scrutinize the intricate details of how and why everything works. They're brilliantly invaluable in scientific and other technical areas. Their fear of missing or overlooking something can make it difficult for them to relax, trust their instincts, and step back far enough to see the bigger picture.

Banner Carrier. On the front lines of battles against what they perceive as injustices, banner carriers will picket, demonstrate, and lobby, whatever it takes to fight their idea of "the good fight." The challenge for the banner carrier is to learn that they can make their point more effectively with tact and moderation than with divisive fanaticism. The 1960s were rich with such banner carriers as Abbie Hoffman, Jerry Rubin, and other well-intentioned radical anti-war activists.

Builder. Builders are the "wind beneath the wings" of society, the often invisible but essential cogs that keep the wheels of accomplishment turning. Builders aren't those who march across a stage to accept a trophy; they're those who played a major part in paving the road to that stage. They can feel unappreciated for not getting the credit they rightfully deserve, but they need to remember that the rewards for taking on and gracefully mastering the builder theme lie in the accelerated advancement of the spirit on its path toward perfection, which is far more valuable than any trophy could ever be.

Catalyst. As the word suggests, catalaysts are the movers and shakers, those who make things happen and mobilize inactivity into action. They're energetic, enthusiastic, and seem to excel particularly in stressful circumstances. They feel empty and depressed without a goal to tackle and conquer.

Cause Fighter. If there's not a social issue to champion, the cause fighter will create one. They're the generals who command the banner carriers—vocal, active, and passionate about their efforts toward a better world, sometimes at the expense of their own and others' safety. At their most undisciplined, cause fighters run the risk of vying for a bigger spotlight on themselves than on the cause they're promoting.

Controller. The most successful of the controllers are those who are brilliant at taking charge of every task at hand through wise, discreet, supportive supervising and delegating. The least successful are those who feel compelled to dictate and judge every detail of the lives of those around them. Ironically, the biggest challenge for the controller is *self*-control.

Emotionality. People born with an emotionality theme have an extraordinary capacity to deeply feel the highest of highs, the lowest of lows, and every shade of emotion in between. Their sensitivity is both a gift and a burden, and they need to recognize that balance in their lives is unusually important.

Experiencer. Experiencers insist on trying any pursuit or lifestyle that happens to catch their eye. They'll move seamlessly from managing a retail store to joining an archaeological dig in Peru to trying their hand at street performing to attending blacksmith school, not out of aimlessness but because of a need to live life as an active, varied series of participation events. Excessive self-indulgence to the point of irresponsibility is the biggest hurdle for the experiencer.

Fallibility. The theme of fallibility is usually undertaken by those who were born physically, mentally, or emotionally challenged. It's an extraordinary spirit who chooses fallibility as a theme, and at those times when they find that choice discouraging, they need to remember what an inspiring example they're setting for the rest of us as they face and triumph over their special hurdles.

Follower. Followers are, in their way, as essential to society as leaders, since without them there would *be* no leaders. Offering strong, reliable support can be a follower's greatest and most generous contribution on this earth. What the follower has to keep in mind at all times, though, is the importance of carefully selecting whom and what to follow.

Harmony. Peace, calm, and balance aren't just the top priorities of people with a harmony theme, they're the *only* priorities, and they'll go to any extremes to maintain those priorities. On the plus side, they're wonderfully cooperative and can have a quieting effect in chaotic situations. On the minus side, they can find it very difficult to accept and adjust to the inevitable bumps, bruises, and stress life has to offer.

Healer. Healers are often but not necessarily drawn to the physical or mental healing professions. Their chosen theme of healing can express itself in a variety of forms, all of them involving the easing of pain and the improving of a life's well-being. It is imperative that healers learn to protect themselves from empathizing too closely with those they're trying to heal, and to pace themselves carefully to avoid an overload of the stressful problems their theme has drawn them to.

Humanitarian. Humanitarians, by definition, are born to extend themselves toward humankind. Instead of addressing life's wrongs and inequities through sit-ins and protests, humanitarians step past the protestors to directly feed the hungry, house the homeless, bandage the wounded, teach the uneducated, and generally address the world's ills head-on. They face a twofold challenge: knowing there's an infinite amount of work to be done, but also knowing when and how to stop and rest and keep themselves from burning out.

Infallibility. This theme is exemplified by the people who are seemingly born with everything—looks, talent, intelligence, privilege, wit, grace, etc. Believe it or not, theirs can be an unusually difficult theme. Their problems are rarely taken seriously. They are often resented for their advantages and can easily feel secretly unworthy from not having had to earn their privileged place in society. It's not unusual for them to be uniquely drawn to such excesses as obesity, promiscuity, and substance abuse, almost as if they're trying to balance the scales by creating difficulties they weren't born with. Because many things have come easily to them, they can feel emotionally inept in situations that challenge their character.

Intellectuality. The best expression of this ultimate thirst-for-knowledge theme is the person who studies throughout his life and continuously uses her wealth of education to inform, improve, nourish, and expand life on earth. The worst expression of this theme is the many versions of the "professional student" whose sole purpose is the self-directed goal of knowledge for its own sake, hoarded instead of shared, which is of no use to anyone but the one who possesses it.

Irritant. For such a difficult theme, it's amazing how many people seem to have chosen it, don't you think? Irritants are the constant, deliberate pessimists, the fault finders, those who are never at a loss for something to complain about. They're very helpful in teaching us patience, tolerance, and a refusal to engage in negativity, while the irritant struggles to overcome the very negativity their chosen theme demanded they embrace.

Justice. People with a justice theme are in an active, lifelong pursuit of fairness and equality. Some of our greatest presidents and activists such as the Reverend Dr. Martin Luther King Jr. are exquisite examples of the justice theme at its finest. Sadly, at its worst, when it's misguided and without God as its center, this passion for righting a wrong can result in riots, anarchy, and vigilantism.

Lawfulness. Law enforcement and the practice and teaching of law are among the professional expressions of the lawfulness theme, which revolves around a concern with safeguarding the line between legality and illegality. Elevated, those with this theme are devoted public servants who fiercely help to maintain order and balance in this world. If corrupted, and abusive of their power, they're an insult to the theme they chose.

Leader. Oddly, people with a leader theme might be very gifted at their ability to lead, but they're almost never innovative, instead choosing to become leaders in already established areas—for example, lawyers who gravitate to highly publicized cases and thrive in the resulting spotlight, instead of devoting their expertise to making significant improvements in the judicial system. Their best efforts at perfecting this theme would be to change their priority from their own success to expressing their leadership through exploring new, more socially relevant frontiers.

Loner. Loners can often be socially active and visible, but they tend to choose careers and lifestyles that will allow them to be isolated. They're content alone and usually enjoy their own company, and they often struggle to overcome feeling drained and irritated when other people spend too much time in their space.

Loser. The loser theme is essentially the fallibility theme without the physical, mental, or emotional challenges. Those with a loser theme have many advantages and good qualities, but because they're determined to feel sorry for themselves they insist on disregarding them. They seek attention through being martyrs, and if there's no melodrama in their lives, they'll create it. Like irritants, they can inspire us to be more positive and to dislike their behavior without judging them as people.

Manipulator. The manipulator theme is a powerful one and not necessarily negative. Manipulators approach their lives and the people in them like a one-sided chess game, able to control them to their advantage and often with remarkable talent. When this theme is devoted to the highest, God-centered good, the manipulator can have an enormously positive impact on society. When the theme is abused, manipulators are too self-absorbed to concern themselves with anyone's well-being but their own, at everyone else's expense.

Passivity. Passive people are sometimes perceived as weak, when they're more accurately described as uncommonly sensitive to emotional disruption. They have opinions but express them most effectively in a nonconfrontational forum, and when they take a stand on issues they are strictly nonviolent. It is difficult for those with a passive theme to cope with extremes, but a little tension can be a valuable tool for spurring them into their form of action.

Patience. This is one of the more challenging themes, since patience takes constant effort in a world in which impatience is almost considered an admirable coping skill. The choice of the patience theme indicates an eagerness to move more quickly on the spirit's journey toward perfection than someone who's chosen a less difficult theme—in other words, patience, in a way, indicates a spiritual *im*patience. Along with their ongoing battle against snapping at stress, those with a patience theme frequently fight the guilt of occasional lapses in efforts toward their goal and of the anger they feel their theme demands they suppress. Recognizing how hard their choice of themes really is can help them be more forgiving of themselves.

Pawn. Pawns are essential in the advancement of the universal spirit, since their role is to be used as the fuse that ignites something of great magnitude, either positive or negative, to emerge. Possibly the most classic historic example of a pawn is Judas, whose betrayal of Christ was ultimately a critical element in the birth of Christianity. People who choose the theme of the pawn, important in their way as they are, have to be vigilant in aligning themselves with only the worthiest, most loving causes.

Peacemaker. Unlike the themes of passivity and harmony, the peacemaker theme is typically accompanied by a surprising amount of aggression—peacemakers can be downright pushy in their zeal to stop war and violence. Their allegiance to peace is far greater than their allegiance to any group or country, and they're not opposed to achieving a bit of celebrity in their noble, highly visible cause.

Performance. People who choose a performance theme might pursue careers in the entertainment field, but they're just as likely to be content with being the local life of the party, office, or classroom. They're nourished by the spotlight, however large or small it might be. Too often they form their opinions of themselves exclusively through the eyes of others, which they need to combat by reserving some of their considerable energy for introspection and learning to provide their own spiritual and emotional nourishment.

Persecution. Another unusually difficult theme, the persecuted are not only constantly braced for the worst possibility, but they're convinced they've somehow been singled out for special bad luck and negative attention. Happiness is frightening for them, because they're sure they'll have to pay too high a price for it or that it can be snatched away from them at any moment. Overcoming the persecution theme takes enormous strength, but the reward for overcoming it is remarkable spiritual advancement.

Persecutor. Persecutors are typically aggressive, self-justifying sociopaths who will abuse and even kill without guilt or remorse and without the mitigating factor of mental or emotional illness. Obviously, it's almost impossible to understand the purpose of this theme in the span of a single lifetime; but they can inadvertently test, challenge, and inspire progress in our laws, our judicial systems, our forensics techniques, our moral boundaries, our social consciousness, and the unity of humankind.

Poverty. The challenge of the poverty theme is apparent, prevalent in third world countries but almost more difficult in the midst of affluence, where privilege can look mocking and unfairly imbalanced by comparison. Even the advantaged can exhibit a poverty theme, perpetually feeling that no matter how much they might have, it's not enough. Endurance, hope, and a perspective on the universal irrelevance of material possessions can provide brilliant spiritual growth for those who choose the theme of poverty.

Psychic. You'd think this would be my primary theme, but no, that's humanitarianism—psychic ability is not the great "who I am" in my life. People who choose a psychic theme often choose strict childhood environments at the same time, where their ability to sense things far beyond "normal" sense perceptions is met with severe disapproval. The life journey of the psychic theme is to learn to accept the ability not as a burden but as a gift and to put it to its highest, most unselfish, most spiritual use.

Rejection. The rejection theme is another extraordinarily difficult one, usually taking root with alienation or abandonment in early childhood and proceeding with those same patterns right on through school, adulthood, and relationships. Hard as it is, the challenge here is to recognize rejection not as a burden beyond your control but as a theme chosen specifically to learn that when the spirit is whole and self-reliant for its identity, it can no longer be held hostage by the acceptance or rejection of others.

Rescuer. If you aren't a rescuer, you've undoubtedly seen one in action—someone who gravitates toward victims, wanting to help and save them, even if the victim has obviously created their own crisis and/or doesn't particularly want to be saved. Rescuers are typically at their strongest in the presence of the weakest or most helpless, and they're highly empathetic. The rescuer can end up being victimized if they don't maintain a safe emotional distance from those they're trying to rescue.

Responsibility. Those who've chosen a responsibility theme embrace it not as an obligation but as a form of emotional nourishment. They find joy in active, hands-on accomplishment and feel guilt if they're aware of something that needs to be done and let it go untended. Their challenge is to become unselfish enough to remember that often the people around them need the nourishment of assuming responsibility, too, and want to share in the process of accomplishing something.

Spirituality. People whose theme is spirituality will spend a lifetime in a fervent search for their own spiritual center, if not as a profession, then certainly as a constant personal drive. The more they search, the more new territory they discover to look into. At its highest potential, the spirituality theme creates boundless inspiration, compassion, far-sightedness, and tolerance. At its lowest, it can manifest itself in narrow-mindedness, judgmentalism, and the dangerous isolation of fanaticism.

Survival. Yes, to a degree, as long as the survival instinct is alive and well, we'd all seem to have a survival theme. But to those who've actively chosen a survival theme, life is a relentless, ongoing struggle, something to be endured despite the fact that the odds are stacked against them. They usually excel in crisis situations, but they have trouble distinguishing between a true crisis and their grim view of common everyday challenges. They should all be given, and take to heart, a bumper sticker reading, "Lighten Up!"

Temperance. The temperance theme is typically accompanied by an addiction to deal with and overcome. Even if the actual addiction never manifests itself, people who choose this theme have to fight a constant sense of vulnerability to potential addiction, whether it's to a substance, sex, a lifestyle, or another person. They also have to avoid the opposite extreme of becoming fanatically or psychotically repelled by the object of what they perceive to be a potential addiction. The key to the progress of the temperance theme across the board is moderation.

Tolerance. You name it, the person with a tolerance theme feels compelled to find a way to tolerate even the intolerable. Obviously, this can become a pretty untenable burden, to the point where they'll eventually focus all their energy into one area they feel they can universally tolerate most easily, while becoming either narrow-minded or oblivious to everything else around them. Their growth can be accomplished by recognizing that the theme can cause an unrealistic and indiscriminate view of the world and learn that being magnanimous is worthwhile only when its target is worthy.

Victim. These by definition are life's sacrificial lambs, and their purpose among us is to throw a spotlight on injustice and inspire us to take action and make changes for the better. Abused and murdered children, targets of hate crimes, and those who've been wrongly convicted of violent felonies and then subsequently proven innocent are among those whose victim theme is devoted to the interest of the highest good.

Victimizer. The victimizer is here to collect and achieve absolute control over as many victims as possible, for the purpose of being surrounded at all times by visible proof of their own power. The will and feelings of their victims are meaningless unless they're in perfect agreement with those of the victimizer, and the only compassion they're capable of is toward their own hypersensitive, insatiable ego. On a small scale, they're the controlling lover or spouse, the stalker, the pathologically overzealous parent, etc. On a larger scale, they're Jim Jones of the People's Temple, "Bo" and "Peep" orchestrating the Heaven's Gate mass suicide, David Koresh of the Branch Davidians—anyone who demands such slavish devotion that even children, who are given no options, are sacrificed not in the name of God but in the name of the victimizer.

Warrior. Warriors are our fearless risk takers, our soldiers, our pioneers and astronauts and firefighters and countless other unsung heroes with the courage to step up to a physical, moral, and/or spiritual challenge from the mundane landscape of everyday life; to the front lines of wars against crime, drugs, natural disasters, and homicidal tyrants; to the vast unconquered worlds in space. Without direction, the warrior's aggression can be destructive. But when focused, especially with a secondary humanitarian theme, those with a warrior theme can make historic contributions of global significance.

Winner. The winner theme differs from the infallibility theme in that winners have an active, pervasive compulsion to achieve and triumph. They're perpetual optimists, always believing that the next business deal, the next relationship, the next roll of the dice at the crap table, the next lottery ticket or sweepstakes entry, the next job, or even the next marriage or child will be the one they've been waiting for, that will make all the difference. In its finest form, the winner's unfailing optimism and ability to pick themselves up from every failure and move on with confidence is inspiring and exhilarating. Without frequent reality checks, though, the winner can squander their money, their security, and their lives with too many impetuous, undisciplined, and uninformed decisions.

Again, identifying our primary and secondary life themes can clarify the paths we have chosen. Just knowing we chose them, instead of having them randomly inflicted on us, can be of enormous comfort. Because our life themes are choices we made on The Other Side before we embarked on this incarnation, based not only on what we want to work on but also on what we've experienced in past lives, we cannot change our life themes. But we can strive to perfect them at their most positive and overcome them at their most negative or destructive.

BIRTHMARKS

Life themes are only one facet of the research I have had the joy of exploring during past-life hypnotic regressions. Another area that came to light more recently is the fascinating study of birthmarks. The credit for my interest in whether or not there might be some actual significance to birthmarks goes to a neurologist friend whose curiosity and love of research are as insatiable as mine. He was convinced that birthmarks aren't always haphazard or simple genetic flukes, and he had been trying with no success to find a connection between birthmarks and certain congenital illnesses. Frankly, until that conversation I'd never given any particular thought to birthmarks one way or another. But he was so sure that birthmarks had some significance that he encouraged me to see if I could uncover any clues though my readings and past-life regressions.

I can honestly say that I had no expectations when I started exploring the subject of birthmarks. I was an open-minded skeptic as I met my next hypnosis client the following morning. It's not at all unusual for me to ask a client during a past-life regression about any serious wounds or illnesses they had in that past life and how that life had ended. But this time, when the client was fully "awake" again at the end of the session, I asked him if by some chance he had any birthmarks or unusual skin discolorations or moles that he'd been born with. He nodded and showed me a brownish-red birthmark on the back of his right calf, about three inches below the knee. I stared at it, and the poor man misread the stare as horror, mumbled some apology about his skinny legs, and self-consciously rolled down his pant leg again.

When I explained my reaction and played back a portion of his regression tape for him to confirm it, he ended up staring at that birthmark with the same amazement I'd felt. He'd described how, in his previous life, he had bled to death from a knife wound "in the back of my right leg, two or three inches below the knee." In the exact same spot as his birthmark.

If that "coincidence" had just happened once or twice, I would have reported back to my neurologist friend that I'd had no more luck than he did on the birthmark issue. But I repeated the same experiment time after time after time, and nine out of ten clients were born with some kind of visible marking that corresponded exactly to a past-life wound or unnatural cause of death.

One woman whose hands were cut off during her past life in Salem in the unspeakable days of witch hunts was born into this life with distinct broken red lines circling both wrists. A man with a lifelong brown discoloration in the middle of his chest had died in the late 1600s when a spear pierced the breastplate of his armor. Another man who had been hanged in 1879 for stealing a horse had a pronounced white birthmark across the side of his neck. The examples continue to this day with such frequency that it has now become rare to find clients who aren't bearing a trace of another incarnation.

Looking back, I'm not quite sure why this was such a surprise to me at first. In chapter 4, I discussed cell memory—our cells' ability to retain all sorts of information from past lives. So it makes all the sense in the world that our bodies would carry over some physical evidence of a traumatic or lethal injury from a previous life.

My six-year-old granddaughter Angelia provides a variation of the past-life/birthmark connection. Angelia is, quite literally, the reincarnation of my beloved, psychic Grandma Ada, who died almost forty years before Angelia was born. We've never told Angelia she's Grandma Ada. We've never had to. She's young enough and psychic enough that she has vivid memories of her life as my grandmother.

Grandma Ada used to run a boardinghouse and spent a large percentage of her time in the kitchen, between cooking, cleaning, and keeping her boarders supplied with unending cups of coffee. Angelia was visiting my office recently, watching my assistant Michael rinse out the coffeepots, and nonchalantly informed him, "When I was Ada, I used to do that kind of thing all the time." Another time she started giggling, and when I asked her what was so funny, she replied, "Remember when I was Ada and I made you that nightgown with the ruffled collar and you hated it?" (I did hate that thing, too. Not only was the collar ruffled but it was very high, and it felt like something was either crawling up the back of my neck or trying to strangle me.) A few months ago, we were driving through my old neighborhood in Kansas City. My son Christopher, who is Angelia's father, was driving. Without warning Angelia yelled, "Daddy, stop the car!" He did, alarmed by her urgency. She turned to me and pointed out the window with great excitement, " Bagda!" (She's called me Bagda since she was first able to talk. It turns out to be a Farsi word meaning "wise woman." Do you think any of us speak Farsi, or had ever heard that word in our lives until Angelia came along? But I digress . . .) "Bagda, look! Remember when I was big and you were little and I used to carry you across this street to the grocery store?" Of course I remembered Grandma Ada doing that. And for the record, the grocery store of my childhood had been long gone by the time Angelia hit town.

In any case, on the inside of her right upper arm Grandma Ada had a birthmark that was very sensitive to the touch. I was eight or nine years old when she told me it was from being badly burned with a fireplace poker in a previous life. (So why did it take me another thirty years to catch on to the past-life/birthmark connection? What can I say, as a child I was so busy adjusting to being psychic that I didn't have the time, energy or interest to spend on this reincarnation thing, so it just didn't register.) Angelia was born with an identical birthmark on the *outside* of her right upper arm, exactly across from where my grandmother's was. It was as if Grandma Ada was saying, "Hi, Sylvia, I'm back!" Also, it was an indication that the spirit is in the process of releasing that long-ago burn, since the "scar" had moved from the inside to the outside of the arm and, on Angelia, no longer causes discomfort when it is touched.

HOW TO DISCOVER YOUR OWN PAST LIVES

There's no question that in countless ways our past lives can provide useful keys to a greater understanding of the lives we're living now. There's also no question that you can be guided to your past lives by a reputable regression hypnotist and/or psychic.

Or, with patience, persistence, and an open mind, you can guide yourself on that same thrilling, enlightening tour of where and who you've been before. Remember, all knowledge of your past lives is stored in your spirit memory, which is alive and well in your subconscious. The process of revealing that knowledge to your conscious mind amounts to following directions to that "storage room" and then gently, methodically working to unlock its heavy door.

A few suggestions before we start:

I urge you to tape the following pages, or ask a friend whose voice you find soothing to tape it for you.

Feel free to play quiet, calming instrumental music in the background while you record, to help you focus on the tape when you listen to it and create an atmosphere of peaceful beauty for the journey you're about to take. It's not absolutely necessary to make this tape. You can give yourself the instructions as you go along. But I think you'll find this experience much more rewarding if you can devote your mind to enjoying the trip and let an external voice do the work of reading the map.

If at any point in this journey you find yourself stuck, or up against an unexpected barrier you can't get past, relax! You'll get past it easily next time you try, or the time after that. Remember, there's no hurry and no pressure, and parts of the experience may be new to you. Like so many other new experiences, the more you practice, the less self-conscious you'll be and the more free and confident you'll feel. So please be patient with yourself.

There may be moments as you travel back in time when you feel as if you're not just remembering a past event, you're reliving it so clearly that it frightens you or causes you pain. If that happens, step back from it, relax, and then approach it again from a distance so that you're simply observing it. Throughout this experience, keep reminding yourself that the events you're recalling are in the past, and so are any pain and fear they might have caused.

If it won't inhibit you in any way, don't hesitate to have a friend with you to take notes while you take this trip. It's not unusual to forget some of what you say, see, and feel once you've "come back," and I don't want any part of your mind to be preoccupied with trying to remember as you go along.

This experience requires spontaneity. Your motto during the whole journey is: "Don't think! Don't edit yourself! Just say it!"

And finally, I promise, it's absolutely safe to let yourself go in this journey. There's no danger whatsoever of not being able to find your way back the instant you choose.

The Journey to Your Past Lives

Sit comfortably in a quiet place where you feel safe, secure, and free of distractions. Place your feet flat on the floor, and let your open hands rest on your thighs, palms upward, ready to receive God's divine energy and grace.

Ask God to surround you with the white light of the Holy Spirit. Feel its loving warmth embrace you, absorbing your worries and burdens into the cleansing, healing glow of its power.

The light caresses your feet. Each muscle relaxes at its touch: the soles . . . the insteps . . . each toe, one by one, releasing pain and tension . . . calming . . . quieting . . . unhurried . . . the cells remembering their healthiest, most vital age and returning to it as the light slowly moves up. . . .

The ankles, the calves, the knees are relaxing, releasing, rejuvenated . . . no tightness . . . no stress . . . blood circulating free and healthy, bringing oxygen, bringing life. Your breathing slows, becomes deeper, more rhythmic, the peaceful breathing of sleep, as the light continues. . . .

Through the thighs, the buttocks, the abdomen . . . cleansing . . . easing . . . taking away all pain, nourishing every organ, every muscle, every vein, every cell . . .

Breathing deeply, unlabored, rhythmic, each breath a divine, healing release . . .

The white light of the Holy Spirit massages the stomach, the chest, the shoulders, relaxation becoming its own energy force, surging through organs, muscles, bones to the spine, the body's lifeline, inch by inch, blessedly slow, a loving, cherishing purge of all negativity, all burdens. . . .

Down the arms, the wrists, the hands, the fingers . . . releasing, relaxing . . . breathing quiet, easy . . . you feel fluid, alive, free of stress . . . muscle by muscle, tendon by tendon, finger by finger . . . no hurry . . . no cares . . . no tightness anywhere . . . so content . . .

Up the neck, absorbing all tension, muscles and nerves letting go, relieved . . . the head, the temples . . . breathing rhythmic . . . eyes closed . . . the white light soothing, divine unseen hands lingering over each feature . . . mouth relaxing . . . forehead . . . nose . . . lines easing . . . jaw unclenching . . . skin softening . . . blood coursing, pure and cleansing . . .

Breathing deepens. With your eyes still closed, look up at the bridge of your nose, for a count of twenty . . . no longer, so you won't fall fully asleep . . .

Now . . . eyes closed, breath slow and rhythmic, travel back in your mind to the age of twenty . . . a birthday, Christmas, your wedding, the first day of school, any event or day that stands out . . . If no particular day becomes obvious and the details don't come right away, gently ask yourself, without pressure, "I know I was twenty, so what was going on in my life in general then?" If nothing still comes this time, it will the next time. . . . Where you lived, what you were doing, who was around you, what car you owned, some detail, however large or small, will eventually open like a flower to release a whole scene, as clear as a movie, as vivid as if it's happening right now. . . . Look all around you, notice every color, every smell, what you're wearing, how you feel. . . . If the memory is a happy one, relive it. . . . If it's a memory that upsets you in any way, simply observe it. . . . There's no hurry. . . . Stay as long as you like, exploring the reality of being twenty again. . . . Then say to yourself, "Any negativity, conscious or unconscious, that I'm carrying from the age of twenty, let it be resolved into the white light of the Holy Spirit, to the age I am now and throughout my happy, healthy, productive, innovative spiritual life. . . ."

Now move on in your journey to the age of ten, when your real identity begins to take shape. . . . Another Christmas, another birthday, another first day of school, meeting a new friend, a special day at camp, any day at all you can find your way to, and the same process if nothing comes. . . . What grade were you in, what school, who was your teacher, who did you sit beside in class, where did you live . . . ? Be patient . . . Let it come at its own pace, and another scene, another vivid movie will eventually reveal itself. . . . Explore it, notice everything . . . Relive the happy, just observe the sad . . . This is your journey, you're safe and in charge, no pain or sadness can interfere. . . . Re-

peat, as before, "Any negativity, conscious or unconscious, that I'm carrying from the age of ten, let it be resolved into the white light of the Holy Spirit, to the age I am now and throughout my happy, healthy, productive, innovative spiritual life. . . ."

Then, with quiet, unpressured patience, return to the moment when you were conceived. Reassure yourself that you can do this. You'll just be using sensory perceptions you're not accustomed to calling on. Don't think. Accept the first thing that enters your mind, painting pictures with the subconscious verbalization that's waiting inside you to be unlocked. You may encounter nothing but darkness at first. Let it happen. Let the darkness and the images unfold at whatever pace your mind reveals them. Slowly, peacefully, you're traveling from your conception through the quiet of the womb to your birth, with an important reminder to yourself: "Any negativity, pain, or fear I might encounter during my birth, let me not relive it but simply observe my entrance into this world."

Now you're traveling through a beautiful, ornate, glowing, calming tunnel, a time tunnel, with pages of a calendar drifting past you in a sweet-smelling breeze, back, back, back, the dates on the pages becoming earlier and earlier. . . . You move willingly, happy and exhilarated, toward the pure white light ahead of you . . . toward it . . . stepping through it, knowing you're safe . . .

Instantly you're bathed in a magnificent glow of purple light, the color of spirituality. You bask in it, aware that this light of purple that surrounds you is opening and sharpening your awareness. . . .

A glorious, brightly colored map of the world appears before you on a screen. You step to it eagerly, saying, "Wherever I have validly been before, through the grace of my soul's memory, let my hand be guided to that place on this map." Without thinking, without looking, without interfering in any way, let your hand touch the map, guided instantly and instinctively by your spirit.

You look to see where your hand has landed on the map, and you have the faith and the confidence not to question it, wherever it is. With total acceptance say, "My spirit remembers. My spirit will take me there, to that place, and that time. . . ."

And suddenly you're there, in this place and time as familiar to your spirit as the place and time you left behind. Fascinated, energized, you start to notice details. . . .

What do you have on?

If you can't immediately see what you're wearing, look around for a place where you can see your reflection . . . a mirror . . . a store window . . . a pond or stream . . . Step to it and describe what you see . . .

Now what do you have on . . . ?

Are you short, are you tall, are you medium height . . . ?

Are you slender, or round and heavy . . . ?

Are you male, or are you female . . . ?

What color is your hair . . . ? Is it long, or short, or are you balding . . . ?

Are you wearing a hat or a scarf, or are you bareheaded . . . ?

What do your shoes look like . . . ?

Don't think! Accept your first answer. The more you let your answers flow, the more easily the descriptions will come. . . .

What year is this . . . ?

How old are you . . . ?

Who is your family . . . ?

Where do you live . . . ?

Who are your siblings? Do you have siblings . . . ?

Who are your parents? Are they both living . . . ?

Take your first answer . . .

Is there anyone around you—mother, father, siblings, friends—who's in your present life . . . ? See through their gender and their physical appearance to the essence of their spirit, the reality of who they are. . . .

Who are they in your present life . . . ?

And now it's five years later . . .

Where are you now . . . ?

Are you married . . . ?

If you have a spouse, what does he or she look like . . . ?

One by one, describe any children you have . . .

Where do you live . . . ?

Do you have a job? What do you do? How do you spend your time . . . ?

Describe your home, and the view outside its biggest window . . .

Are you happy ...? Sad ...? Anxious ...? Fulfilled ...?

Do you know your spouse or any of your children in the life you're living now ...?

Who are they in your present life ...?

Are you repeating the relationship now that you had with them then ...?

Your immediate thought is the right one ... Answer without thinking ... There are no wrong responses ...

Now ...

Take yourself to the moment that life ended, the moment of your death ...

You're only observing it, not experiencing.... There's no fear, you're just watching yourself go Home....

What did you die from ...?

Who was around you ...?

Was it painful ...?

Who came for you from The Other Side ...? Do you know that person now ...?

What illness, or what birthmark, or what remnants of that death have you carried into this life ...?

Looking back on that life, what was its purpose? What was its primary theme? What was its secondary theme? What were you there to work on, and what did you learn ...?

Take your first answer—which of your lives have you just seen? And how many lives have you had ...?

Now, slowly, peacefully, bathed in the loving white light of the Holy Spirit and a rich green light of heal-

ing, with a calming sense of well-being flowing throughout your body and spirit . . .

Quietly return to this life and, happy and refreshed, thanking God for your safe journey and the reunion with your own eternity, open your eyes. . . .

If you don't have a friend with you to write down your responses as you went along, immediately record, in a journal or on tape, everything you remember about the experience you've just had, in as much detail as you can recall.

Repeat this exercise as often as you like, with the probable surprise in store that you will return to a different time, place and life on each journey.

When you've practiced enough to become comfortable with the process, you can refine it and put it to use for any number of specific purposes. Are you curious about the source of a birthmark, or illness, or unexplained fear? Do you wonder if you have known a best friend, or the love of your life, or your child before? Is there someone you find you cannot get along with no matter how hard you try, and you'd like to explore the possibility of some bad experience with them in a past life that you're finally trying to resolve? Do you have a chronic aversion to some place, or culture, or subject that you don't understand and want to overcome?

Any questions you have, any curiosity you want to satisfy, can be explored with this same exercise. Just tell yourself and God before you start what it is you want to know and then ask for the time tunnel to guide you to the life that holds the answer, with the white light of the Holy Spirit surrounding and protecting you every step of the way.

Life, after life, after life.

* 6 *

Hauntings: What They Are and What to Do

"I don't believe in ghosts," a client once told me, "but I've been afraid of them all my life." That's a pretty fair summary of the general attitude I've run across since I started formally investigating hauntings in 1974, the year I created the Nirvana Foundation for Psychic Research. Some of those "hauntings" turned out to be wayward rodents, faulty wiring, optical illusions, overactive imaginations, and a few pitiful attempts at out-and-out hoaxes. No wonder hauntings have such a dubious reputation.

But I've also encountered my share of very real ghosts, spirits, imprints, and kinetic energy, and by learning what each one is and the differences between them, I have found even more affirmation of the eternal power of the soul.

GHOSTS

Ghosts absolutely exist. I've met them, I've talked to them, I've even developed relationships with a few of them. And the one sad, fascinating thing they all have in common is that none of them know they are dead. For their own distinct and very personal reasons, ghosts refuse to transcend to The Other Side and insist on staying earthbound. In their confused, deluded minds, they are as alive and real as we are. Because they are stubbornly clinging to this dimension after death, they are the easiest residents of the spirit world for the rest of us to hear and see.

One of my unbreakable rules is that I never do research before I investigate a haunting. If I did, my objectivity might be compromised by some predisposed expectation. For that matter, a psychic could just fake a sighting, with a few impressive researched facts—and eventually be exposed as a fraud. That's not for me, thanks.

So when the TV series *Unsolved Mysteries* asked me to explore widespread rumors of a ghost at a cliff-side restaurant in northern California called the Moss Beach Distillery, I arrived knowing nothing but the fact that countless owners, chefs, waitresses, and customers had heard and seen the form of a woman wandering anxiously around its rooms and the nearby beach. Popular local wisdom, I found out later, held that she was the legendary Woman in Blue, a regular at the Distillery during its previous incarnation as a speakeasy in the late 1920s. As the story goes, she was cheating on her husband with the resident piano player and was accidentally stabbed to death one night on the beach, trying to intervene in a fight between the two men.

Ghosts tend to enjoy attention, or maybe just our reactions to them, and this one was no exception. With *Unsolved Mysteries* cameras rolling, she quickly made herself apparent to me. But instead of an unfaithful flapper, I found I was talking to a sad, anxious ghost, indeed dressed in blue and a large hat tied with a scarf, who introduced herself as Mary Ellen Morley. She'd been in a terrible car accident near the Moss Beach Distillery, she told me, and was roaming the area to search for and comfort her three-year-old son. Her hairstyle and clothing had been outdated decades ago, but she clearly thought only minutes had passed since the accident. Time has no meaning after death, even for those who don't move on through the light to The Other Side, where they belong.

Only after my part of this *Unsolved Mysteries* segment was finished did their cameras accompany a couple of the Moss Beach Distillery's employees to the local library, where, after poring through old newspapers, they discovered the obituary of a woman named Mary Ellen Morley. Cause of death: a car accident. She had been survived by her husband and a three-year-old child.

That ghost stayed behind in the delusion that her child was still three years old and needed her. Another heartbreaking ghost stayed behind for a far different reason: His faith and trust had died years before he did.

A CBS news crew was with me in 1984 when I went to Alcatraz, years after the notorious island prison had closed its doors to inmates, to explore what were described as "odd disturbances." The night ranger who'd first reported these disturbances joined us, as did a former inmate named Leon Thompson.

It was no surprise that the atmosphere inside Alcatraz was mean, hollow, and doomed, a jarring assault on the senses. Early in the tour I had a particularly strong reaction to a stark cell in the prison hospital. I "saw" the letter S just as the empty walls appeared to be full of what looked like notes and cards. That cell, it turned out, had been occupied for more than ten years by Robert Stroud, the famous "Birdman of Alcatraz." Contrary to popular belief, he never shared his cell with actual birds—only with hundreds of notes and cards about them, tacked to his walls.

A horrible sense of some past violence hit me the instant we entered the prison laundry room. A moment later, a ghost appeared, tall and bald, with small, wary eyes. The initial M immediately came to me, but he told me they'd called him "Butcher."

I reported all this to my increasingly unnerved little team, and Leon Thompson, suddenly looking as if he was longing for the good old days when his fellow inmates at Alcatraz had all been *live* felons and murderers, inched forward. He remembered "The Butcher," a convicted hitman named Abie Malkowitz who'd been killed by another prisoner in that laundry room.

The least we can do for the ghosts we meet is try to convince them they're dead and urge them toward the light. Spirits on The Other Side, in the meantime, are aware of these earthbound souls and make every effort on their part to bring them Home as well. Basically, while we push, The Other Side pulls, and sooner or later, in minutes or hundreds of years, ghosts will find their way to the light.

And so, genuinely wanting him out of there as much as I wanted out of there myself, I began telling poor Abie Malkowitz that his life had ended, that he was free to go home now and find peace in the Holy Spirit. He began walking toward me, watching me but refusing to listen to a single word I had to say.

I hate losing, especially when someone's soul is at stake. Instead of backing off, I summoned my ever-present "ace in the hole"—my Spirit Guide, Francine. While I entered a trance state, she spoke to him through me:

"Don't be afraid. We're not here to hurt you."

He'd heard that before. She was sure he had, countless times, by people who'd inflicted deep pain. Keeping her eyes directly on his, she went on.

"When I leave Sylvia's body, I'll be returning to The Other Side. Please come with me. There are people there who care about you and want to help you."

He considered that, and her, through a long silence. When he finally spoke, it was to offer a simple, final response that was probably the only reliable position his life had taught him: "I don't believe you."

Abie Malkowitz is still a prisoner there, an earthbound ghost in that deserted hell by his own misguided choice. There are still strange disturbances in the dark nights of what's now a state park called Alcatraz. I still pray for him all these years later, asking the white light of the Holy Spirit to take him Home.

The Other Side and I did have one success I've never forgotten, because she was probably the most frightened, desolate ghost I'll ever meet. I won't mention the name of the San Francisco museum that called me to investigate reports of disembodied footsteps, moving shadows, and the occasional vague echo of a woman crying. They've never included the word *haunted* in their brochures, so I assume they'd rather be known for their exhibits. It was built on the site of a nursing home run by nuns, though, and I found one of those nuns still wandering the museum halls, a nun whose brief life was ended by the multiple tragedy of an illegal abortion.

I couldn't imagine the nightmare she had gone through, and I begged her to let it finally end in the peace and comfort The Other Side was waiting to give her. She believed me about that. After all, she was an expert on the subject of transcendence and life after death. But that's exactly what was stopping her: She was convinced that the sin she'd committed was so unforgivable that she'd forfeited her worthiness to face God, let alone ask for His compassion.

Fortunately, I was raised Catholic, so I was able to talk to her using our common vocabulary. It took several visits, a lot of prayers, and a few sacred rituals, but finally Francine and I restored her faith in herself as a child of a perfect, loving God and, with the rite of Extreme Unction, sent her willingly to the light. (By the way, for anyone who's ever wondered why I believe guilt is such a destructive force, let that particular ghost story answer the question.)

Then there's my nominee for the "Ghost With the Best Timing" award.

A Los Angeles TV show called *Evening Magazine* asked me to take a ghost-hunting tour of a bizarre, fascinating place called the Winchester Mystery House, conceived in the late 1800s as a collaboration between Sarah Winchester and a team of spirits she contacted every night in her small blue seance room. Sarah, heiress to the Winchester weapons fortune, had been told by a medium that a curse had been placed on her by everyone who'd been killed with a Winchester rifle, and that her only hope was to build a house so vast and complex that the evil spirits sent to exact punishment couldn't find her.

It's been estimated that at one point Sarah and her nightly team of spirit architects managed to have some 750 rooms built, torn down, redevised, rebuilt, and torn down again, all for the purpose of keeping her hidden from the curse. She slept in a different bedroom every night, refused all human contact except for her endless construction crews and caretakers, surrounded herself with secret passageways and trapdoors for quick escapes. Still she couldn't avoid death, which came quietly in her sleep at the ripe old, uncursed age of eighty-five.

The Winchester Mystery House today resembles an unfinished 160-room jigsaw puzzle, deserving its official designation as a historical landmark. Miles of hallways creep through it, some ending in closets or blank walls, others only two feet wide and leading into the back of a walk-in freezer. Sarah had heard that spirits enjoy traveling by chimney for easy access, so she built 47 of them. Obsessed with the number 13, she insisted on 13 cupolas in the greenhouse, 13 palms beside the driveway, ceilings with 13 wood panels, 13 drainage holes in the kitchen sink, and 13 lights in the chandeliers. One night, convinced she'd seen the devil's handprint in her wine cellar, she ordered the room sealed and walled in so securely that almost a hundred years later it still hasn't been found.

By the time the L.A. television crew asked me to escort them to the Winchester Mystery House, I'd already been there myself, more than once, with research teams who found the prospect of a house built by ghosts for ghosts as irresistible as I did. The first night I spent in the dark house—much of it has never been wired for electricity—was busy and tense. There were inexplicable blasts of ice-cold air everywhere. A wildly animated light show appeared, flared brilliantly, and then disappeared just as quickly. Two huge globes of angry, fiery red confronted us in midair before exploding back into the darkness. We all heard the sounds of carpenters' hammers on pipes and wood, doors opening and closing by themselves, footsteps and rattling chains that had been widely reported by other visitors, but I also heard organ music that none of my companions heard until we discovered it was perfectly audible the next day on the tape we'd made of that long night.

All I knew about the house when I stepped through its doors for the first time was that it was huge, Gothic, built by a woman named Sarah Winchester, and must have been a nightmare to clean. So when a ghost couple appeared, accompanied by their big Labrador retriever, and told me they were the resident caretakers, I tried to imagine anyone staying behind after death to do more housework. She was Hispanic-looking. Her name was Maria. He had red hair, and both of them wore work clothes from the turn of the century. They weren't threatening, but they definitely resented having strangers in their mistress's house.

Subsequent research revealed that for all her eccentricities and antisocial reclusiveness, Sarah Winchester was a fair, kind, and very generous employer during her thirty-eight years in that house, and these two fiercely loyal servants had refused the light on The Other Side for the sake of protecting and preserving Miss Winchester's compulsive need for privacy.

I obviously couldn't promise that the two caretakers would put in an appearance for the TV camera crew that had driven several hours from Los Angeles in the hope of capturing them on film. But I was rooting for them to give at least a small jolt to the segment's on-air host. I won't mention his name—I don't want to embarrass him. (Actually, I do, I just promised myself I'd be ladylike about this.) I didn't have to be psychic to tell from his attitude that this was not exactly his dream assignment. As far as he was concerned, he wasn't paid enough to follow some loony woman around a house looking for ghosts that every sane person knows don't exist in the first place. I'm sure he was silently composing his letter of resignation while we waited . . . and waited . . . and waited . . . and the cameras kept rolling. . . .

Finally, he'd had it, and announced to everyone within earshot that he'd be waiting outside in the unlikely event that anything interesting happened.

Just as he turned away to leave, someone even I didn't know was within earshot apparently decided this man could use an attitude adjustment—not either of the caretakers but the ghost of Sarah Winchester herself, who, right on cue, in his line of vision and captured on film, moved in a graceful, unmistakable white mist past the outside of a second-story window, then vanished again, her job done, and done well. Once our host calmed down and was able to form complete sentences again, he was attentive, humble, and stuck to me like glue for the rest of the night.

Thanks, Sarah. If I wasn't afraid you'd waste it adding yet another room, I'd send you a check for that appearance.

Without a doubt the most stubborn, ornery, and argumentative ghost I've met resides in Sunnyvale, California, at the local Toys 'R' Us. In the summer of 1978, the store employees and customers began to notice that something awfully strange was going on. Lights and water faucets were turning off and on at random. Footsteps and loud banging noises echoed from empty rooms. A defective, totally silent, talking doll began screaming "Mama!" at the top of its pretend lungs when it was put back in its box to be returned to the manufacturer. During the night, when no one could enter or leave the store without triggering a sophisticated timer alarm, toys were systematically removed from their shelves and arranged on the floor in deliberate, intricate patterns. Stacks of paper nowhere near a fan or air vent would suddenly waft to the floor, one page at a time. Well-secured displays crashed, wall hangings began swinging wildly back and forth all by themselves. . . .

Finally one day my phone rang. The store manager, reluctantly convinced he had a haunting on his hands, had contacted a popular TV show called *That's Incredible*. The show, hoping to increase their odds of capturing the specter on film, invited me to be their on-camera "ghost-buster."

A few Toys 'R' Us employees had done some research, trying to find the possible identity of their ghost. Their likeliest candidate was Martin Murphy, the wealthy, gregarious founder of Sunnyvale who died in 1884 and, legend had it, could still be seen wandering his beloved Santa Clara Valley when the moon was full. They fondly referred to the ghost as "Martin" when they told me about him.

I'd done no research myself, of course, so I was equally prepared for Martin Murphy or no one at all when a few employees, the TV crew, and I were locked in the store for the night, the alarms set to prevent anyone from entering or leaving until morning.

Shortly after we'd settled in, a maverick herd of beach balls suddenly propelled themselves from the shelves of one aisle to the floor. Soon after that a weighted ball toppled from the back of a shelf. But that can happen—not easily, but it can—so we returned it to its spot and secured it in place with a heavy box. Then it fell again, and we found the box carefully moved aside. Then a large bean bag executed an utterly graceless swan dive from its home on a high platform to the freshly waxed linoleum below.

Shortly after midnight I saw the ghost for the first time. He was pumping imaginary water from a fresh stream that seemed to be gushing up out of a corner of the room. His leg was injured and bloody, causing him to limp.

It wasn't Martin Murphy.

He told me his name was John Johnston, but people called him Yon or Yonny. He was a circuit preacher who boarded with the family who owned the property we were standing on. He loved a woman named Beth, daughter of a wealthy, prominent Sunnyvale couple, but she'd broken his heart by marrying another man and moving to Boston. Johnny, as I've come to call him, was staying right there where Beth could find him when she inevitably realized her mistake and came back.

The next day a research team from *That's Incredible* uncovered, in *The History of Santa Clara County*, the account of a circuit preacher named John Johnston, who customarily boarded with his parishioners, and died a bachelor after bleeding to death from an ax wound in 1884.

Martin Murphy, incidentally, died that same year, leaving behind several children, including a daughter Elizabeth, whom everyone called Beth.

In 1884 there was an orchard where the toy store stands today, with a stream running through what's now the corner of the store where I saw Johnny Johnston pumping water.

A lot of photographs were taken that night in the Sunnyvale Toys 'R' Us. Those using infrared film clearly show large, unexplainable blobs of light in midair. My favorite is a distinct backlit image of Johnny himself, leaning against the shelves in a deserted aisle, watching us.

I've tried many times to explain to him that his lifetime as Johnny Johnston has ended, and that if he'll just go through the light he'll find Beth on The Other Side. But he finally got so tired of my nagging him about it that he gave me an ultimatum: "If you tell me I'm dead one more time, I'm not going to talk to you anymore."

Since then, when I take my granddaughter Angelia to see him, we find other things to chat about, while he clings to what he believes is still an orchard, tending to it to earn his keep, waiting for Beth to come back. One day he complained about all these noisy children who keep showing up for no good reason, particularly a loud, unruly set of twins—that the Toys 'R' Us employees complained to me about later that same day.

Someday, when he finally does find his way to The Other Side, I hope Beth will be the first to welcome him Home. Everyone at the Sunnyvale Toys 'R' Us will miss him, and so will I. We've been able to hammer out a sort of quasi-friendship, and my little granddaughter seems to get a kick out of him when I take her there to visit.

Because ghosts think they're still alive, they firmly believe they're entitled to the spaces they're inhabiting, and we're the intruders. After all, they were there first. Asking a ghost to quiet down or leave is like being a houseguest and asking your host to shut up or get out of his own home. It simply won't happen.

I've met dozens of them, and sooner or later they'll all transcend, with a team effort between us and The Other Side. In the meantime, they deserve more compassion than fear. After all, we might not be so easy to live with either if we didn't know we were dead.

SPIRITS

Spirits, on the other hand, have already accepted their death and transcended to The Other Side. When they visit us, it's from another dimension, which generally makes them more difficult to see and hear clearly. Perceiving the spirit world through my eyes and ears is a little like seeing and hearing a room full of people through a sheet of waxed paper and a pair of earmuffs—not that I've spent a lot of time trying to do that. But that's why it's usually easy to distinguish spirits from the human-like clarity of ghosts. The longer it's been since their last incarnation, the faster and higher their vibration. This isn't a complaint, and I mean no disrespect, but Francine, who hasn't been incarnated in nearly five hundred years, sounds just like one of the Chipmunks.

That difference in the pitch of most spirit voices can make for some interesting challenges during readings. A delightful man came to me several days ago, hoping for some sign that his dear, deceased wife was around him. I saw her immediately, a radiantly happy brunette with small, deep-set eyes and a strong jaw. He validated my description of her right away, but then, just to satisfy himself once and for all, he asked for the pet name they used to call each other.

It is important to mention that as a medium, I'm just a wire connecting you to The Other Side. I have no business editing what I'm given, even when I'm sure it can't possibly be right. So I listened very closely and then, with as much conviction as I could muster, I said, "It sounds like . . . 'smooshie'?"

Close enough—it was "wooshie." He was ecstatic. Not only was it a detail I couldn't possibly have known; it was one I wouldn't have guessed if he'd given me a week to come up with it. After four husbands and more relationships than I care to remember, I would have bet I hadn't left a single pet name unturned. I would have lost. "Wooshie" was a new one on me.

An easy way to picture the difference between the vibration frequency of ghosts and spirits is to look at an electric fan. When it's turned off, you see its still blades. That's us, in this dimension. Turn the fan on low, and the blades whirl just enough to make each individual blade harder to make out but not impossible if you concentrate. That's the ghost's dimension, less distinct than we are after their death but still visible. Turn the fan on to its highest speed, and the blades move so quickly that they become almost invisible—we can look right through them as if the blades themselves have disappeared. That's the spirit's dimension, existing in a speed/vibration that the normal human eye can't perceive. The next time you wonder why you should believe spirits are around when you can't see them, ask yourself if you stop believing a fan has blades every time you turn it to high.

Luckily some spirits, especially if they died recently, are powerful enough and their desire to visit strong enough that they can slow down their vibrations and be seen, heard, and perceived as human for very short periods of time. My Grandmother Ada is one of those, as she first proved in the fall of 1954, two years after she died.

Grandma Ada Coil, brilliantly psychic since her birth, was my mentor, my heroine, and a loving, patient confidante for this child who couldn't always tell the difference between psychic gifts and insanity. Grandma Ada calmly explained the voices and visions no one seemed aware of but me. She told me what Spirit Guides are when I ran screaming from my first encounter with Francine. She shaped my life, by teaching me that being a psychic isn't a burden but a sacred blessing. Grandma Ada always hoped and believed I would become a teacher. It's an understatement to say at times during my high school years that looked really unlikely, and I was only eighteen and a freshman in college when Grandma Ada's great heart gave out and broke mine in the process.

One month short of my twentieth birthday, I started my teaching career at a small Catholic school in Missouri. Not a day went by that I didn't wish Grandma Ada had lived long enough to hear this classroom full of students address her little Sylvia as "Miss Shoemaker" (my maiden name).

My phone rang one Saturday afternoon in November, two months into the school year. It was Sister Regina Mary, the principal. She had never called on a weekend before, and she sounded upset. I, of course, still living in the vise-like grip of Catholic guilt, immediately assumed I'd committed some mortal sin and started wracking my brain trying to figure out what it was. As a stall tactic, I asked if everything was all right. She said she wasn't sure.

She'd been alone at the school earlier, catching up on paperwork in the rare silence of the unoccupied building. The alarm was on and the entrance and classroom doors were all locked. When she first heard a noise coming from downstairs, she dismissed it as imagination. After all, no one could have come in without setting off the alarm. But the more she listened, the more sure she was of hearing footsteps on the cold tile floor of the "lower level," her polite term for the basement that housed the furnace, air ducts, and my classroom. Brave and Catholic to the core, Sister Regina Mary grabbed her crucifix and tentatively headed down the stairs to explore.

Despite the fact that both she and I had confirmed that my classroom door was locked when we'd left the night before, she found it standing open when she arrived in the basement. Inside my room, gazing around, was an elderly woman.

Startled and relieved at the same time, Sister Regina Mary greeted her with a tentative "May I help you?"

"No, thank you," the woman answered. "I just stopped by to have a look at Sylvia's room. Please tell her I think she's doing fine."

Sister Regina Mary promised she would and asked the woman's name, but she simply replied, "Never mind. She'll know."

The phone rang, and Sister Regina Mary left the room to answer it. When she returned moments later, the woman was gone—impossible without being seen and without setting off the alarm.

I asked what the woman looked like.

"She was tall, about five feet seven, with pure white hair in a kind of Gibson girl style. She wore a blue dress, and she smelled of lavender. Do you know her?"

It was one of the most comforting, affirming moments of my life. "Yes, I do," I said. "She's my grandmother."

"But how did she get in and out?"

I was grinning by now. "It was easy for her. She's dead."

Sister Regina Mary managed an insincere, barely audible "I see" and never looked at Miss Shoemaker quite the same again.

That was the spirit, not the ghost, of my Grandma Ada. Not lost, delusional, and earthbound, but powerful and purposeful enough to appear, make sure I was in a good place and deliver her message, and then go home again to The Other Side.

When I tell a client I can see their deceased loved one right beside them, and confirm it with a description, I completely understand the look they give me. I've smiled that smile myself. I never add, "Congratulations, they're not a ghost," because it would take the rest of the reading to explain. But ghosts, stuck in our dimension, are also stuck with one of our most basic laws of physics: They can't be two places at once. They can't wander Alcatraz, or the Moss Beach Distillery, for example, and visit loved ones at the same time.

Spirits can, and do, move freely among us without our time and space constraints. There are no such things on The Other Side, where life is viewed in terms of eternity and infinity. Francine never becomes more impatient than when I press her on the subject of "when?". In her world there's no difference between a hundred years and the blink of an eye. Instead of answering with, let's say, "A week," she always includes the words "*What you call* a week."

As much as we might wish spirits to visit for the purpose of giving us specific messages like, "The insurance policy is in the green hat box in the attic," I rarely see that happen. Most often they come here to let us know they're with us, they love us, and they're very much alive.

For the most part, they're well and happy, too, although I've seen exceptions, and those are invariably caused by us. The most extreme was a client whose life had come to a complete stop since the death of her daughter a couple of years earlier. Her daughter appeared standing right behind her, sobbing. When I asked her why, she told me, "My mother won't let me go." This woman, it seemed, had manipulated her daughter throughout her life, and even though the daughter had transcended to The Other Side, the mother was still demanding the same absolute obedience. When I explained what was happening and the profound unhappiness she was causing, the woman calmly replied, "Of course I won't let her go. I have no intention of letting her go." I'm usually pretty objective and unemotional during readings. Not that time. That woman and her self-centered need to control her child got a face full of me before she left.

This isn't to say we shouldn't grieve the death of a loved one. A few years ago I lost nine people very close to me, including my father, whom I adored, in a three-month period. There were many days when I didn't particularly want to take my next breath, let alone get out of bed. Grieving is instinctual, necessary, and unavoidable—even animals grieve. But next time you decide to be nasty, or selfish, or greedy in the wake of a loved one's death, don't bother wondering what they would say if they were still around watching you. *They are.* And our behavior can absolutely affect the peace of mind they're entitled to as they go about their lives on The Other Side.

Spirits are much more subtle and considerate than ghosts about revealing their presence. They'll leave an unusual number of dropped coins for you to find. They'll move a photograph, particularly one of themselves, just enough for you to notice. They'll give you a hint of their favorite fragrance. They'll gently disturb your hair on the back of your neck, or give you that odd feeling of being watched when you're alone in a room or in your car. One of my father's most reliable signals is playing a music box of mine that I haven't wound in years. They're fond of creating odd behavior in anything involving electrical currents, particularly TVs, telephones, clocks, lights, and small appliances, especially in the early hours of the morning, for a logical but unromantic reason. Electricity and pre-dawn air heavy with dew both act as perfect conductors for them to "ride in" on. Unlike ghosts, spirits are aware that they're only guests in our dimension, so if you politely tell them they're disturbing you, they'll stop. They don't want to frighten us; they're just trying to share the amazing, reassuring fact that they're right here among us, literally inches away.

Often when they appear during readings, they don't speak at all but instead communicate by pantomime, like a divine game of charades, and while I can see and describe their gestures clearly, I don't always know how those gestures are significant.

A woman once asked me to contact her deceased husband, whom she'd loved very much. He was standing right behind her, plain as day to me, and I described him to her satisfaction, to verify we had him and not some other spirit who had stopped by to show off and get attention. Then, to my confusion, he started repeating the same gesture over and over again—a clasped hand, touched to his chest, several inches below his throat. Often a spirit's gestures are meant to indicate their cause of death, but since his clasped hand was touching a spot too high for his heart and too low to indicate strangulation or a trachea problem, he had me stumped.

Fortunately, I don't do guesswork, and I'm not shy about saying, "I don't know," or I might have made a fool of myself blathering about her dead husband's sternum or something. Instead, I simply gave her the same gesture he was giving me and said, "He keeps doing this. I don't know what this means."

I'll never forget the joy that suddenly lit up her face.

Unbeknownst to me or anyone else, she had recently started wearing his wedding band on a chain around her neck, and it touched her chest at exactly the same spot his clasped hand was touching his. That small gesture I didn't understand was all the proof she needed that he was watching her and was very much with her. She left me that day with the peace of mind she'd been praying for since the day he died.

Watch and listen closely for spirits' efforts to communicate with you, without demanding they be dramatic about it, or that every message they send has to involve major news. Let it be enough that they're with us, and watching us with eternal love.

IMPRINTS

I still get a knot in my stomach when I remember my first encounter with an imprint, which unfortunately happened before I even knew what an imprint was. I was on my way home to northern California with one of my ex-husbands after a few days in Palm Springs. In the strange, soft light of early evening, we reached an area of Highway 152 known to the locals as Pacheco Pass.

Suddenly, without a flicker of warning, I was hit with a wave of what I can only describe as panic, pain, and absolute terror. I've never felt anything, before or since, that tore through me as deeply and with more power. I felt as if my soul was being assaulted. My immediate instinct was to pray, but I honestly couldn't remember a single word beyond "Our Father . . ." A prayer would have been drowned out anyway, it seemed, by the bedlam of voices that started crashing into me, wordless screams of rage and violence and agony, what we have all imagined hell would sound like.

I found out later that I grabbed my husband's arm and yelled, "Help me!" and that he tried to pull over but couldn't on the narrow road. All I remember is that the farther he drove, the more visions appeared, relentless freeze-frames of brutality—Indians circling a terrified child in a covered wagon; Spanish men in cloaks mercilessly beating Indians bound with chains; Mexican and American settlers in vicious battles; crowds gathered around a corpse hanging by a noose from a tree, flaming torches igniting crude wood cabins, trapping helpless families inside. Even when I closed my eyes trying to escape the carnage, I was still assaulted by the acrid, suffocating smells of gunpowder, fire, and blood.

Many miles later, and I don't know how much time, my panic finally started to subside, leaving behind a deep depression I didn't recover from for days. My family and friends were sympathetic and tried to reassure me that it was just an especially intense series of the psychic impressions I've had all my life. But I knew it was more than that, and that I couldn't be the only person who'd been ambushed by something horrible on that road. I put out a call through the local radio station asking to hear from anyone who'd noticed anything unusual in Pacheco Pass.

My office at the Nirvana Foundation was flooded with calls and letters that I still have on file. The wording was different, but the experiences were all the same: "desperate anticipation" . . . "lost, panicked, and very dizzy" . . . "extremely frightened" . . . "totally alone and alienated, and felt I couldn't get away" . . . "a state of sheer panic" . . . "I can never remember feeling such terror" . . . "I truly felt my death was imminent . . ." California Highway Patrol officers reported a well-above-average number of accidents, violent quarrels, fistfights, suicides, and a belief that "they're all trying to die quick up there." One CHP lieutenant added, "I know people who won't even drive through Pacheco Pass because they're scared to death of it."

A few people even mentioned a distortion of time: "We gained forty-five minutes going one way through Pacheco Pass and lost an hour coming back." Too curious for my own good sometimes, I made myself go there again and went through the same horror as before. Sure enough, I lost an hour as well.

Pacheco Pass, cutting through the Coast Ranges between Interstate 5 and Highway 101 and named for landowner Don Francisco Pacheco in 1843, has absorbed more than two hundred years of unspeakable tragedy. Indians, chained and beaten and killed as slaves of the existing Spanish feudal empire in the early 1800s, called it the "Trail of Tears." Mexican bandits and Indians freed from bondage murdered each other and the American settlers who flocked there during the gold rush later in the century, and the settlers fought savagely back.

I became both a victim and a student of imprints, all thanks to what I thought would be a boring, uneventful drive home from Palm Springs.

Basically, an imprint is an energy vortex, a kind of emotional Bermuda Triangle. It is caused by a highly concentrated collection of intense feelings—such as rage, violence, grief, terror—gathering in a specific area and then becoming self-contained and self-sustaining over the years. The entire atmosphere in and around it, acting almost like an invisible veil of soft wax, becomes warped and indelibly "imprinted" as the vortex continues to turn in on itself and intensify by pulling in any other emotional energy that crosses its path. We feel the power of the imprint's concentrated emotion and react profoundly, and our profound reactions help feed the imprint and make it stronger.

Since that unforgettable night more than twenty years ago, I've encountered and been affected by imprints all over the world. So have you, possibly without understanding any more than I did at first why their impact was so deep and hard to shake off. Battlefields, concentration camps, any specific sites of the worst of man's inhumanity to man have caused that same intense panic, disorientation, and depression I remember so well. But it is not always violence that creates an imprint, as you know if you have ever stood near the Wailing Wall, or the Vietnam Memorial, or made the pilgrimage to Lourdes or Fatima or any of the sites of great healing miracles.

It might exist even in a house that happens to be in the wrong place, as a house of mine in Kansas City was. It was brand-new, the tract house my first husband proudly bought for his wife and their infant son Paul to prove we were upwardly mobile. The moment we stepped through the door I knew something was very, very wrong in that house, and it wasn't just my husband. That place didn't terrify just me; it terrified my baby, my German shepherd, and my sister Sharon. I became so ill there that I ended up in five hours of surgery. My marriage disintegrated. My husband lost his job. A tornado roared through town and didn't touch any other house but ours. Glowing blue apparitions appeared on the wall. Our German shepherd was thrown through a screen door with no one near him. The house caught fire with no apparent cause.

Francine sent me to the local library, where old land grants and maps led to the discovery that our brand-new house had been built on what was once a sacred Indian burial ground, which should never, ever be disturbed. Until Pacheco Pass, I thought we'd been the victim of a haunting. Since Pacheco Pass and all the research it inspired, I now know we were living squarely in the eye of an imprint.

The subject of houses reminds me that another powerful emotion—joy—can create an imprint as well. Once I took a brief trip home to Kansas City with my two young sons and decided to take them to see the house I grew up in, a house I adored despite some difficult times there. (Aren't you tired of people complaining about what "dysfunctional families" they had? The truth is, who didn't?)

After the current owner opened the door and I started to introduce myself, she cut me off with a friendly, "I know exactly who you are. I hear that voice around here every day of my life." These days I'm accustomed to people recognizing my voice, which I appreciate as distinctive—every doctor I meet insists on checking me for throat cancer. But this trip home happened years before I'd ever appeared on television.

I asked her what she meant as she graciously invited us in, and she explained that my voice, and particularly my laugh, drifted through the house on a subtle but regular basis. She'd quickly become used to it and found it too friendly and harmless to be frightened of, although she did seem relieved to discover that the voice belonged to a woman who was very much alive.

Frankly, my being alive was what threw me. I'd already had countless encounters with disembodied voices, but they'd all come from the deceased. But she erased what doubts I had when she added, "I can even tell you which bedroom was yours—most of your laughter seems to come from there." She escorted us to the first bedroom on the right at the top of the stairs—too good a guess in a sprawling four-bedroom house.

A whole lot of experience and research later, I know that the living can and do create imprints at places in which they've invested intense emotion. I'm not quite sure how I feel about that. On one hand, I love the fact that we can leave happiness and laughter stamped into the atmosphere we leave behind without having to go through the inconvenience of death to do it. On the other hand, assuming it is not always happiness and laughter we leave behind when we move on, sticking our successors with a negative imprint to deal with seems like a dirty trick. Obviously when John Donne said, "No man is an island," he *really* wasn't kidding. We are all affecting each other all the time, whether we've met or not. And to that lovely woman in my old house in Kansas City, what more can I say but thanks for being such a gracious hostess to my imprint, and I'll try to keep it down.

KINETIC ENERGY

The Donning International Encyclopedic Psychic Dictionary defines *kinetic energy* as "the movement of objects spontaneously, unwilled and without mundane means." In other words, unlike psycho-kinetic energy, which is the deliberate mental manipulation of tangible objects, kinetic energy can be just as powerful but unconscious, qualifying it as another phenomenon often confused with a haunting. A number of frauds have created a host of skeptics on the subject of psycho-kinetic and kinetic energy, but it exists. Take it from me. My older son, Paul, and my granddaughter Angelia are both gifted but untrained with it. So here's my invitation to anyone who says there's no such thing: Fine. Then *you* come clean up the trail of chaos they cause without meaning to. Paul's an adult now and much better at controlling it. Angelia's only six and still understandably thinks it's funny to walk into a room and crash every computer, fax machine, and copier in sight. Neither my other son, Christopher, nor I have kinetic ability, but I must admit if I did have it, I might get a little playful with it myself.

If objects fly across rooms at your house, or your appliances seem to go insane all at once, or pictures crash to the floor while your favorite afghan suddenly leaps up and drapes itself over your head, it might not be a ghost or a spirit or an imprint at all. You might just have, or be living with someone who has, kinetic energy. In that case, I cannot recommend strongly enough that you be as patient and understanding as possible. Unless a kinetically gifted person has been diagnosed and trained by a reputable parapsychologist, they're not causing all that racket and running up your repair bills deliberately, and, in the long run, they're in more potential danger than you are. It's not unusual for people with strong kinetic energy, even when it's well trained and controlled, to be subject to health problems, particularly heart attacks, due to the "power surge" the body goes through during a kinetic exercise.

As if hormones don't already complicate our lives enough, kinetic energy reaches its peaks during times when hormonal levels are fluctuating at their wildest. Prepubescent and pubescent teenagers and women who are either pregnant or menopausal are especially vulnerable to uncontrollable kinetic outbursts, and those moments just before sleep, when the conscious mind is handing control over to the subconscious mind, are typically the most chaotic.

When my son Paul was entering his teenage years, I kept hearing a long series of loud thudding noises coming from behind his closed bedroom door every night after he'd gone to bed. It sounded exactly like he was in there with sneakers on, tap dancing on the walls. (And in this family, how big a surprise would that be, really?) After several annoying nights I finally found out what was going on. My kinetically gifted, prepubescent son was unconsciously causing every shoe he owned to careen wildly around the room every time he started to doze off. Obviously he wasn't doing it on purpose, so there was no reason to punish him or give him one of those long, boring lectures we parents are so crazy about. Instead, every night from then on when the racket started, I just knocked loudly on his bedroom door and yelled, "Paul, wake up and stop that!" And it worked, every time.

You might be wondering if kinetic energy is hereditary. Maybe I can answer that question by tracing my own recent family history. My maternal grandma Ada had a psychic gift but not a kinetic one. My mother wasn't psychic or kinetic, nor was my father. I'm psychic but not kinetic. My sister Sharon isn't psychic or kinetic. My son Paul is kinetic but not psychic. My son Chris is psychic but not kinetic. My granddaughter Angelia is both psychic and kinetic, but she's not Paul's daughter, she's Christopher's. Christopher's other child, William, is neither psychic nor kinetic, he's just the cutest, happiest baby ever born. Does that help?

I didn't think so.

CLEANSING AND BLESSING YOUR HOME

I wish I had learned these lessons a lot earlier than I did, like maybe while I was plopped there on that Indian burial site all those years ago feeling so helpless and assaulted. Francine must get so tired of watching me try to figure things out for myself before I finally get around to asking her. But I perform rituals now, for myself and for clients in an emergency, and they really do help. They take much less time and effort than the routine cleaning we do around our homes every day, and the results can have a lot more impact on the physical, mental, and spiritual health of ourselves and our families.

I recommend these tips for everyone, but I strongly

urge them if you have any reason to believe you're cohabiting with a ghost, a spirit, or the effects of an imprint. I refuse to plant any negative ideas by specifically naming houses and other locations I worry about because of imprints, but please, if you're living, building, or working in or near a scene of violent death, pay particular attention to these simple suggestions and take a few minutes to follow them.

House Hunting. This applies whether you are buying or renting, in the market for a studio apartment or a mansion. We get so focused on the price, the square footage, the number of bathrooms, and the view, we forget another consideration: What is the history of the place and the land it was built on? We think nothing of asking about any past problems with rats, mice, cockroaches, and termites. But what of the spiritual atmosphere we are about to ask our family to call "home"?

If you can take the time to step into each room to explore the closet space and carpet color, you can take an extra minute in each room to ask yourself, "How does it feel in here?" and then pay attention to the first answer you get. As I said, I knew something was wrong with that first tract house the instant I stepped inside, but I didn't act on what I knew, and my child, my dog, my marriage, and I all paid the price. I learned from that mistake, and I hope you will, too. If something about a place feels bad or "off" or creepy or any other word that implies negativity, walk away. You can count on someone to tell you you're being hypersensitive, ridiculous, and/or crazy. Who cares? There's nothing hypersensitive, ridiculous, and/or crazy about protecting yourself and those you love.

Furnishings. Let me make something clear right up front: I love antiques. I buy antiques. I would never discourage anyone from buying antiques, or from accepting hand-me-downs and inherited items from family and friends. But I would never bring any of those objects into my house without touching it and spending several minutes with it to concentrate on how it "feels" and how I feel near it. A ghost can get attached to an object and believe it's still theirs. A spirit might have a lingering fondness for an object and want to come visit it, wherever it is. And every object is capable of holding an imprint that may or may not be a happy one. Your five senses have had their turn. Now give your sixth sense a chance to do its work. It warns you when there's tension and negativity in the air, and it can do exactly the same thing when you're shopping.

In fact, I take the same approach with new items too, and so do you; you just may not have stopped to notice what you were doing. You see something you like in a store, you pick it up and hold it, and all of a sudden, for "no reason," you decide you are not interested after all. There's just something about it that doesn't quite feel right. It's not important to identify what that something is, it's enough that you felt it and left without it. So what I'm recommending is really just to become aware and make a habit of an instinct you already know you have. There's enough negativity in our lives as it is. We certainly don't need to be buying and bringing home even more.

If your instincts give you the go-ahead, or you feel nothing one way or the other from the item you're considering, great. If it gives you even a hint of warning, ideally you'll leave it right where it is and move on.

But from time to time, if you're like me, you'll get that feeling that something's wrong, decide you still want that item more than life itself, and buy it anyway. But before you bring a new or antique object into your house to stay—in other words, let's not get nuts and start doing this with our groceries—you can bless it, or give it a "spiritual bath," in less time than it takes to brush your teeth.

The Spiritual Bath. Either visualizing the object or standing beside it, imagine a bright white light, the brighter the better, flowing over it until it seems the light has completely surrounded it. Then, holding that image, ask God to surround it with the white light of the Holy Spirit and release any negativity it might be holding into His loving care.

It's that simple. Believe it or not, it really does make a difference. And no, it is not too late for the house full of "unbathed" belongings you already own. You can go through your home blessing them piece by piece, or you can bless your entire house or apartment and everything in it all at once, through a different, more infamous technique.

The Exorcism. I'll discuss in chapter 7 why I don't believe people can be possessed, but I know our homes can be. Exorcising them, which just means cleansing them of any negative spirits and imprints that might have taken up residence there, is as easy as it is worthwhile. Whether it is a place you are about to move into or a place you've lived in for years, it can always use a good spiritual freshening.

If you would prefer to ask your minister or priest or rabbi or spiritual teacher to perform the exorcism, by all means go ahead. But in God's eyes you're just as elevated and worthy as all His other children, so there's really no reason you can't do it yourself.

Frankly, when Francine first suggested I perform an exorcism and told me how to go about it, I rolled my eyes and said it sounded pretty hokey to me. Since the same thought might occur to you, I'll pass along her answer: Ancient rituals sacred to any religion are powerful precisely because they carry the sanctity of the ages with them.

I still doubted it until I tried it. Sure enough, she was right again.

All you need is salt, a white candle, and holy water. Salt is an ancient symbol of purification, and the white candle simply represents positive spiritual energy.

I know, you're fresh out of holy water. But the truth is, you can make it yourself. Just let ordinary water sit in direct sunlight for three hours, and three times during those three hours make any sign over it that has spiritual meaning and power for you. I, for example, make the sign of the cross.

Starting at night, on the stroke of a third, or Trinity, hour—3:00, 6:00, 9:00, or 12:00—light your way with the white candle and spread the salt around the outside of your house until it's completely encircled. (When your neighbors ask you what on earth you're doing, just tell them you're killing snails.) Pause at each of the doors and windows and sprinkle them with holy water, again making the sign of your faith or carrying its symbol.

Once you've finished enclosing your house in a circle of salt and sealed its openings with holy water, move inside and go from room to room, still carrying the white candle. Bless every room with more holy water and the sign of your faith or its symbol, and keep repeating the same prayer from one end of the house to the other:

"Beloved Father, cleanse and purify this room with the white light of the Holy Spirit. Purge all negativity from within and fill it with Your loving grace. Amen."

✱ 7 ✱

The Dark Side: Protecting Ourselves from the Evil Around Us

The Dark Side wasn't one bit happy about this chapter being written. The first night Lindsay and I sat down to put our work session for it on tape, with the same recording equipment we'd used for every other chapter, we ended up with three hours of my voice drowned out by a weird, screeching static. Refusing to accept defeat, we took the tapes to an audio engineer, who was confident he could salvage them for us. A few days later, though, he called to announce that he was sorry. He'd tried every professional trick in the book, but those tapes were still as worthless as when we'd brought them in.

So we settled in for a second stab at taping "The Dark Side" chapter. For the duration of our work session that night, every ten minutes or so, for fifteen or twenty seconds at a time, the lights went out in the room we were working in, and *only* in the room we were working in. We have witnesses. Even the lights in the adjacent bathroom stayed on, just to give us a pointed, childish signal that the Dark Side didn't appreciate being talked about—or, more to the point, exposed.

It's typical of dark entities to be petty and selfish enough to try to interfere with a book they'll never read. And believe me, any book that explores and cherishes our spiritual essence would be of no interest to the Dark Side. In fact, if you find yourself wondering as you read this if you might be a dark entity, I can assure you you're not, or you wouldn't be reading this in the first place, let alone wondering. Dark entities never spend a moment wondering if they are dark—not because they already know they are but because, unlike the rest of us, they simply don't care.

Throughout this chapter I'll be discussing *dark entities, white entities,* and *gray entities.* Dark, white, and gray are just adjectives referring to the amount of God's light a spirit has let in. If it even enters your mind that the darkness, whiteness, or grayness of the human spirit has any connection to race whatsoever, shame on you, and give me a break.

WHAT IS THE DARK SIDE?

God didn't create the negativity, chaos, and evil that characterizes the Dark Side. In order for Him to create those things, part of Him would have to *be* negative, chaotic, and evil, and we know that's not true.

The reason a Dark Side exists is that God endowed the spirit with free will, and some spirits have exercised their free will to reject the light and embrace a Godless darkness instead. God never turns away from anyone, but He won't stop anyone from turning away from Him.

When God saw that some of His children had chosen the Dark Side, He sent Lucifer, one of His most beautiful, beloved, and powerful Angels, to watch over them. Lucifer is neither dark nor fallen. He wasn't rejected by God, or banished from the light. Actually, the name Lucifer *means* "light." It was because God didn't want His prodigal creations on earth to be abandoned and alone that God entrusted Lucifer with their care.

I don't happen to buy that there's such a thing as "the devil." I don't believe there's some evil, horned, red-suited, pitchfork-carrying menace named Satan. For that matter, I don't believe in a fiery eternity called hell, either, where some mean-spirited god supposedly dooms everyone who gets on his nerves. If that were true, what about all the Catholics who went to hell for eating meat on Fridays? Now it has been decided Catholics *can* eat meat on Fridays if they want. Do the Catholics in hell get to come back up now, or are they still stuck down there, or what? And since the Baptists think dancing is a sin, where does that leave poor Fred Astaire or Gene Kelly? I'm sorry, but the more you apply simple logic, the more this whole hell thing falls apart as far as I'm concerned.

But, most important, the God who created us doesn't judge, doesn't punish, and certainly doesn't condemn. We're all His children. His love for each of us is unconditional and eternal. Yes, there are consequences for rejecting Him and His love. But He doesn't doom those who refuse to reciprocate that love and would rather live in darkness. They doom themselves. So please, while we discuss the Dark Side, don't picture some legion of evil creatures flying in and out of hell like bats at Satan's command. It's a scary image, and it looks great in movies, but it's just not real.

The Dark Side exists in both human and spirit form, just as white entities exist in both human and spirit form. Those who live among us in human form can be a family member, a neighbor, a lover, someone you work with, a supposed friend. When "dark" humans die and their spirits leave their bodies, those spirits' negative energy can deeply affect us without our even realizing what is happening (including, to name a couple of instances off the top of my head, stunts like ruining audiocassettes and switching lights off and on). But whether they are in human form or spirit form, the dark entities of the Dark Side all share the same basic qualities:

First of all, they have no conscience, no sense of responsibility for their actions, and no remorse. They take all the credit and none of the blame for everything that happens around them. As far as they are concerned, if they hurt you, it's either your fault or you made them do it. In graphic terms, if they stab you, it's because you ran into the knife. If you criticize them, it is not because they deserve criticism—you are either too stupid or too shallow to understand and appreciate them. Self-justification is as natural to them as breathing. In their eyes, you are lucky to be among the chosen few they have decided to grace with their time and attention. And trust me, any relationship like that is demeaning and unacceptable to begin with.

In psychiatric terms, dark entities in human form are the true sociopaths among us. They can mimic human emotions brilliantly without ever really feeling them. They can seem incredibly charming (all the better to seduce you into their proximity); they can seem deeply sensitive, compassionate and loving; they can seem genuinely sorry after they've wounded you, to keep you off balance about their true nature. They can feign interest in anything that interests you—including God and spirituality—in order to create the illusion that you and they have something in common. It is all a performance, and they drop the act when they're convinced that their control over you is secure.

Sadly, we white entities, because our emotions and faith are genuine, have a tough time grasping the concept that it is all performance. So rather than walking away from the dark entity once they have "removed their mask," we stay with them, trying desperately to rescue that wonderful person we are sure is in there because we saw them with our own eyes. It is almost impossible to imagine that that wonderful person isn't lost but instead never really existed in the first place. But in the case of a genuine dark entity, it is the cruel, bleak truth.

Second, dark entities don't genuinely get to know or care about the people around them. What they do care about is the reflection of themselves that they get back from the people around them. As far as they're concerned, white entities are walking mirrors in which to admire themselves. As long as their reflection through our eyes is flattering, we're of value to them. But the minute we catch on that we're only looking at a disguise, and that whatever character and integrity they possess exists only because we "filled in the blanks" ourselves, they will react in one of two ways. Either they'll distance themselves, or they'll repeat the performance that won our approval in the first place, to try to win it again.

Third, dark entities live by their own arbitrary, self-serving rules, which can change without warning at their convenience and which don't necessarily apply to anyone else around them. In their minds, their behavior is always acceptable, but they may become outraged or deeply wounded if someone else aims that same behavior at them. White entities invariably try to make sense of all this and adjust accordingly. That's logical. It's also useless. The rules and behavior that please a dark entity on a Tuesday might throw them into a tantrum on a Wednesday. The result is that the white entity is kept constantly off balance and confused, which gives the dark entity that much more control and power.

The goal of the dark entity is not to turn a white entity dark. That can't be done. Their goal is to destroy the white entity—not physically, necessarily, but certainly emotionally. Let's face it, the only way for darkness to survive is to extinguish light, so that's their purpose and their pleasure. They go about it by trying to create as much emotional turbulence, self-doubt, guilt, and depression as possible in as many white entities as they can lure into their dark grip. They insult, they demean, they threaten to end a relationship if the white entity doesn't "shape up" while insisting that no one else would even want a relationship with someone as worthless as the white entity anyway. They promise to take away anything that's truly important to the white entity if they do leave. In other words, they will do anything that makes the white entity feel insecure and, as a result, eliminate any power the white entity might have.

The problem is, white entities have a conscience. We are sensitive and compassionate, and we take our moral responsibilities seriously. We have a natural tendency to believe the best about the people we care for. Those are the very qualities that attract dark entities in the first place. They love the flattering reflection of themselves through our eyes, and they know we're likely to perceive their darkness as some kind of sadness or pain and try to help. You may have heard the saying "No good deed goes unpunished." I have a feeling that saying was coined by a white entity who tried to rescue some supposedly troubled, misunderstood dark entity. If you're trying to rescue a dark entity in your life with your love and/or friendship, please ask yourself this simple question: Which do you feel you get more often as a reward for your efforts—appreciation or punishment?

Turning your back on another of God's children is probably contrary to your upbringing and your humanitarian instincts. But I promise you, you have more valuable ways to spend your time and energy than trying to help or save a dark entity whom you are sure will be a wonderful person if they'll only "change" (a goal white entities refer to often when talking about a dark entity in their lives) and let in the light you have to offer them. A dark entity can't be turned white, any more than a white entity can be turned dark. You can't appeal to a conscience that doesn't exist, and make no mistake about it, dark entities have no conscience. Besides, how are you going to inspire genuine remorse in someone who doesn't believe anything bad is their fault? I say this as both a spiritual psychic and as a person who learned the hard way: If there's a dark entity anywhere in your life—a friend, a lover, a spouse, or a family member—follow the advice of Christ: "Shake off the dust from your feet [and] leave."

I started this chapter with a few illustrations of the petty ways dark entities in spirit form tried to interfere with this chapter. Only because it might be helpful, I'll give you an example of a dark entity in human form: My mother was a dark entity. She was a physically and emotionally abusive parent, with every one of the qualities I've mentioned. Once I reached adulthood, I finally stopped trying to "help her" or make her happy or find some common spiritual ground where we might connect. I gave up arguing with her as a waste of my time and breath, I resisted the temptation to reciprocate her emotional abuse—and I avoided getting anywhere near her on a personal level for the rest of her life. I struggled with my guilt over that for years until I had a talk with my Spirit Guide, Francine, about it. I pointed out that, after all, one of the Ten Commandments is, "Honor thy father and mother." She calmly replied, "Of course. *If they're honorable.*" From that moment on, I never again felt guilty about keeping my mother at arm's length. To the end of her life I helped make sure she was taken care of, but I did it from a distance.

I wrote my blueprint for this life before I came here, which among other things means I chose to be born to a mother who was a dark entity. When I was younger, I jumped to the obvious conclusion—while I was writing my blueprint, I was clearly out of my mind. But looking back, I really do understand why I made that choice. Everything I know about being a good mother, I learned from her—whatever she would have done in any given situation with her children, I do exactly the opposite. I don't mean that facetiously. Not only have my sons assured me many times over the years that I did just fine with them, but they've also honored me by closely involving me in their own children's lives.

Another quote from Francine I need to add: "One white entity can dispel a thousand dark ones." Please note the word *dispel.* Not *save,* not *transform,* not *rehabilitate.* Just *dispel.* Deflect and send elsewhere. The negative energy from a dark entity, in either human or spirit form, can debilitate a sensitive, caring white entity. Later in this chapter I'll give you some specific tools for spiritually protecting yourself from dark entities. But in general, the safest option for dealing with the human ones is a firm "No, thanks!" as you break for the nearest exit.

No discussion of what dark entities are would be complete without making clear what they *aren't.* Not all murderers and other criminals are dark entities. Not everyone who's ever turned you down or broken up with you is a dark entity. Not everyone who criticizes you is a dark entity. Not everyone who hogs the remote control, or cuts you off in traffic, or tries to sneak twelve items through the Ten Items or Less line at the grocery store is a dark entity. Not everyone who dislikes you is a dark entity. Not everyone you dislike is a dark entity. I'm not talking about labeling people, or judging anyone, or becoming a spiritual snob, which is obnoxious. Recklessly categorizing people as "dark entities" without thinking the matter through completely is to trivialize a distinction that deserves to be taken seriously.

The distinction is more complicated than it looks. Take Judas, one of the most notorious people in history. A beloved disciple of Jesus, who betrayed Him for thirty pieces of silver. One of those most responsible for the crucifixion of Christ. Judas played a major role in extinguishing probably the purest, most brilliant light this world has known. An entity can't get much darker than that, right?

Yet that betrayal was essential to the birth of Christianity. Jesus even foretold it during the Last Supper. Someone had to fulfill that destiny. Someone had to write it into their blueprint to be Judas, the man who made the agonizing decision to turn over his most precious, adored friend to the soldiers who would lead Him off to be killed. Once Jesus was in custody, Judas was so horrified and grief-stricken at what he'd done that he refused to keep the thirty pieces of silver, and then he hanged himself.

That is not even close to the behavior of a dark entity. A dark entity would have kept the money and happily strolled away without a twinge of guilt in search of some other white entity to destroy.

So you can't simply point a finger and say, "Okay, that person did something despicable, so they're a dark entity. Next?" Also, the Dark Side doesn't include the mentally ill or genetically chemically imbalanced, either, which makes the distinction even more complicated. I happen to believe that one of the most important verses in the whole Bible is, "Judge not, lest ye be judged." I can't stress enough that the purpose of explaining and exposing the Dark Side isn't to name names or initiate some new spiritually elite party game. The purpose is to identify the common characteristics of dark entities so that we can learn how to spot them, understand how they operate and what their goal is, and avoid them like the flu.

If someone in your life makes you feel drained, depressed, diminished, tired, insecure, inadequate, weak, pessimistic, confused, helpless, even nauseated or headachy, I won't say they're definitely a dark entity, but you should get away from them just in case. Dark entities thrive on depression, fear, turmoil, and emotional chaos. Those are the symptoms an unprotected white entity will usually experience if they spend too much time with a dark entity. The weaker your emotional resistance is, the easier it is for a dark entity to manipulate you. Their negative energy can be as real and powerful as a white entity's positive energy. So once they've caused any or all of those negative symptoms in you, the more power they'll have over you, and we white entities just can't give them that satisfaction.

Dark entities don't happen by accident, of course. There's a logical reason for how spiritually hollow they seem, and even though there's no such thing as hell, they do pay a high price for choosing darkness instead of light.

THE DARK SIDE BETWEEN LIVES

Before I started studying the Dark Side in depth, I used to wonder what on earth I would do if a dark entity came to me for a reading. I wasn't afraid of them. Thanks to my mother, I'd had plenty of experience with darkness. But for some reason I didn't understand, I didn't think there would be anything for a psychic to read.

Many years of research later, I understand why.

There's a right door and a left door on The Other Side.

White entities go through the right door when we "die." It's usually such a direct trip that we're rarely even aware there's a door at all. We just joyfully step through it as we follow the light.

Dark entities, on the other hand, go through the left door, into an abyss of nothingness, devoid of hope, in a blackness that is the spiritual opposite of God's pure white light of unconditional love. Again, not for one moment has God sent them through the left door.

"Left door people" are separate from God only because they have chosen to turn away from Him. Nor do they stay there for long. From the black, hopeless, loveless void behind the left door, dark entities go right back in utero again for another lifetime on earth, in a kind of perpetual "horseshoe" pattern.

That explains why I always had that sense that there was nothing for me to read about a dark entity. There isn't! They recycle, life after life after life, without a blueprint, without Spirit Guides, without Angels, without the benefit of the peace, wisdom, insight, reunions with loved ones, perfect love and joy in God's light that the rest of us have to look forward to on The Other Side.

For example, I am convinced that my mother went from this earth through the left door to the darkness, and then right back into the womb of some poor unsuspecting woman in Ethiopia. About twelve years from now you'll hear about a violent uprising in Ethiopia, and you'll just nod to yourself and say, "Sure enough, it's Sylvia's mother."

Not even dark entities are doomed to an eternity excluded from God's presence, though. Sooner or later the powerful white entities on The Other Side are able to catch these dark entities in transit from one dimension to another and bring them Home, to be embraced into the white light of the Holy Spirit. But until then dark entities proceed on their own dark, uncharted, chosen, Godless journey that we can't imagine or salvage.

Like white entities, some dark entities remain earthbound for a while, not realizing they are dead; others visit earth in spirit form in their brief time between lives. Given a choice, I'd rather deal with a dark entity in ghost or spirit form than a dark entity in human form any day of the week. But again, in any form, they can create all sorts of major and minor chaos with their negative energy. They can tamper with cars, phones, appliances, computers, TV sets, anything mechanical or electrical. They can also affect the general atmosphere in a room, so that suddenly, without knowing what hit them, even the happiest, most pleasant people can become depressed, anxious, and cranky enough to start snapping at each other.

In this situation an important step is to open your mouth and talk about it. If dark entities are at work on a group, there's a very good chance that you are not the only one who's feeling the assault. Announce that your car's acting up for no reason, or you have a sudden headache, or that you're in a nasty mood. You'll be surprised at how often you hear a chorus of "Me too!" from everyone you are with.

Talking helps dispel the confusion and helplessness you are feeling, by putting the blame where it belongs—on the negativity of dark entities. Nothing makes them disappear faster than being dragged out into the light of white entities.

Speaking of exposure, I want to clear up a few myths about dark entities in spirit form, because in some cases they've been given credit for more power than they have.

1. They can't physically hurt you. At their worst, they can only cause enough confusion that you become careless and accidentally hurt yourself.
2. They can't will you to kill yourself. At their worst, they can only cause enough depression that you might fall off track, but *it's only temporary,* and *it's not your fault*! Don't you dare give them the satisfaction of diminishing your light. We white entities need each other, and together we're more powerful than they will ever be.
3. They can't put a curse on you. As we'll discuss later in this chapter, there is no such thing as a curse. Period.
4. And above all, *they can't possess you.*

I don't believe in demonic or evil possession. Mind you, I've performed my share of exorcisms in my day, but only if I'm working with someone who is so convinced they are possessed that nothing short of an exorcism will make them believe they are "cured." Even then, during the exorcism I reassure them that there is no devil, and there are no demons—and if there were, they wouldn't have the power to actually invade your mind or body anyway.

I have it on expert authority—my Spirit Guide, Francine—that no spirit, either white or dark, can actually possess your mind. She and I have talked about possession many times, and she always comes back to the same bottom line: The spirit world can affect our minds, but they can never enter and overtake our minds. Yes, our human minds can be brainwashed. But they're still our own "brains" being "washed," not some dark entity's "brain" that has replaced ours.

I am a trance medium. That means that by going into a trance, I can "step aside" and allow my Spirit Guide to use my voice to communicate to other people. Some trance mediums allow spirits to actually inhabit their bodies during seances and channeling sessions. I personally don't permit that myself—which is more proof against possessions. Any trance medium will back me up on this: The spirit world can use only as much of us as we *allow*. So if a white entity can inhabit a trained trance medium only when we let them, there's not a chance that a dark entity can possess someone with no permission at all.

I'm not saying that people who claim to have been possessed are making it up. If they believe it, it deserves to be taken seriously and dealt with. What I am saying is that there are other phenomena that can be easily mistaken for possession.

For one thing, they don't call it the "power of suggestion" for nothing. Being raised in a culture or religion that believes in possession can be enough all by itself that anything from PMS to serious mental illness can pass as a "possession." But just identifying with a person or special interest can lead someone to affect the symptoms of a possession if it's been suggested to them strongly enough. You'll notice that people with devout religious backgrounds are always sure it's Satan they're possessed by. A person with an avid interest in history may think it's Napoleon, Theodore Roosevelt or Marie Antoinette. Literary buffs are convinced it's Shakespeare, Ibsen, Poe or Dickens. Aviation enthusiasts go for Amelia Earhart, Charles Lindbergh or Wilbur Wright. Come to think of it, I have yet to run across someone who claims to be possessed by a person no one has ever heard of.

Some people are so sensitive to negative energy that they become overwhelmed by it, to the point that they feel they've lost their own identity. That isn't a possession. We all feel lost and "not ourselves" sometimes, and the more sensitive we are, the more often it can happen. But again, unless we make a conscious decision to let another spirit take over, being "not ourselves" doesn't mean we're "someone else." It just means we need extra spiritual attention from ourselves and our loved ones to help us find our way back to our safe, familiar path again.

Kinetic energy can also cause the dramatic physical chaos we picture when we think of a possession. Remember that kinetic energy occurs when the mind spontaneously and undeliberately manipulates tangible objects. Times of extreme emotional or spiritual turmoil can trigger spasms of kinetic energy—electrical power surges, objects flying across the room, appliances going insane, pipes bursting, etc. Since the turmoil that unleashes kinetic energy is often the same turmoil we've come to associate with a possession, it's no wonder the two get mistaken for each other. But there's one major difference: Kinetic energy is real. Possession isn't.

GRAY ENTITIES AND THE HOLDING PLACE

In any world where white and dark both exist, there are bound to be shades of gray. And that's just as true in the spirit world as it is here on earth.

Gray entities are kind of the "fence sitters" among us. They can be deeply influenced by both white and dark entities, so they're not quite sure where they belong. It's not that they're weak necessarily; they're merely confused and trying to find a place where they fit.

If we're honest with ourselves, we white entities have to admit that at least once we've wondered if the Dark Side is having more fun than we are and given "dark" behavior a try. Unless you've never, never, ever done something you knew was wrong, but you did it anyway with some lame excuse like "because I felt like it" or "it just happened," in which case I'm guessing you're too young to be reading this. We're usually miserable failures at "dark" behavior, and sooner or later we make complete idiots of ourselves. We know deep in our hearts that we've crashed a party where we don't even want to belong, and with varying degrees of embarrassment and remorse, we crawl back to the "whiteness" that's the only real comfort zone we have. Again, white entities can't be turned dark. It's as if we suddenly decide to try on a whole new wardrobe that looks more exciting than ours, but the novelty wears off when we finally have to admit to ourselves that those other clothes just don't fit.

Gray entities are right in the middle, in search of their own style, able to wear either wardrobe but never sure which one feels better. A gray entity can be turned either white or dark, so they feel as if they're being pulled in both directions.

They're the criminals who, unlike dark entities, *can* be rehabilitated. They're lost children, still looking for an identity that will win them the most attention and approval—the Dark Side's favorite targets. They may have run into the "wrong" white entities too often and started wondering if there's really any sincerity, integrity, compassion or hope to be found in "whiteness." Or they have lived good, decent lives until too much bad luck or too many tragedies made them wonder what the point is. Substance abuse, physiological chemical imbalances, mental illness—any number of forces can pull an innocent spirit into a gray wasteland.

There are a couple of things we white entities here on earth can do to help steer gray entities away from the Dark Side.

One is to avoid the white entity's occasional habit of being "all talk and no action." We've all seen it. And let's face it, from time to time we've all done it. We make loving God and living the life of a true white entity sound great when we describe it. But after we change out of our church clothes, we can be just as miserable and rude and dishonest and judgmental as we preached against being. How appealing is this to a gray entity if we don't live what we believe? We can't merely talk about the joy and hope that comes from embracing God. We have to show it, or the gray entities are going to think there's nothing for them but empty hype.

And by all means, we can pray for them.

The importance of that was really driven home for me by an experience I had while writing this book. I'm not much of an astral projectionist. I don't let my spirit travel around without my body very often, but one night, through astral projection, I ended up in what my Spirit Guide later explained was the Holding Place.

I was surrounded by people who had died. They

never said a word to me, but I could tell they were in deep despair. The air was thick with sadness, and the people, who ranged in age from early teens to elderly, kind of shuffled when they walked and kept their eyes downcast, so that even their body language conveyed hopelessness.

Beyond the area we were in, I saw a pitch blackness that frankly terrified me, and I wasn't about to go anywhere near it. That's when I realized that I'd stepped inside the left door of The Other Side, and that the blackness beyond us was full of dark entities about to return to earth in utero.

I also realized that the people I was with still had the free will to choose. They could go on into the blackness, or they could go through the right door into the light of God on The Other Side. They weren't trapped in this Holding Place; they were there waiting to make that choice.

Their faith wasn't gone; it was just as heartbreakingly lost as they were. Purely on instinct, I started approaching them one by one, begging, "Please say you love God. Please say you have hope. Believe in God and you can get out of here." They still didn't make a sound or even raise their sad eyes to look at me, and I remember becoming weaker with the despair I started to absorb from them before I finally got out of there.

I squared off with Francine, my Spirit Guide, the next day and demanded to know why she'd never told me about the Holding Place before. She said the same thing she always says in those situations: "Unless you ask the question, I won't give you the answer." I hate it when she does that.

But she also told me I'd managed to get through to two of the spirits among the thousands that were there. Two of them had left the Holding Place and stepped through the right door into the light of The Other Side after I'd gone.

Since that night I have included those sad, lost Holding Place spirits in my prayers. I hope you'll do the same. If they can't summon the faith to get safely Home to The Other Side, the least we white entities can do is help them along with our faith, since we're lucky enough to have plenty to spare.

SUICIDE

Even though none of those spirits ever spoke to me, I did "know" why some of them were in this Holding Place, and Francine confirmed it. Because of that, I want to get a few facts straight about the confusing, tragic issue of taking one's own life.

I was taught growing up that "people who commit suicide go to hell." Period. Case closed.

That's not true. And, I might add, what an ugly, cruel, guilt-provoking lie to dump on the loved ones of suicide victims. Again, there is no "hell," and no way God would condemn any of His children to an eternity in it even if there was. And while in general suicide is a broken contract with God and with our own spirits, since none of us write suicide into our blueprints, there are exceptions to that. So, as always, we have no business making a blanket judgment like that.

Suicides resulting from extreme mental or physical illness are as likely as we are to go to the light and be embraced on The Other Side.

Suicides resulting from hopelessness and despair, I now know, go to the Holding Place. In fact, if you've ever talked to someone who had a near-death experience during a failed despair suicide attempt, they describe finding themselves in a place of overwhelming sadness, not in pitch blackness but more as if they're "away from the light." They're either surrounded by silence, or they're being mocked and scorned by the other spirits around them, with no compassion to be found anywhere. Sure enough, that's the Holding Place. Yet that also means they still have the option to choose to join the dark entities in the blackness or to go to God's unconditional love through the right door on The Other Side. Again, our prayers can make all the difference.

Those suicides from despair and other gray entities who choose the Dark Side go directly back in utero again, just as dark entities do. Unlike dark entities, though, they won't be dark in their new incarnation. They will be gray again, with a new life and new chances to choose the light and overcome the hopelessness that defeated them last time.

Other suicides, though, are motivated by revenge, self-pity, or just plain meanness to punish those around them for not paying enough attention or for other alleged slights. Those are the only suicides that go directly through the left door into pitch blackness and then directly back in utero again. They won't necessarily be a dark entity in their next incarnation, they won't have a blueprint, Spirit Guide, and the whole range of help The Other Side provides. That next incarnation is guaranteed to make that revenge/self-pity/meanness suicide seriously not worth it. And again, it's never a case of God depriving those suicides as a means of punishment. They deprive and punish themselves, while God waits as always with His arms eternally extended to embrace them.

Because suicides are usually deaths by trauma, their spirits can be shocked by the suddenness of it, even though it was by their own hand, and remain earthbound for a time, not realizing they're dead. The same rules for what to do about ghosts apply to earthbound suicides. Keep telling them they're dead and urging them to go to the light. Above all, pray for them. If they're white or gray, you can make all the difference in helping to send them Home. If they're dark, it's a great way to protect yourself from them. After all, in any situation there's no better protection than God.

Here is a perfect example of a suicide inspired by pure meanness and revenge that resulted in a haunting: A distraught woman asked for my help in identifying and getting rid of the ominous presence she felt in every room and every corner of her house. Its source was immediately apparent. Her late husband had been abusive and pathologically possessive throughout their sixteen-year marriage. She had finally started to defy his demands and signed up for night school in spite of his outraged, brutal objections. On her first night of classes, moments after she managed to escape the house and his wrath to head off to school, he took a shotgun from his hunting rack, stretched himself out on her side of their bed, and blew his head off. As if he had not already caused her enough grief during his lifetime, he remained earthbound, watching her, haunting her and keeping her constantly frightened and miserable.

Understandably, it wasn't all that easy to convince her to set aside her resentment and join me in praying for him and insisting that for his own benefit, he needed to accept that he was dead and let God bring him Home. The fact that when she did pray with me it was more to get rid of him than to bless his spirit was perfectly fair. A few weeks later, between our prayers and my talks with him, he did move on. He still chose to turn away from God, go through the left door and horseshoe right back in for another dark incarnation. That was his choice to make, not ours, and we still accomplished our goal for her. She was finally free of him once and for all, and she is now happily and peacefully remarried to a kind, gentle man.

PSYCHIC ATTACKS

No, I'm not referring to a situation in which you get attacked by an unruly mob of psychics. Psychic attacks are one of the insidious ways in which the negative energy of the Dark Side tries to extinguish the light of white entities. They are aimed directly at our consciences, and at our sincere concerns about our contributions to humanity and to God.

Ask yourself if any of this sounds familiar:

"I don't know why I ever thought I could make any difference on this earth. I thought I'd worked hard and tried hard, but look at me. I haven't accomplished anything worthwhile at all. I've just been kidding myself. If I never bothered to get out of bed again, or just vanished into thin air, it wouldn't make any big difference to anyone."

Those words, or a version of them, are the definition of the classic psychic attack. They are assaults by the negative energy of the Dark Side, seemingly out of nowhere, on our mental and emotional well-being. They are the Dark Side's way of throwing a bushel over our light, so to speak, and trying to destroy our power by debilitating us with depression, self-doubt, and hopelessness. No matter how real the implanted thoughts of a psychic attack might seem—they're not, I promise you. A lesson I learned firsthand.

Several years ago I got hit right between the eyes by every one of the negative thoughts I described. I felt like a complete failure and phony, not as a psychic but as a worthwhile human being. As far as I was concerned, anyone who said they appreciated or admired or even liked me was either just being polite or I'd tricked them into thinking I had some value. I felt numb and powerless, too insignificant to deserve any special attention from God.

One night in the middle of this "spiritual desert," I

was speaking to a congregation of about one hundred fifty at my church. I decided that, not as a play for sympathy but as a debt of honesty, I owed it to these people to drop my act of having something valuable to say, so I confessed what I was feeling. I started right down the list of all those negative thoughts that were plaguing me. What I expected to see was a sea of shocked, disappointed faces.

What I saw instead, to my amazement, was a sea of unanimous nods, understanding, and even some audible sighs of relief.

It turned out at some time or other, every other person in that room had felt exactly the same way I was feeling with the same thoughts of failure, phoniness, and worthlessness. They'd been too self-conscious to admit it while they were suffering. Needless to say, even at my lowest, I can't claim that self-consciousness is among my problems.

That night was the beginning of my research into psychic attacks. It was also the beginning of the end of the psychic attack I was going through—proving once again that *we have to talk openly and honestly with each other*! Just finding out that it wasn't just me, and that people I loved, who weren't failures or phonies or worthless or anything of the kind, had survived this same emptiness, set us all free.

Most important of all was the discovery that when a psychic attack hits, *we're all hearing the very same "tape."* Clients around the world, in the widest possible variety of circumstances, find that same tape playing in their heads at some point or other in their lives.

So here's what I want you to try the next time you find yourself in the midst of a psychic attack. Don't worry if you feel silly doing it. Feeling silly beats feeling numb, depressed, and worthless.

The instant negative thoughts about yourself enter your mind, don't dignify them for one second wondering if they are true. Remind yourself that it's just the Dark Side again, slipping another one of those ridiculous tapes into your head to try to upset you and turn off your light. You're smarter and stronger than the Dark Side, and you're not going to fall for this stupid prank again.

With your forefinger, reach up to a spot on your forehead between your eyebrows and about an inch and a half above them, where your "third eye" is, and picture an "eject" button there. Push that eject button while saying, "I refuse this tape and the Dark Side, and I release its negativity from my mind into the white light of the Holy Spirit."

The simple act of hitting that eject button will remind you that those negative thoughts really are just an annoying tape that we all get stuck with every once in a while. Remember that and you'll never feel so helpless and assaulted during a psychic attack again.

CULTS AND CURSES

There are several reasons I lump those two into the same category. They're despicable enough to answer sincere spiritual questions and needs with nothing but self-serving, manipulative lies, and they flourish during times of heightened fear and uncertainty—such as, for example, a new millennium.

I'm not sure what it is about new millennia that makes everyone a little nuts. If God has written somewhere that He's going to wipe us all out on a date with three zeroes in it, I must have missed it. What I *have* read is that in the last moments of the year 999, thousands of people ran screaming into the streets, convinced that the world would end at the stroke of midnight. I've always wondered: How long did they stand out there before they felt sheepish enough to scuff back home and go to bed?

At any rate, since cults, curses, and scams are going to be particularly prevalent around the year 2000, and since they can cost you dearly in financial, emotional, and spiritual terms, please be especially vigilant and especially clear in your loud, resounding "Stop!"

Cults. They are almost always started by a dark entity disguised as a white entity in order to lure and destroy other white entities. It has become illegal to deprogram cult victims—"freedom of religion," you know. I passionately believe in freedom of religion. Yet I also passionately believe that any group that promotes suicide, isolation, and the molestation, endangerment, or sacrifice of innocent children has one hell of a nerve calling itself a "religion."

What is particularly heartbreaking about cults is that by definition they victimize people who are on an earnest, well-intentioned, humanitarian spiritual search. If you're on that search and think you have found the answer in a person or group to which you're considering devoting your money and/or your life, I truly hope you'll sit down with someone you trust *outside that group* and discuss the following issues:

Ninety-nine times out of a hundred there's a person (or, very occasionally, two people) at the head of the group who requires that, in order to be accepted into the group, you recognize that person as your God center. That means you are dependent on them for your proximity to God, because they are closer to God than you are, and they alone determine who does and who doesn't deserve the ultimate rewards God has to offer.

All of that is a lie. No matter what your personal belief, *you* are your God center. Any time anyone demands that you look anywhere but inside your own divine spirit for your God center, your own closeness to God, and your own birthright to the rewards God offers every one of His children, *get out of there*!

Cult leaders devise all sorts of excuses for why their particular group should isolate itself from the rest of society. I don't care how articulate, or even spiritual, those excuses might sound. The truth is, they're all just clever rhetoric for the real reason a cult leader wants you isolated: Cults don't bear up under scrutiny from "outsiders." In the bright light of day, someone just might take a look at the leader and point out that "the emperor has no clothes" (but maybe *does* have a criminal record, in which case you'll hear one of two excuses—he has repented, so his past doesn't count, or, she has conveniently renounced "the arbitrary laws of government and mankind").

Or, someone might wonder why, in some cases, a group that embraces pacifism and nonviolence has more guns than many small countries.

Or, someone might want to look into why the cult members have either "donated" or willed all their money to the group and/or its leader. Cults isolate themselves from society, so we know the money isn't being used for reputable charities or the good of humankind in general. And cults aren't exactly known for living in luxury, so not much of the money is being spent on them. A popular claim is that the money is "for God." What use does God have for money? What exactly is He going to do with it? Next time you see God at the mall or the grocery store, for heaven's sake, call me! I don't want to miss that!

So if all that money isn't for the benefit of humankind, and it's not being spent on the membership, and God doesn't need it, where do you suppose it's going? Or, to put it more accurately, to whom?

If after honest soul-searching and getting straight answers to the hardest questions you can ask yourself, you still decide that a cult is what you want in your life, I really do wish you Godspeed. Please, though, don't drag your children into it. If what you are getting into is really such a worthwhile, God-centered pursuit, they can sign up when they are old enough to make their own decision. If you have the right to choose, they should have that same right someday too. In the meantime, stop and think. You know that the parents who joined the People's Temple and the Branch Davidians didn't start out believing that they would ultimately condemn their children to a death sentence. Your life is yours to do with as you please. But every child deserves a chance to grow up safe, so that someday their lives will be theirs to do with as *they* please.

Curses. They are another insidious way of separating you from your money through fear and a supposed hotline to God and/or the spirit world. Those who are vulnerable to the threat of a curse usually have a run of bad luck and want to find out why it is happening and put a stop to it. Those who claim to have the answers call themselves many things, from psychics to mediums to fortune tellers to spiritualists, but they all have one thing in common. They are liars.

Here's the truth: The only person who can put a curse on you is *you.* No one else has that power unless you give it to them, and even then you have to actively make the curse work.

I'm living proof that curses are powerless without your permission. I've helped police and district attorneys bust any number of these despicable scam artists, so you know there are Sylvia dolls all over the world getting pins stuck through them twenty-four hours a day. If curses were real, my life would be nothing but a series of pained jerking motions and a nonstop scream of, "Ow, ow, ow, ow, ow . . . !"

In the old days, and in a handful of cultures even today, if someone put a curse on you, they would announce it by laying a dead chicken on your front doorstep. You'd be paralyzed with fear at the news that you'd been cursed, take to your bed, refuse all food and water in case it had been poisoned, and, within a relatively short time, you'd die, and the myth of the curse would carry on.

Or, maybe the reason was that after depriving yourself of food and water for days on end, of *course* you died! If any version of that ever happens to you, get up, eat, drink plenty of water, go on about your business, and for God's sake, get rid of that disgusting dead chicken on your doorstep.

Isn't it a coincidence that the only way to get rid of every curse, no matter what it is or who's behind it, is money? Your money? Sure, okay, sometimes it might be your car, or your jewelry, or your house, but what do those really boil down to? Hand over your money and/or valuables to the fortune teller who uncovered the curse and, like magic, the curse will be gone, along with your money and/or valuables—and the fortune teller.

For the sake of discussion, even though these curse busters come in both genders, we'll call ours Madame Zorro—"Madame" because they are basically prostitutes (although I have more respect for prostitutes, who at least provide an actual service for your money), and "Zorro" because Z seems to be a popular letter with that crowd and many of them seem to believe they look good in capes.

The Madame Zorros of this world have thought of enough ways to separate you from your money to fill a book. But they invariably start with one basic assumption that gives them an edge before you even walk through the door. If things were going well, you wouldn't be there. You want to know why, and you want to put an end to it.

Madame Zorro's answer to why is always "a curse." She might call it a dark cloud, or the evil eye, but a curse by any name will still cost you. Remarkably, even though you have never met her before, so she can't possibly have had anything to do with putting the curse on you, she just happens to be the only person who can make it go away. Is it just me, or does that make absolutely no sense?

Her usual prey are those who were raised in a culture—particularly Hispanic and the West Indies—that embraces curses and superstitions as a natural part of its belief system. But even those of us who scoff at the very idea of superstition (usually while wearing our lucky socks) can be thrown off balance enough to wonder, if only for an instant, "What if she's right?" So if you're thinking as you read this that you could never be that gullible, guess again.

According to Madame Zorro, the curse was usually inflicted on you by a dark-haired woman who is probably a distant relative or a former co-worker. That should cover every job you have ever had, every remote branch of your family, and your in-laws, whom you have never particularly trusted anyway. But wherever the curse came from, she sadly informs you that she can't rid you of it for the basic price of the reading, which is always deceptively low—she relies on volume business.

Her "curse cures" are always visual, hyperemotional, and expensive, with enough urgency to prevent you from having time to regain your balance and think clearly. If you won't take her word for it that the curse exists, she'll prove it with some sleight-of-hand or special effects you could duplicate with a good book on magic and a child's chemistry set. She's invariably good at it, so never believe your eyes. Remember, David Copperfield once very convincingly made the Statue of Liberty disappear, but last time I looked, about a week ago, it was still there.

If Madame Zorro is a small-time scam artist, she will banish the curse by lighting ten candles at $80 apiece or selling you a small vial of "potion" for $50. If she's after bigger game, and planning to leave town very quickly, she'll soon "discover" that it is your jewelry, or car, or house, or anything of value you own that is cursed. And no matter how artfully she might put it, she always has the same four-word solution for this cursed item that's causing your life to fall apart: "Give it to me." What I've never understood is, if it really is cursed, why does she want it?

Never forget, whether she pretends to set fire to it, bury it, or throw it off a bridge, the moment it leaves your hands, you'll never see it again. Being scammed has nothing to do with her being smarter than you. She's simply put the same energy into learning how to manipulate you that you've put into being a decent, caring person.

Her biggest gun is her curse of curses—you're suffering because God is angry with you. If you can't think of anything you've done to deserve His punishment, you obviously did something in a past life that He's still fuming about. And if you thought a curse from a dark-haired relative was expensive to get rid of, brace yourself for the cost of the prayers it's going to take to get back on God's good side again.

If you doubt everything else I ever tell you, don't doubt this. God never was, never is, and never will be angry with you. God's love is perfect and unconditional. God is not sitting off somewhere with a clipboard giving us demerits every time we're naughty—correct me if I'm wrong, but I think that's Santa Claus.

Even if He was angry with you, which will never happen, would He choose Madame Zorro of all people to complain to about it?

And since when does God give a higher priority to prayers that are accompanied by cash? No matter what variations and smoke screens and deceits the Madame Zorros of this world devise, there are three simple facts that can save you a lot of money and even more pain:

1. *Anyone* who tries to turn your fears against you to make you even more afraid is out to control you, not help you.
2. There is never any reason why a reading with any psychic, medium, fortune teller, or spiritualist should cost you one penny more than the price you agreed to pay at the beginning.
3. The moment you hear any reference to a "curse," "hex," "bad mojo," "dark cloud," or any other term implying you've been targeted for damnation, leave and do not pay.

I could not be more serious. If you've been scammed by anyone you went to for any kind of psychic or spiritual help, *speak up*! You may feel stupid, or embarrassed, or gullible, but remember, that's exactly what these con artists are counting on, and your silence is the only way they can stay in business.

A formal complaint to your local district attorney will at least get these frauds on file for future reference. And by the way, most of them have no business license, take cash under the table with no receipts, and pay no taxes. I'm sure the IRS would be delighted to have you point them out, too. Every reputable, legitimate psychic I know, including me, has a business license and reports and pays taxes on every dime they make, just like you do.

Do keep in mind, though, that there's not a psychic in the world, including me, who has an accuracy of a hundred percent. Any psychic who claims to be one hundred percent accurate is either lying or just plain nuts. So while inaccurate readings or predictions that don't come true aren't what you hope for, they don't qualify as "fraud." Psychics are only as good as our last reading, and we depend on our credibility and reputations. If any of us let you down in some significant way, spreading the word will put us out of business soon enough.

One last note on the subject of money. Not long ago I was offered a considerable amount of money—$40,000 a week and a sliding scale of 3¢ per call—to create the Sylvia Browne Psychic Hotline. Without a moment of hesitation I turned it down. To borrow a line from *Cyrano de Bergerac*, I intend to go to God with my white plume intact. There is no Sylvia Browne Psychic Hotline, and there never will be. Several national publications have run ads for a "Silvia B. Psychic Hotline," whoever "Silvia B." is, and other supposed hotline numbers have been circulated with my name attached. Law enforcement authorities and I are closing in on the people behind these scams, and we'll get them. Until we do, it's worth repeating: I will never operate, lend my name to, endorse or recommend *any* psychic hotline.

TOOLS OF PROTECTION

Sometimes it seems as if the Dark Side is everywhere, ready to spring out at us from under every rock. Sadly, that's only a small exaggeration. But the good news is, we white entities can win. The Dark Side is already diminished by the fact that they've turned away from God, while we've turned toward Him, and their tricks aren't nearly so frightening when we shine a light on them, talk about them, and fight them together.

The first, strongest, and most powerful Tool of Protection against the Dark Side is: Love and embrace God, and every day say, "No one else but me is or ever will be my God center."

The second is: Never forfeit your free will, your mind, or your common sense to anyone! They're precious gifts, given to you by a loving, generous God who should always be the first and last place you turn for answers.

The following Tools of Protection are in no particular order, and none is more effective than any other. Use any or all of them that appeal to you—the more the better. Any time of day or night is fine. I happen to prefer mornings as I'm getting ready for the day and nighttime as I'm getting ready for bed, but choose whatever times work for you. Get into the habit of using your Tools of Protection, so that a point will come when you'd feel naked without them.

If you doubt that they'll work, humor me and try for a week or two. Trying won't cost you a dime, and it certainly won't do you any harm. The one excuse that just won't work with me at all is, "I don't have time!" If you can spend five minutes shaving, ten minutes on your makeup, fifteen minutes on your hair, or twenty minutes deciding what to wear and getting dressed, you can certainly devote one or two minutes to arming yourself against the Dark Side and its negative energy for the whole day.

The Circle of Mirrors. In your mind's eye, place yourself inside a perfect circle of mirrors, taller than you are, facing away from you. White entities will be drawn toward the mirrors, while dark entities will be repelled by them and avoid you.

The Bubble of White Light. While you should always ask to be surrounded by the white light of the Holy Spirit, here's an image I love that makes it easy to picture. If you saw *The Wizard of Oz,* you remember that Glinda, the Good Witch of the North, traveled from one place to another inside a beautiful transparent bubble. Try traveling through your day and night that same way, inside a bubble made of the glowing, transparent white light of the Holy Spirit, and you'll start noticing that dark entities won't want anything to do with you.

There's another moment from that movie you can borrow that will help you keep the Dark Side in its proper place. When Glinda is confronted by the Wicked Witch of the West, she waves at her dismissively and says, "You have no power here. Be gone with you." Silently project that thought to anyone around you that you suspect is a dark entity. You'll be amazed at how effective it is in reminding you of *your* power while diminishing theirs without ever saying a word.

The Golden Sword. Picture a long, powerful, gleaming golden sword, its hilt beautiful, ornate, and sparkling with jewels. Hold the sword up in front of your body, so that the hilt forms a cross over your "third eye," between and slightly above your eyebrows, and the blade extends like a shield of strength and protection down the length of your body, intimidating and deflecting the inherent cowardice of the Dark Side.

Gold and Silver Nets. The image is a fisherman's net, of gold and silver gossamer, strong but light as air, its fibers braided and glistening with the white light of the Holy Spirit. Drape it over yourself, to cover and protect yourself from head to toe in divine white light. As you move through your day, drape a matching gold and silver net over any dark entities you encounter, to bless them and to contain and neutralize any power they might have.

The Dome of Light. Picture a magnificent dome, its perfect rounded walls and ceiling made of the radiant white light of the Holy Spirit, with you and those you love inside it, safe, warm and basking in God's love, protected from all darkness and negativity.

To show you how handy and effective the Dome of Light can be, I was at a cocktail party recently with a psychologist friend of mine. There was a dark entity working the room, an obnoxious opportunist who'd clearly decided this group of people had assembled for no other reason than to do as many things as possible for him. As we watched him, my friend groaned and worried out loud about how we were going to manage to be polite to this obvious phony. I said, "We won't have to. He won't come anywhere near us." With which I domed the two of us with God's white light.

There were thirty people at that party. The dark entity relentlessly pestered twenty-eight of them. As for my friend and me, he never came within ten feet of us the entire evening.

I *love* the Dome of Light!

All day and all night, throughout your life, may you and the other white entities of this world find each other and walk together safe and unharmed through the negativity of the Dark Side as you make your way Home.

8

Ten Things We Fear and Why We Shouldn't Fear Them

Fear is destructive. It isolates us, shrinks our world, and separates us from our dignity, our self-confidence, and our faith. Fear feeds on itself and becomes a daily, mocking companion if we let it. And sadly, none of us gets through our lifetimes without feeling its grip.

Our fears can be so deep-seated in our subconscious that we are not even sure what they are or where they come from, so we live with a nagging, uneasy sense that something's not right, that we're always in some kind of potential emotional danger we can't quite put our finger on. But how can we fight something we can't identify, let alone defeat it so that it's out of our way once and for all?

The truth is, we can't.

When we hear a noise or see a strange form in the corner during the night, we have two choices. We can lie there in the dark and grow more and more terrified imagining monsters, or we can turn on the light and find out exactly what we're up against. Nine times out of ten it amounts to nothing more than the house settling or a pile of clothes on a bedroom chair.

Even when it turns out to be something more serious than that, I still believe in throwing on all the lights in the house. Knowledge is power. The more afraid we are of something, the more we owe it to ourselves to learn about it. And the more we learn about it, the more confidence we will have in facing it and beating it.

My thousands of clients have come from all over the world, from every possible background and circumstance, and yet the vast majority of them are struggling with the same ten basic fears. That doesn't really surprise me, since I've done battle with some of those fears myself. I know how cold and paralyzing fear can be. I know how much strength, courage, and hard work are needed to conquer it. Most of all, I know that there are few victories in life more liberating than the victory over the low, dark clouds of fear that block our spirits from their rightful place in the sun.

You *can* overcome any of the following ten things we fear. On the surface, some of them may not seem like psychic issues. Yet, they often have deep-seated psychic roots. Sometimes they can be traced to traumatic events in this lifetime, but frequently the feeling of helplessness they cause is multiplied by the fact that we can't figure out what is causing the fear.

The pain from these fears can pierce us to our psychic core. It is that core that needs to be examined, treated, and healed. For example, I'm not exactly calm in the presence of large bugs. I've been known to shriek at the sight of them. But that sort of fear barely scratches the surface of my being, let alone penetrating to my core. Then too, there are ways to keep the large bug population at a minimum. The Ten Fears addressed here can wound our psychic essence, and there's nowhere to run from a fear whose psychic roots are tangled deep inside us.

We don't have to run away, though. Luckily, we can do better than that. We can take a nice big psychic shoe and stomp these Ten Fears right out of existence, with understanding, knowledge, and some well-aimed action.

1. REJECTION
AND
2. ABANDONMENT

These two are so closely related that they are not easily separated. Both can be deeply painful, and both can leave us feeling as if we somehow failed, or fell short in someone's eyes and were discarded because of it.

The fear of rejection and/or abandonment can interfere with relationships throughout our lives. We may refuse to let anyone get too close to cause us that much pain. We might hold on too tightly to someone, inadvertently suffocating them, so that we cause the very rejection or abandonment we fear. We might even seek out those we subconsciously know will reject or abandon us, either to prove the fear is justified or to see if just once we can prove it isn't.

Depending on your experience, you probably have your own opinion of the difference between rejection and abandonment. I've always defined rejection as someone saying, "Go away," and abandonment as someone saying, "Good-bye." You can be rejected by a stranger or by someone you love, in the workplace or at home, or by a friend. Abandonment, on the other hand, implies that love, or the appearance of love, is given and then taken away. In both cases, though, the result is a sometimes devastating sense of emotional loss.

There's a very good, very deeply rooted spiritual reason why rejection and abandonment have such a profound effect on us, and understanding that reason is a huge step toward putting our fear of them in perspective:

The pain of rejection and abandonment is already familiar

to us from the moment we're born, so every time we experience it on earth we're reopening an existing wound.

When we make the decision on The Other Side to return here for another incarnation, we're put through a desensitizing process to help ease the spiritual shock of the transition. In a way, it is the opposite of the orientation we're given when we leave this life and return Home. As part of that desensitizing process, the entities on The Other Side, from our loved ones to our chosen Spirit Guides to our soul mates to our countless other friends and co-workers there, emotionally distance themselves from us. It's an act of kindness purely for our benefit, their way of preparing us for our journey.

Imagine being surrounded every day by a happy, stimulating, productive, openly adoring family, with friends who offer absolute trust, compassion, and an unending supply of unconditional love. Your beloved pets are with you, and the very air you breathe is alive with the power and presence of God. You're living in a state of blissful perfection. But for reasons of your own essential growth and progress, you have made a commitment to your soul to go away to college, or an important job. You know it's the right decision, and everyone who loves you agrees completely. You have been on this journey before and so have they, so you're all aware that, as part of your preparing to leave, they have to pull away from you. If they don't, the departure will be unbearably painful for you, and you won't arrive at your destination as independent and open as you should.

So out of necessity, you start your trip away from The Other Side feeling abandoned and rejected, and every time you experience abandonment and rejection in this lifetime, you are subconsciously reliving the profound sense of loss, emptiness, and separation that made it possible for you to be here in the first place. It's perfectly natural to assign all the pain of earthly abandonment and rejection to the event that triggered it. But the majority of that pain is coming not from that event but from the spirit memory of a far greater loss—and a purely temporary loss—than we will ever experience here.

This isn't to diminish the very real trauma that earthly abandonment or rejection can cause and the importance of reaching out for help to get you through it. I am simply reassuring you that it is not a fresh new wound you are feeling but the aggravation of an old wound that you've already survived. The most effective treatment, of course, is to tend to the original wound—our devastating but essential distance from Home.

The key to that treatment is spirituality. The more energy and passion we invest in our spirituality while we're here, the more connected we feel to everything and everyone we left behind for this brief trip away from The Other Side. It's the surest way of keeping in touch with those we miss the most until we can all be together again. By keeping that spiritual connection alive and well, no one who abandons or rejects us here on earth can possibly inflict pain too deep for us to bear.

3. FAILURE

The fear of failure is almost epidemic, and much of the reason is that life has become more and more complicated. Thanks to everything from constant advancements in technology to the increasing accessibility of the global community to the too-slow-but-sure evolving of equal opportunities for every race, gender, religion, and sexual preference, we find ourselves with more options than ever, more available paths than ever before to choose from during our time here.

But let's cut through the complications right up front. No matter how many options come along, no matter how confusing it all feels sometimes, the real spiritual root of the fear of failure boils down to only one question, whether we are consciously aware of it or not: Am I following my chart?

And the answer is a simple unequivocal yes!

If it's a given that we're all going to follow our charts regardless of how often we screw up, or how lazy we are, or how mean we are, what's the motivation to put out any effort at all? Why not just lie around like a bunch of slugs and let everyone else deal with all that stress, anxiety, and potential failure out there?

Remember, before we come here from The Other Side, we compose a blueprint or chart for our upcoming lifetime, and we also choose a primary and secondary life theme to work on while we're here, compatible with the goals in our chart. No one—not even ourselves—can interfere with those life themes or the unfolding of the charts we've written. We're born already motivated, already driven to purposes of our own design. In fact, believe it or not, if I did a reading for you and told you you are here for no other reason than to lie around like a slug and accomplish absolutely nothing, it might sound like a big relief for maybe five or ten seconds, but I guarantee you, if that information were contrary to your chart and your life themes, you would never go through with it.

The variations in acting out our charts stem from how we deal with the inevitable obstacles we confront along the way and the difficulties we put ourselves through in the process. Let's say, for the sake of illustration, that according to your chart, your purpose in this lifetime is to walk from Los Angeles to New York. It's guaranteed that during your lifetime, you'll get there. The question is, how? Are you going by way of Argentina? Are you complaining about it with every step and making everyone around you miserable? Do you keep putting on tight shoes, or tying your legs together and trying to hop there, to make sure the three-thousand-mile trip is as painful as possible? Are the people you meet on your journey better for having met you? With all the choices in the world, are you choosing to devote your time to people who will treat you well and enrich your trip, or are you seeking out those who'll happily throw all sorts of obstacles in your path or try to convince you that your trip is less important than theirs?

In other words, you will walk from L.A. to New York. You can't fail. You will get there one way or another, so fearing failure means you are fearing something that can't happen.

The sure way to erase the fear once and for all is to concentrate on the quality of your journey. A simple rule of thumb to ensure that quality is to live your life according to an unwritten promise God offers us every time we leave The Other Side to come here again: *"If you take good care of my children, I'll always take especially good care of you."*

Does that mean God withholds His love and care from those who disappoint Him? Of course not. But how easy is it for you to feel loved and cared for by someone if you ignore them or continually push them away?

Humor me. For the next three months, make a point of one prayer a day to keep you connected to God and one kind act a day to keep you connected to His children. Chances are, the two of them together will take less time than your morning shower, or brushing your teeth. Three months is just long enough to create a habit, so that a day without a prayer and an act of kindness would feel strange and unpleasant. That you are doing it for a seemingly selfish reason won't count against you. You are ensuring yourself a life in which the word failure will never enter your mind again.

As for making sure you make regular progress at following your blueprint, try sitting down once a month for a few quiet minutes and giving honest answers to these basic questions:

- How are you dealing with the inevitable negativity you came here to confront? Are you making a genuine effort to overcome it, and helping those around you overcome it without judging them when they need you? Or are you perpetuating negativity, wallowing in it, and/or getting attention by allowing yourself to be victimized by it?
- Are you using, or abusing and wasting, the gifts you were given?
- Are the lives you touch richer or poorer because of you?
- When you have caused someone pain, can you truthfully say that it was not your intention?
- Does your day-to-day life genuinely reflect your values and beliefs, or are your values just a handy yardstick you use for measuring everyone else's life but your own?
- When you make mistakes, do you take responsibility for them and do everything in your power to apologize and make things right again, or do you immediately start looking for someone else to blame? Are you as quick to forgive other people's mistakes as you hope to be forgiven for yours?
- No matter what your age, when is the last time you made an effort to learn something?
- No matter what your age, are you putting equal daily effort into your mental, physical, and spiritual health?
- How often do you stop to listen to—and thank—The Greater Wisdom and your spirit helpers on The Other Side who never abandon you, even in those dark times when you abandon them?

Clients frequently ask for my help in getting their lives back on track, which of course really means getting back in synch with their blueprints. One of my favorites was Pam, a struggling single mother in her early thirties who had resorted to becoming a stripper to make ends meet. I have nothing against strippers. The problem was that Pam hated every minute of it, knew it was a wrong choice for her, and wanted me to guide her in a happier direction. The answer came to me clear as a bell. "You need to write children's books." She was shocked. She loved children, but she had never tried or even thought of writing. But I was so sure that she promised to give it a try and let me know what happened.

She called six months later. She had written several children's books, and not one of them had been published. But a literary agent had taken an interest in her work, and then in her, and the two of them had fallen deeply in love and were planning their wedding. And, by the way, her career as a stripper was permanently behind her.

A case in point that there are all sorts of unexpected rewards for finding your way back to your blueprint.

One of the questions I am asked most often during readings is, "What is my purpose in life?" Since life is so complicated, we tend to overcomplicate the answer to that question. But here is the simplest answer of all, one that applies to all of us, regardless of our blueprints:

Love God,
do good,
then shut up and go Home.

4. SUCCESS

Forgive me for stating the obvious, but the main reason people fear success is that they are afraid it will be taken away from them. That's why some people cling to their version of failure. At least when you fail, you have the comfort of knowing there is nowhere to go but up.

It's sad, really, how frightened we get of success. If you don't believe me, ask yourself which is easier for you—telling someone that something nice happened for you, or telling them that something bad happened? And when you talk about something nice happening, do you knock on wood, or worry about jinxing it by talking about it, or almost find yourself apologizing for it and/or interjecting some minor bit of bad news into the conversation to balance out the good news?

No one likes a braggart, that is true. Yet there is a difference between sharing good news about yourself and clubbing people over the head with it. Next time you have good news to share, try it without the apologies and the superstitious frills, say out loud how grateful you are and then change the subject. If there are people around you who can't be happy for your success and/or seem to resent you for it, stay away from them. Period. If you wanted to put up with relationships that only go smoothly when you seem to be failing, or that make you feel guilty when success comes your way, you'd only hang out with your enemies.

The same goes for people who are quick to remind you that good times and success never last. That is a fact only if you believe it is a fact. If you believe with all your heart and soul that bad news always follows good news, or that the next logical step after success is failure, you'll move heaven and earth to make it happen. So be careful not to shoot yourself in the foot, and don't let anyone else do it to you either.

But then, a lot depends on your definition of success. I don't happen to believe it has a thing to do with money, job description, the size of your house, the brand of your clothing, or the kind of car you drive. I've known wildly successful people who were filthy rich and wildly successful people without a dime to their name.

Success lives in the spirit. Nowhere else. If you define yourself by anything other than the integrity, activism, courage, depth, curiosity, and compassion of your spirit, you still have some work to do before you can truly call yourself successful. A good way to measure your progress is to ask yourself who you'd be if your career, your marriage or romantic relationship, your savings account, your house, your car—anything external by which you might be trying to identify yourself—vanished tomorrow. If you don't know the answer to that question, you'll find it only by exploring, nurturing, and expanding your spiritual self. That's who you are. That's your identity. The rest is just wardrobe and makeup. Having a happy, healthy, active spirit is the greatest sense of security you'll ever experience, because it's the one mark of success no one can ever take away from you.

Another helpful yardstick to measure your real success, by the way, goes like this: You reap what you sow.

If you hear that and think, "I hope so!"—good for you, you are on the right track.

If you hear that and think, "Uh oh!"—I'd get busy turning that around if I were you. No matter what you have done, it's not too late. As long as you are still breathing, it is never too late.

One final bit of proof that I'm not just making all this up:

Ask anyone you know who's spiritually happy, healthy, and active if they ever experience a fear of success.

They won't have a clue what you're talking about.

5. BETRAYAL

This subject is a tough one for me, since I know first-hand what it's like to be betrayed by someone who swore he loved me while, at the same time, almost destroyed me.

What is the most devastating form of betrayal, though, is the betrayal of self. We can betray ourselves in any number of ways, by either ignoring signals from ourselves or by letting ourselves be swayed by something I call "determinism." Simply put, determinism means letting someone else determine supposed facts about you, whether there's any evidence to support those "facts" or not.

For example, one of the many "facts" my mother told me about myself when I was growing up is that I wasn't cut out to be a career woman; my only hope for success was as a housewife and mother. Certainly I love cooking and baking and decorating and caring for a home and all those other domestic things, and being a mother and grandmother is the great joy of my life.

But imagine how I would have betrayed myself and my spirit if I had allowed her "determinism" to keep me from my almost fifty years with all of you. I heard a psychic on TV the other day refer to doing readings as "a living." I almost put my foot through the television screen. A living? It's an honor! It's a gift from God! To have let that gift go unexpressed—even for the sake of being a housewife and mother, which I found very worthwhile and fulfilling—would have been my ultimate self-betrayal.

It's betrayal of self to let anyone, including yourself, arbitrarily define who you should be and what your supposed limits are. It's betrayal of self to let anyone, including yourself, demean you, abuse you, or make you doubt your goodness and potential. It's a betrayal of self to let anyone, including yourself, separate you from your gifts and your dreams and the joy of God's power in you.

Here is a simple exercise to ease you toward the habit of paying attention to yourself and refusing to allow self-betrayal. Every time you hear yourself say or think any sentence that starts with the words, "I always wanted to . . ." write it down. Keep adding to the list until there are five items on it, whether that takes hours, days, or weeks. Then, in a few peaceful minutes, go down the list one item at a time and underneath it write the *honest* answer to the question, "Why haven't I?" Beneath that, write the *honest* answer to the question, "Why don't I do it now?" You'll immediately spot the difference between legitimate reasons and lame excuses. Keep right on adding to your list as time goes by. If nothing else, the exercise will be a great way of keeping in touch with your dreams and goals and reminding you that it doesn't have to be too late to pursue them.

It takes work and discipline and faith in yourself and God, but you *can* prevent and/or overcome self-betrayal.

Overcoming betrayal by someone you loved and trusted isn't so easy. I wish I could promise you that if you're smart enough, or alert enough, or careful enough, or a good enough person, you'll never be betrayed. As it is, I can only promise you that you can, will and must survive it if it happens to you—if only to keep your betrayer from getting the added satisfaction of destroying you. Unfortunately, good people are the easiest to betray, for a perfectly logical reason. Because we see the world only through our own eyes, and we assume that everyone thinks just like we do, it doesn't occur to us to stay on constant alert for deceit and lies and back-stabbing, particularly from someone we love who claims to love us.

Francine, my Spirit Guide, told me years ago that all

betrayals boil down to two basic motives—greed and vanity. I tried arguing with her and proving her wrong; but when you really cut through all the twists and turns of every betrayal story, she's exactly right, it is always greed or vanity or both. Most of us would never value greed and vanity over love. There are those, however, who just don't get it that love, when felt and expressed in its most divine state, automatically shrinks greed and vanity to the petty, shallow, shortsighted nonsense they really are. I don't know about you (actually, yes I do), but when I take my last breath on this earth and head Home, I'm looking forward to the peace of knowing that I loved and loved well. I find it hard to imagine any peace in lying there thinking, "Well, I may be alone, everyone I ever cared about may hate me, but at least I was greedy and vain."

Sadly, I doubt that you need me to give you examples of betrayal, since you have probably experienced it on your own. If my clients are any indication, it happens every day, to some of the nicest, brightest people. There is the spouse who leaves for a younger and/or wealthier alternative. Greed and vanity. There is the best friend who violates your confidence behind your back, invariably to damage your reputation and enhance their own as the possessor of privileged information. Greed and vanity. There is my experience, the estranged husband who without my knowledge used my name and reputation to illegally seduce investors into a supposed "can't miss" business venture. Greed and vanity. (For the record, I have since paid back every single dime to those investors.) The stories are endless. And apparently, I regret to say, so is the inevitability of betrayal at some point in our lives.

Recovery from betrayal is very much like recovery from a loved one's death. You go through denial, grief, anger, self-pity, self-recrimination. They can't be avoided, but keep an important goal in mind—let yourself feel them for the purpose of getting them out of your system, not for obsessing over the betrayal to the point that you can't move on. There *is* life after betrayal, take it from me. Here are a few tips, some of which I learned the hard way:

- The answer to "How could I have been so gullible/stupid/blind?" is, "By believing that everyone's mind and heart work like yours." They don't. It's that simple. There are other good people like you out there, and the sooner you pick yourself up and walk away, the sooner you'll find them.
- The answer to "How could they do this to me if they loved me?" is, "Their spirit has a longer way to go on its journey than yours does, or they wouldn't put so little value on love." It's their lesson to learn, which they may or may not accomplish in this lifetime. It's not your job to teach them whether they want to learn it or not. They won't learn until they're ready, any more than a kindergarten student is ready to learn nuclear physics. Take a long, honest look not at who you wanted him to be but at who the evidence proves he really is; recognize that his spiritual limits, not yours, caused the betrayal to happen—and let it go.
- The adage "Actions speak louder than words" has become such a cliché that we forget how important it is. When there's a contradiction between what someone says and what she does, ignore the words—the truth is in the behavior every time. Hearing "I love you" from someone who's plunging a knife between your shoulder blades does *not* mean, "Love is a knife between the shoulder blades." It means, "This person is deliberately hurting me, and that's not love!"

Revenge may be fun to fantasize about, but it's out of the question to act on it. There's a saying from Oriental philosophy I love: "If you set out for revenge, you might as well dig two graves—one for the other person and one for yourself." The major problem with revenge is that it requires your time, thoughts, and energy. When someone's betrayed you and caused you all this pain, don't you think you've devoted quite enough time, thoughts and energy to them already without prolonging it and giving them even more power while you try to get even? Make no mistake: as long as someone is a focal point of your attention, you are giving them the message that they have power and importance in your life. The biggest insult you can pay someone isn't hatred, after all—it's apathy.

Let's get something straight about the issue of forgiveness. Being a good spiritual person does *not* require you to forgive anything and everything someone does to you. Don't struggle with the unreasonable expectation that you can't move on or find peace about a betrayal until you've forgiven it. Yes, you can. The way you move on and find peace is to include in your prayers, "This one's too big for me, God. *You* handle it."

He will. You can count on it. In the meantime, you'll be busy elsewhere, because you have far better things to do than waste one more minute on someone who had their chance with you and blew it.

6. LONELINESS

People who fear loneliness always have trouble believing what I'm about to say, but it's the truth. And anyone who doesn't have a problem with loneliness will back me up on this:

The cure for loneliness has absolutely nothing to do with other people. The cure for loneliness is inside you. So why on earth be afraid of something that you can control?

Don't confuse the words *aloneness* and *loneliness*. You can be alone without feeling a twinge of loneliness, and you can ache with loneliness in a room full of people. One of the first questions I ask clients who want to learn to explore their spirituality is, "Can you spend time alone?" If they can't, that's the first thing we have to work on, because the ability to be alone means you know and like who you are, without having to look to other people for your opinions or your very identity. Only when you arrive at the threshold of spirituality as a whole person can you fully receive the joy, love, peace, and power spirituality has to offer.

Chronic loneliness is a blank space in your spirit, and no one can fill it but you. That is not to imply that we don't all get lonely from time to time, for a specific person we love, for a familiar voice, for the laughter and stimulation and healthy input our friends and loved ones have to offer. But chronic, pervasive loneliness means you haven't begun to find out how interesting and funny and powerful and curious and loving and insightful and entertaining and creative *you* are, all by yourself, whether anyone else knows or not.

There are two compelling reasons for overcoming the fear of loneliness, besides the fact that it can lead to depression, anxiety, and illness.

First, depending on other people to identify who you are puts you in the horrible position of only having an identity at someone else's convenience. What if you call everyone you rely on to establish your persona and they're all busy and not at home? Do you cease to exist until someone returns your call? Or what if they're in a bad mood and blow up at you for no reason? Does that mean you're a worthless idiot until they snap out of it? How many people do you know who are that dependable in the first place, or whose opinions are always that much more brilliant and accurate than yours?

Second, if you think loneliness can be cured simply by having someone around, you're not likely to be as discriminating as you should. I shudder to imagine who you might put up with for the sake of not being alone. Look at it this way—if you don't truly know and like yourself, it means that whenever you are alone, you're stuck spending time with a stranger you are not especially wild about. Rather than compounding the problem by dragging in still more people you don't know and don't like, why not make friends with yourself?

Along the way you'll discover an amusing irony. The more you enjoy being alone, the more other people will want to spend time with you. Complaining about how lonely and depressed you are is a way of advertising that you are really pretty dull company, which isn't likely to attract a stampede of friends. When it is apparent that you're quite comfortable being alone, people get the message that you may be an interesting, stimulating person who warrants a closer look.

All you need is a gentle shove in the right direction to get you started, and a reminder that making friends with yourself is even easier and cheaper than making friends with other people. You don't have to coordinate schedules with anyone, and there are no toll charges involved.

Every day, while you're in the shower, or driving to work, or cooking dinner, or anything else you do alone that doesn't require much thought, ask yourself five "pop quiz" questions that you might ask anyone you are interested in getting to know. Any subject at all is fair game. The only rule is, *no peeking at anyone else's answers*! We don't care about what other people think for this exercise, understood? This is about you. If the answer to any question is "I don't know," keep thinking about it until you do know. That's the whole point—to help you learn not only that you do have your own opinions but also that they're as valuable and interesting as anyone else's.

I'll get you started with some sample questions and then trust you to take it from there, five a day, until it's become a habit you actually look forward to:

How do you feel about capital punishment? Why?

Who's your favorite artist? (If "I don't know," there must be a museum or gallery nearby, or some lovely art specials on A&E. If "I hate art," have you honestly seen enough of it to take that position?)

What's the best book you've read in the last six months? What did you like about it? Have you read anything else by that same author, or about that same subject matter? If not, this might be a nice day for a trip to the bookstore or library.

What are your three favorite TV shows? Why? Do you have friends who enjoy those shows, too? Why not take turns having potluck and watching them together?

Do you like rap music? (If "I hate it," have you tried listening to it, or have you simply formed an opinion on something you know nothing about?)

If you could take a vacation to any place on earth, where would you go? Why? Have you studied anything about it? If the language there is foreign to you, how about buying or renting a Berlitz tape and learning a few basic words and phrases, just in case?

Who do you think makes crop circles?

Are there any sports you'd enjoy learning to play?

Name three things you're especially good at.

Name three things you especially enjoy doing. How long has it been since you did any or all of them?

What historical figure do you admire most? Why?

Who's your favorite comedian?

How do you feel about opera? (If "I hate it," have you ever listened to it?)

Do you like Thai food? (If "no!", have you ever tasted it?)

What questions do you have about God? What are you doing about trying to find answers?

What's your astrological sign? Do you believe in astrology?

You get the idea. No subject is too large or small, no answer is wrong, as long as they're your answers. Five questions a day, every day, and not only will you learn a few things about yourself, but if you keep at it you'll actually start to make friends with yourself and enjoy your own company.

And when that happens, you have my word, you'll never be afraid of loneliness again.

7. ILLNESS

We discussed this subject in far greater detail in the "To Your Health" chapter, but here is an important point about the fear of illness. You can make a potential illness worse by worrying about it, adding unhealthy stress and anxiety to what your body is already trying to fight off.

Illness is such a natural part of the life experience that we include it in our charts before we come here. Like all the other negativity written into our charts, we challenge ourselves with illnesses to learn to overcome them, both physically and spiritually—not to wallow in them, obsess over them, or assume them as part of our identity.

I'm sure you've met people who almost introduce themselves with whatever's wrong with them. "Hi,

I'm Susie. Sorry about the limp, I have a herniated disc." "I'm John. You probably noticed my handshake's a little weak, I have carpal tunnel syndrome." Don't you feel like coming back with, "Who asked?" In a widely reported case in California someone fought for the right to have his license plate read "HIV POS." The supposed issue was whether or not it was in poor taste: The *real* issue is, the more you declare any illness or physical problem to be a part of you, the more you'll hang on to it and refuse to let it go, because we never willingly forfeit anything we've woven into the fabric of our identity.

Please don't misunderstand—I'm not saying for a moment that you shouldn't take your illnesses seriously. Follow the advice of the best doctors available to you; have regular physicals; educate yourself on health issues; eat sensibly, exercise, and listen to your body when it tries to tell you it needs some kind of special attention. But keep health in perspective. "You" are not your body, any more than "you" are the car you travel in or the house you live in. Can you imagine introducing yourself with, "Hi, I'm Susie. My radiator's on the blink"? or, "I'm John. I need a new roof"?

Fearing illness or making it a regular topic of conversation is exactly like the quoted instruction: "For the next five minutes, don't think about elephants." You probably won't give as much thought to elephants in your entire lifetime as you'll give them during those five minutes. Remember, everything you hear—including your own words—registers in your mind and affects it. So reinforcing, over and over, everything from, "I'm not feeling well," to "I have this ache or pain," to "You know me, I catch every cold and flu that goes around!" tells your mind, over and over, to cue your body to act as ill as it keeps hearing it is. Even trying to be positive and repeating, "I refuse to get sick, I refuse to get sick, I refuse to get sick!" sends the word *sick* constantly to your mind and on to your body. Change that to: "I will be healthy, I will be healthy, I will be healthy!" and your mind and your body are guaranteed to reward you for it.

Here's a quick exercise that can help you through a physical problem until you can get whatever medical attention you might need, and it's also a great way to remind yourself that "you" and your body are two separate things. I used this myself recently. I won't bore you with the details, but I think a combination of the words *root canal* and *airplane* will give you the general idea. If not for this exercise, I would have either hijacked the plane to the nearest dentist's office or offered the flight attendants any amount of money to do me a favor and just cut my head off. As it is, I managed to survive without causing any international incidents.

When that kind of pain or oncoming illness hits you, first, don't clench! Relax and breathe. Relax and breathe. Relax and breathe, as you ask God for the protection of the white light of the Holy Spirit until you picture the light completely surrounding you. Then, in your mind, slowly turn the glowing white light to a warm, healing green. Once you're embraced by this green light, form the pain or illness into a ball of fire in your mind's eye and let it float out of your body into a lead box a few inches away from you. As soon as the ball of fire is safely inside the lead box seal the box securely, light a fuse leading into that box, and explode the pain or illness right out of existence. The lead box will protect you and the people around you, and, by externalizing your pain or illness and detonat-

ing it, you'll be taking action against it to make it more manageable.

Don't get me wrong: The pain was still there, and I've never been so happy to see my dentist in my life as I was when I floored it from the airport to his office the minute we landed. But I promise you, if not for that exercise, I would have been carried off that plane unconscious.

Again, there's much more on the subject of illness in chapter 4. The more you read, the more you'll be assured that you have more control over illness than you might think. And it's simple logic: We don't fear anything we know we can control.

8. AGING

Just as we can refuse to identify with our illnesses, we can refuse to identify with our age, especially since people like John Glenn, Betty Ford, Walter Cronkite, and countless others have proven that there's no such thing as "what being old means."

I once asked my Spirit Guide why we get old at all. Why we don't choose a pleasant, vital age—like thirty, for example—and stay there until we drop? I've never forgotten her answer: "Those who wrote old age into their blueprints did it because aging makes you tired enough to want to go Home." That's not to imply that we should all go cartwheeling into our caskets yelling, "Yippee!" when the time comes. But at sixty-two years and counting, I'm starting to understand what she meant.

I'm not tired yet, or ready to leave. I still have a lot of work to do, and grandchildren to spoil. If I went today, though, I can honestly say I'd head Home without a single complaint. It's been an amazing ride, without one day wasted, and that's one of the best ways I know to thumb your nose at a fear of aging. Spend each day as if it's your last on this earth and you'll eliminate any possibility of an old age full of regret.

There are some things I like a lot about growing older that no one bothered to mention to me ahead of time.

When I was in my teens, for example, I loved to go out dancing until two or three in the morning. In fact, I was pretty sure that dancing until two or three in the morning was right up there with oxygen as a basic necessity of life. My grandmother was in her eighties at the time and was usually in bed, sound asleep, while I was just starting to decide what to wear for the evening. I adored her, and I felt so sorry for her. Poor Grandma Ada. She must have wanted so desperately to go out dancing, since who in their right mind didn't want to go out dancing? Yet she never did, obviously because she was too old and couldn't handle it anymore. How heartbreaking and unfair getting old must be.

I have since discovered another possible reason why Grandma Ada wasn't fox trotting her way through senior citizenship—she couldn't have been less interested. Even now, twenty years younger than she was when I was wringing my hands feeling sorry for her, I'm sure I could still find my way around a dance floor. But a noisy, crowded club at two or three in the morning? Like Grandma Ada, I'm not too old. I simply don't want to. I have other interests that excite me every bit as much.

Isn't it lovely and spiritually graceful that we really do season and deepen with age? Isn't it wonderful that we think hide-and-seek is the height of fun when we're five, but we don't exactly have friends over to play it on Saturday nights in our thirties? Isn't it a luxury to be old enough that, unlike when we're in our teens, our lives are no longer held hostage by our hormones? Nor will anyone say to us again that we're too young to know what love is. Don't you appreciate the slow but inevitable realization that what other people think of you doesn't count nearly as much as what you think of yourself?

Aging also provides a terrific, inarguable excuse for getting out of things you don't want to do. I've trudged around all over the world trying to prove what a good sport I am as a parent. As a grandparent, when I don't happen to feel like scaling ruins or taking hang-gliding lessons, I can get out of it with a simple "Thanks anyway, but I'm not a kid anymore."

I'm very careful to use exactly those words. You'll never hear me say, "I'm too old," or, "At *my* age?!" as if my age is limiting or something to apologize for. I'm proud of my age. I've earned every minute of every day of every year of it, as I'll keep right on earning my time here until I go Home. If it seems hard to believe that what you say out loud about yourself can have a dramatic effect on how young or old you feel, that's okay. Just try, for three short months, taking the position that you're exactly the age you want to be, whether you mean it at first or not, and I think you'll find that it does make an exciting difference in your enthusiasm for getting out of bed every day.

Obviously part of the fear of aging involves concerns about our bodies developing mechanical problems, and God knows none of us wants to be incapacitated. But aging is another good reason to remind ourselves that "we" are not our bodies. "We" are spirits that have been here many times before, that wrote the blueprint we're living now, and that hold the divine promise of the eternity in God's love that awaits us on The Other Side.

As for these bodies we're traveling around in—yes, just like cars, they do take more work as they continue to accumulate mileage. And if you know me, you know I'm not opposed to keeping the paint job up to date and the dings and dents hammered out. To be honest, it's less of an effort to look younger than a refusal to put up with anything that makes me self-conscious if something can be done about it. So until they start putting age limits on my brand of hair color, nail color and makeup, or passing laws against plastic surgery for anyone over fifty, I'll insist on considering myself a work in progress.

9. LOSS

If you have experienced the loss of a loved one, you know how devastating it is. Though I am certain about life on The Other Side, I have been decimated by grief, too, not for those who've gone Home but for myself, separated from them by different dimensions, temporary as that separation is.

Riding the dark horse of grief is excruciating, hollow, numbing, enraging, and a deeply private process. It takes as long as it takes—no more, no less. That's not news, just a reminder if you're trying to help someone who is grieving. The word *should* means nothing—how they "should" be feeling, what they "should" be doing, how far along they "should" be toward recovery, when they "should" feel like socializing again. I understand the urge to try to alleviate a loved one's grief, but at its core is the fact of human nature that it's painful and scary to witness grief, and often our efforts are more for our comfort than for theirs. No, the most helpful thing you can do for a loved one who's grieving is, with respect, ride that dark horse with them so they'll have something to hold onto until they're ready to dismount and walk again.

Ending grief before it's been fully expressed and experienced can be dangerous to your health, too. I tried it once many, many years ago. I decided I was too strong and indestructible to hurt that much, so I stuffed the pain deep inside and overloaded my schedule with all the trivial busy work I could get my hands on. I paid for it with a horrible kidney infection. Like every other powerful emotion, the energy of grief has to go somewhere, and if it's not worked through completely and released from the body, you can count on it to take its toll sooner or later one way or another. So be patient with grieving, in yourself and in those around you.

I remember driving away from the hospital after my father died and wondering how all those people on the street could go about their business so casually, as if this were another ordinary day, when my world had totally collapsed. I remember going to the grocery store on my way home and moving through an aisle like a zombie until a stranger stopped me with a loud, goofy, probably well-intentioned, "Hey, cheer up!" I would have run him over with my cart, but there were too many witnesses.

To be fair, how could he have known? But to this day I find myself thinking we should bring back mourning clothes, or black armbands, or some way for the grieving to identify themselves on sight, so that others can give the dignity, the space, and the special consideration mourners deserve.

As agonizing as loss is, the more we understand the spiritual perspective of what has happened, the more at peace we can be and the less we'll blame God for snatching away someone we love. It makes God sound so arbitrary and selfish to say, "He took them," especially when it's a child. That's not the way it works. Even the tiniest of babies house ageless spirits who composed their blueprint on The Other Side before coming here, and that blueprint includes their death. Their choices and the reasons for them aren't ours to understand. They're simply ours to respect as best we can, cruel and unfair as they might seem. God doesn't "take" any of us or loved ones against our eternal will. He simply helps us compose and live out our blueprints, and loves us enough to walk with us and keep our spirits safe along the way.

I've had countless clients who are so afraid of losing those they love that emotionally they stay at arm's length to protect themselves from the pain of loss. In the end, they deprive themselves and their loved ones of the joy of spiritual intimacy, and instead of being protected when the loss occurs, they're left to struggle with the guilt and regret of everything they missed out on. It's not unlike being so afraid of earthquakes that you spend your life in a door jamb, or living in the southwest corner of your basement in case a tornado comes. Lives ruled by fear—even the fear of something as devastating as loss—are lives robbed of the peace, freedom, love, and compassion this world has to offer, if we'll just be patient and demand nothing less.

One client in particular who deeply moved me was a man named Bernie, who was grief-stricken by the recent loss of his wife of thirty-two years. Adding to his profound sorrow was the fact that even though he had deeply loved his wife, he had always kept himself at a slight emotional distance from her and had never once actually told her how much he loved her. In the course of the reading I uncovered the reason for that. When Bernie was a child he had told his mother one day how much he loved her. Three days later she died, very suddenly. Without realizing it, he had concluded that loving someone and telling them meant they would disappear. So throughout his marriage he deprived himself and his wife of true emotional intimacy, for the ironic reason that he loved her so much. The good news, of course, was that it is never too late to tell our departed loved ones everything that is in our hearts. He was skeptical about that, but he promised to try. A week later he had what he described as a dream about his late wife but what was really a visitation from her, during which he expressed the depth of his feelings for her and how happy she had made him. In his "dream" she assured him that she had never doubted it for a moment, which finally put his mind and his heart to rest.

It's true that there's comfort in knowing that our loved ones live on in our memories and in our hearts. But I find even more comfort in the fact that we actually take on qualities we admire most in everyone who touches our lives. We're all gatherers, absorbing the best and rejecting the worst of those around us. We do better than just remembering loved ones. We're living, active tributes to them, and the void they left behind can be eased enormously if we pay attention to the many ways they're alive and well as part of us. I'm enhanced every day by my father's sense of humor, my grandmother's wisdom and closeness to her grandchildren, and my late great friends' uncommon compassion, generosity, unique insights, laughter and courage. I'm even enhanced by those departed spirits who were, to be kind, flawed. Whatever I've done right as a parent, for example, is due largely to thinking what my mother would have done in the same situation and then doing exactly the opposite. When we look at ourselves as mosaics, combining our own brilliant colors with those we miss to make an evolving whole, we realize that we never really "lose" anyone at all.

The truth remains, though, that we can't prevent the losses we'll have to confront during our lives. Yet there are a few wonderful things we can do to keep ourselves prepared for loss that will help make us strong enough to get through it intact.

One is to keep our relationships with our loved ones current and as devoid of unfinished business as possible. Don't do it for your loved ones, do it for yourself. There *is* no unfinished business as far as our loved ones are concerned once they're on The Other Side. Regrets, resentment, anger, and negativity don't exist when they are Home. But it breaks my heart to hear clients say, "Did they know how much I loved them?" or, "I meant to apologize for that stupid argument we had. I just never got around to it, and now it's too late," or, "I'm so afraid they're still upset with me." Please don't do that to yourselves! Express your love and make your peace today, while you're both here in the same dimension to reap the benefits.

The second thing we can do is to keep our relationship with our spirituality—with the divine presence of God that lives in us—alive, active, and readily available. The more in touch we are with our spirit lives and our awareness of God's love and wisdom, the more easily we'll remember the truth each of us knows in the depths of our souls, that even the cruelest, most devastating loss is temporary. As endless as it seems while we're trying to recover from it, it's the blink of an eye in eternity, and only moments from the unimaginable joy of the reunions we have to look forward to when we're all Home together on The Other Side again.

10. DEATH

You know what's really goofy? I know our spirits transcend death. You know our spirits transcend death. Almost every religion on earth knows our spirits transcend death. But what's our biggest fear about death? Annihilation. The fear that when we die we'll cease to exist.

What is that about, for God's sake? We *know* better! Or what, we think that everyone else's spirits will transcend death, it's just ours that won't? As if the Bible says, "that whosoever believeth in Him shall not perish but have everlasting life—except you, you get about five minutes, then you're over with!"? Isn't that silly? There's no such thing as the annihilation of our spirit, period. So we can put that out of our minds right now.

We also seem to believe that death is, by definition, this hideous ordeal that's so awful it literally kills us. But here's something fascinating I've learned through thousands of regressive hypnosis sessions. Every single client I've ever worked with isn't nearly as traumatized by the memory of their death in a past life as they are by their birth into this one. Picture the birth process if you think I'm just saying that to make you feel better. One minute you're in this dark, safe, warm place, sleeping and eating and minding your own business. The next minute you're being squeezed through this tiny space, grabbed by cold hands or cold steel and yanked out into these bright lights with a room full of total strangers yelling, whooping, and staring at you, until one of them spanks you and then cuts off your feeding tube. You've already been through that or you wouldn't be here. What is the moment of death compared to that?

We also worry needlessly about *how* we're going to die. It's important to realize that when we chart our blueprint before we come here, we write five "exit points" into our charts—five different opportunities to exit this life and go Home again. Here's a simple analogy: You decide to leave a home you love for an educational field trip. You're not sure how long it will take you to accomplish all your goals on this trip, but you do know that you are not heading out on the trip in the first place until you've guaranteed your return home again when you're ready. Before you leave home, you arrange five options for that return, at various stages throughout the trip—let's say, a plane reservation after a week; a train ticket after a year; a bus ticket at the five-year mark; a rental car twelve years into the trip; and reservations on a cruise ship after twenty-five years. You have made a promise to yourself that no matter how much you yearn for home while you are gone, you will see this trip through until you have fulfilled your prearranged goals. If that turns out to be only a week, you will board that plane. If it takes as long as twelve years, you will hop into that rental car, etc. In other words, the five exit points are simply the five means of transportation you reserve for yourself before you leave Home, and it is your choice to decide which of those five to take along the way, depending on when you feel you have learned all you needed.

Some exit points are obvious. A serious accident, a severe illness, even a near collision you narrowly avoided or a fall from your crib two inches from a sharp corner that would have killed you are perfect examples. But other exit points are so subtle you might not have recognized them for what they were—a sudden "wrong" turn or freeway exit in your car, a last-minute flight change or cancellation, something as seemingly trivial as a series of silly delays that keep you from leaving your house when you'd planned to. Whether or not you're ever aware that one of your exit points has come and gone, it's part of life's magic, and God's, that there really are no "accidents."

During his recovery from a serious motorcycle accident, a dear friend of mine asked me to hypnotize him and guide him back through the details of the accident, since he had no conscious memory of how and why it happened. Under hypnosis he remembered two fascinating details. One was his absolute awareness of having *chosen* to veer off the road and over an embankment rather than allow what would have been a fatal head-on collision with the truck that was speeding toward him in the wrong lane. The other was the voice (his Spirit Guide, it turned out) that whispered to him as he regained consciousness in the ambulance, "That was number four."

Please don't panic if you think back on the exit

points you've had and realize there have been four of them and you're now facing the fifth and final one. You didn't space them out evenly when you wrote your chart. Decades can pass from one exit point to the next. I had my third and my fourth exit points in the same year. That was twenty years ago, and my Spirit Guide tells me that the fifth one isn't even on the horizon yet.

As she also points out, whichever of the five exit points you choose to leave on, you also have a choice about how long to hang onto the rope that holds you here. With or without life support equipment and other "heroic measures," it's ultimately our decision and ours alone, with God's blessing, when to release ourselves to the peace and joyful reunions waiting on The Other Side. We're conditioned to hold on, for the sake of loved ones. But it's an act of great, unselfish kindness if you can bring yourself to tell someone you love whose time has come to let go, move toward the light, and go Home.

I want to stress one other point—with a few exceptions, suicide *is not an option as a potential exit point*. Suicide, most of the time, is a broken contract with ourselves, our own blueprints, and with God. That does not mean God condemns suicide victims to an eternity in hell. There is no such thing, and God would never do that. But as you saw in "The Dark Side" chapter, the long-term consequences for most suicides can last for too many lifetimes to be worth the momentary relief.

I'll bet you thought I was going to tell you not to be afraid of death because it's a "natural transition" and you'll be "going to a better place." Both of those clichés are true, but they're so overused that they've long since stopped giving me much comfort, and I have to assume they're wearing a little thin for you, too. I have the benefit of direct communication with the spirit world, so you don't have to take my word for it that death is fascinating, complex, one more step in a journey through eternity, and a magnificent reunion with Home on The Other Side. Take the word of those who've "died" who, through me, want desperately for you to know that they're happier, healthier, and more alive than ever, in the divine white light of God that's waiting for us all.

Knowledge is power. Whatever frightens you, whether it is included in this chapter or not—please, instead of running from it, arm yourself with knowledge about it and face it head-on. Nothing looks quite as scary under the glare of bright lights. And overcoming fear makes the difference between a life fully lived and a life spent hiding in the dark where the sun cannot reach you.

* 9 *

PREDICTIONS FOR THE NEW MILLENNIUM— 2000–2099

I have known all my life, of course, that part of my psychic gift is an ability to foresee future events for clients, family, and friends. But not until thirty years ago, when the local newspaper in Campbell, California, asked me for a list of predictions for the upcoming year, did I start seriously focusing on that skill for the sake of society in general, and it has become one of my most useful and gratifying pursuits.

I could fill a separate book with my predictions that have come true in these thirty years, and fortunately most of them have been recorded in the media—from television to radio to newspapers and magazines—so that they can be authenticated rather than your having to take my word for it. Many of these predictions have been helpful, as opposed to just random bits of trivia about celebrity scandals and marital problems. They keep me passionate about staying tuned in to what lies ahead. Below are a few examples:

- Six months before the tragedy, I predicted the devastating plane crash at O'Hare Airport in Chicago in 1980. A few days after that plane went down, I got a letter from a man named Kent Herkenrath, thanking me for saving his life. He had been scheduled to be on that flight but canceled when he read my prediction.

- On Leeza Gibbons' talk show I gave Ted Gunderson of the FBI the names of the five men responsible for the World Trade Center bombing while the investigation was in such an early stage that the authorities were still trying to assemble a list of suspects. To be honest, on one of the five names I gave Ted, I was off by one syllable. Luckily, it was close enough that my relationship with the FBI has continued to deepen ever since.
- Immediately after the heartbreaking abduction and murder of Polly Klaas, I announced, on record, the initials of her killer—R.A.D. Richard Allen Davis was arrested and subsequently convicted of that murder.
- I still have thank-you letters on file from people who decided to temporarily relocate when I predicted the unprecedented violence of both Florida's Hurricane Andrew and California's Northridge earthquake.
- Months ahead of time, on *Montel Williams,* I predicted the stock market crash in October of 1997; the three-ingredient protease-inhibitor "cocktail" in the battle against AIDS; a "brief skirmish" with Iraq in late 1998; an erroneous story on *60 Minutes* which would result in their investigators becoming the target of an investigation themselves (a false report on Colombian drug lords, as it turned out, for which the *60 Minutes* producers ultimately had to apologize); the failed attempt to indict Hillary Clinton; etc.

Oddly, other than occasionally either validating or invalidating the predictions that come to me, my Spirit Guide, Francine, has nothing to do with the process whatsoever. She and I both believe her inability to initiate predictions stems from her difficulty in perceiving time in our earthly terms, so that it is very difficult for her to tell the difference between the past, present, and future. But for whatever reason, she leaves the predictions to God, through me. Basically, it is a very simple but exciting exercise. I sit down with pen and paper, focus on one topic at a time—the economy, health and medical breakthroughs, weather trends and natural phenomena, national and world politics, specific people and personalities, almost anything but sports because I frankly could not care less—and give my usual silent "Hit it, God." Next thing I know, my hand is moving across the paper, automatically writing down whatever information I am given, and what comes out is invariably as much of a surprise to me as it is to everyone else.

It was Montel who gently guided and encouraged me to expand the range of my predictions and wondered out loud, privately at first, if I could see ten, or twenty, or fifty, or a hundred years into the future as clearly as I could see one year at a time. With a little practice, more than a little patience, and a lot of willingness to focus on the goal of accepting predictions that far ahead, I discovered that yes, I was just as readily given and able to write down that information.

And so, with some thanks to Montel and all, eternal thanks to God, here are the predictions that have been "dictated" to me for the next one hundred years:

SYLVIA BROWNE'S PREDICTIONS FOR THE YEAR 2000

- Sorry to say there will be three hurricanes that hit in rapid succession in the fall, again around the Bahamas, then Mexico, Florida, and the Carolinas.

- An earthquake hits around the Niagara Falls area, small but significant because of where it is.
- The warming trend continues and climates begin to change drastically even more than we have seen in the last ten years. Temperatures along the East Coast become milder. The West Coast gets colder and more damp, also due in part to the polar tilt.
- The Midwest U.S. has a big uprising because of some kind of pollution waste hazard. This has not been recognized at this point, but begins to surface around Branson, Missouri.
- An airline hijacking is thwarted out of Florida, in August.
- Democrats will win the election with Bill Bradley, with close competition from the Reform Party.
- New York crime continues to be at an all-time low, and crime across the country, including crime in schools seems to reach an all-time low.
- The one thing that is very frightening as we go into the millennium, and even though spirituality is at an all-time high, is that we will see more occult groups arising and people professing to be the Messiah.
- Organized religion becomes gentler and kinder and more liberal, which goes along with spirituality and in keeping with Christ's words.
- Elizabeth Taylor ends up back at the Betty Ford Center.
- Brad Pitt and Jennifer Aniston get married, but it lasts for only a short time.
- Gwyneth Paltrow marries an older man who is in the entertainment business, but not as well known as she.
- David Letterman decides to call it quits from his nightly late show after this year.
- Neither Warren Beatty nor Donald Trump has any success in politics.

- A new injection for diabetes is perfected toward the summer of 2000.
- Alzheimer's is going to see a definite cure from some type of protein enzyme introduced into the body. Protein enzymes, which have been researched for the past ten years, are going to be on the cutting edge of cures for M.S., M.D., Alzheimer's, and most immune deficiency illnesses.
- Genetic research comes to the forefront midyear, not only with earlier detection of possible cancers, strokes, and heart attacks, but also in being able to prevent most cancers by introducing injection. Geneticists will be able to supplant whatever gene is deficient.
- We will see an influenza strain that will start on the East Coast and head across the country by October. The medical profession will be frantically trying to put together a new vaccine that will quell this, which will be almost like the Spanish influenza. There will be a crackdown on better screening of Asian immigrants coming into this country that will help quell this flu virus.
- There will be a nasal spray that will stop the common cold dead in its tracks.

California will experience a drought that lasts from late 1998 until 2000.

New York and the East Coast will take the lead in reducing crime and homelessness in 1999–2000.

Cancer as we know it will be eradicated in the next one hundred years through the use of sound waves, photo-sensitive drug therapy, and "self-addicting" cells.

There will be an abundance of robotic houses, controlled by computerized switchboards. Houses will be made of pressed paper with plastic coatings, and the interior walls will be interchangeable. Many will be three-story homes with roll-back roofs to allow Hovercrafts to come and go.

Electric cars will be perfected, with a flotation ability for water travel to bypass freeways. These electric cars will someday be powered by an atomic battery instead.

Entire human bodies will not be cloned, but separate body parts will be cloned for use in organ transplants.

Dentistry will develop a new form of painless tooth extraction, using a type of suction, with immediate replacement of the extracted tooth.

Diagnostic chambers will map the body's electrical balance to predict health problems before they arise.

Cylindrical rooms will exist in which people can see projected images of themselves in various clothing and colors. Once selections have been made, the body will be scanned for measurements and the new custom-made clothing will be completed two days later.

Invasive surgery by scalpel will become obsolete. A molecular-ionization device will instead remove the afflicted cells and then seal the wound without a scar.

Plastic surgery will advance to allow a simple remolding of the whole facial structure that can duplicate any look the patient chooses.

The office of president of the United States will be eliminated. Our government will instead return to the structure of a Greek Senate system.

Instead of a single pope, a triumvirate of popes will be chosen, each assigned to a specific geographic Catholic population.

Peace in the Middle East will prevail by 2050.

In 2026, the West Coast, parts of the East Coast, and large portions of Japan will be hard hit by devastating tsunamis, or tidal waves. As a result of these tsunamis, a large new land mass will emerge among the Hawaiian Islands.

Atlantis will begin to reappear in 2023 and be fully visible by 2026.

After 2050 we will enter the "Age of the Messiah." People will commit themselves to their spirituality, and peace will reign for many years. Successful communal living will appear in which residents will finally learn to love each other and work together.

Treatment for depression and mood disorders will come from a "control chamber" that gently emits sensory stimulation to the brain, including certain smells and music that elevate a sense of well-being.

Medicine in pill form becomes obsolete. Instead, medications will be delivered through the skin by painless air injection.

Rockets in space will no longer be gas-propelled. Instead, space travel will be accompanied by nuclear-powered cylindrical objects.

A moon base will be created for tourist visits and as a stopping place for further destinations.

By 2055 most cities will be domed due to poor atmospheric conditions.

A virtual-reality headset will stimulate brain waves so that people can learn entire libraries of information in a matter of hours.

Giant fruits and vegetables will be grown in hothouse environments. Their nutrients will be synthesized into a highly condensed injection.

Powerful proteins to enhance the immune system will be developed without animal meat.

A brain stimulant without side effects will successfully eradicate all addictions.

Death-penalty executions will be accomplished by a complete vaporization of the body.

Separate governments will ultimately give way to a single global government.

Before the world finds peace, great earth changes will occur and germ warfare will be used. But from all of the bad, good will come, and the pendulum will swing back to humanitarianism and love.

There will be a lot of civil disorder and small skirmishes between countries. But there will be no further world war and no nuclear holocaust.

Toward the end of the twenty-first century, the veil separating our world from The Other Side will diminish, so much so that most people will easily see and communicate with their Spirit Guides and deceased loved ones.

Many false prophets claiming to be the resurrected Christ will emerge, particularly around the new millennium, and try to lead people astray.

Four more comets will pass within the next hundred years.

Aliens will begin allowing themselves to be seen on earth in the year 2010. They will not harm us. Instead, they will be here to observe what we are doing to this planet. They will also teach us again to use anti-gravity devices, as they did during the construction of the pyramids.

Peace will last from 2050 until 2100.

I see nothing beyond the year 2100, which could mean the end will come "like a thief in the night."

A FINAL BLESSING

It has been my joy to take this journey with you, learning and growing in faith right along with you, celebrating the fact that, as children of God, we are a global family, brothers and sisters, united by our divine heritage and by the very courage it took for us to choose to leave Home and come here again in the first place. I cherish our connection, and the hunger for more knowledge, hope, and intimacy with the God center in each of us that led us to meet inside these pages.

In closing, until we meet again, may we all sit together, hands resting in our laps, not clasped in a "closed" position but open, with our palms facing upward, in a position to receive the grace and joy of God as our spirits unite in a prayer I offer with love from the bottom of my full, grateful heart:

Dearest God,

I stand before You knowing that You know who I am and what I wish to accomplish. Help me each day to stay on my written chart so I can gain my own perfec-

tion and thereby glorify Your holy name. Let me always be aware of the white light of the Holy Spirit surrounding me and the Christ Consciousness guiding me. Should I fall, as we all do, give me Your hand to lead me back onto my chosen path.

I promise to employ my judgment, honor, and righteousness to always follow the path of goodness. I will be cognizant in my actions so that I never intentionally hurt another person. I will give of myself in service to others without expectation of any return for the effort.

I ask for Your light to encompass this world and bring peace and harmony to all people. I ask that we finally live a spiritual life and together make a world free of color, creed, and religious prejudice. I ask that during this year and all the years to come, until we are reunited with Thee, Your love will enter every heart, mind, and soul.

All of us together, God, shoulder to shoulder, will lend our souls to create a giant ladder right into Your heart, from whence we came. If every heart would simply turn and whisper Your name of love, then all the darkness within the world will turn to light.

We can do it.

We must do it.

And we will do it.

For the love of God, ourselves and all humankind.

Amen

Appendix: Affirmations

Prayers are our contact with the God of which we're each a part. Affirmations, on the other hand, are our contact with the God who is a part of each of us. Making a daily habit of both prayers and affirmations really can create miracles in our lives.

Affirmations reinforce those divine elements in us that are our birthright—dignity, self-respect, hope, compassion, peace of mind, and intimacy with the Higher Power whose voice resonates to the depth of our spirits, just waiting to be heard.

Literature is rich with countless beautiful affirmations, from the Bible to the Koran to the Talmud to the writings of Buddhist masters to poetry to anything you yourself have read or written that ignites the fire and truth of the Holy Spirit in some lasting way in your soul. The several I have included here are the ones I use every day in whatever moments of quiet solitude I can find—in the shower, in my car, as I fall asleep, any time, no matter how brief, that I can declare "mine." Affirmations are as much a daily habit in my life as brushing my teeth, and I promise you, they are the one addiction that can bring you true ecstasy and health, without ever costing you a single dime.

"God has granted me the strength and fortitude to survive this day with peace, love, and joy. I am protected from all negativity around me by the shield of the white light of the Holy Spirit."

"Throughout this day I will picture myself and my loved ones safe inside a perfect white bubble of God's light. I will even surround my enemies with that same bubble of light, so that God may disarm and dissolve the negativity and darkness that separates us."

"Today I ask every cell in my body to respond and react as they did at the age I felt my healthiest, most energetic best. I will negate all illness, knowing that my mind is stronger than my body."

"I will move closer today to becoming the person I wish to be. By making a list of all the undesirable things I am not, I will affirm and celebrate all the wonderful things that I am and build on those things toward spiritual perfection."

"On this day I declare with the almighty strength of God's power that I deserve abundance and the financial means to be comfortable, and that I will joyfully share my abundance with others less fortunate than I."

"Today I will exude an aura of beauty and light to everyone around me, with a bright glow of orange radiating from the core of my breast to make others feel blessed and loved."

"I begin this day with the vision of a pure white cloud above my head, and inside that cloud I place all my deepest and most cherished wishes for myself and for those I love. I then ask God to let that cloud gently descend over me, until it surrounds me and becomes a part of me."

"I will listen closely today to this vehicle I know as my body. I will not negate any pain or illness that needs expert medical attention. But any chronic or minor pain or illness I will condense into a ball of fire, release it from my body, secure it in a safe of thick lead, and blow it up into a harmless, impotent vapor."

"I will find a quiet moment for myself today and write a Letter to the Universe, addressed to God, telling Him all my wishes, my heartaches, my abuses, and my joys. I will then burn the letter in a safe place, trusting the fire's energy to carry my words to their divine destination."

"Today at the beginning of each new hour I will remind myself that I am young, I am vital, I can accomplish any goal, and I possess great beauty of both mind and spirit."

"I affirm on this day that my intellect and my emotions will be cemented together as one, forming a perfect funnel through which God's messages and energy flow to heal me and those I love."

"As I start this day I feel a surge of strength that I will devote to following my life's blueprint and perfecting my spiritual purposes."

"I am from God. I am part of God, and God is part of me. Therefore I cannot be diminished. I am strong, I am loved, and I am loving, because I am living this and every day in accordance with God's great plan."

"As I face my grief today, I will not bury it, but instead I will consent to it. And by consenting to it, I ask God to help me draw strength from His divine plan and guidance and surround me with His Angels, knowing the truth that I will see and share eternity with my loved ones again in the perfect joy of The Other Side."

"Today I will not just look at the people around me. I will really see the divine spirits inside them and love them without prejudice as the children of God I know we all are. I affirm that my greatest purpose is not to expect love but to give it freely, asking nothing in return."

"I will love myself completely today, regarding myself with pride and honor. Because my soul and my spirit come from God, I cherish myself too much to let anyone deface or defame me in any way."

For nine nights, at precisely nine o'clock, light a candle and repeat:

"I am a blessed child of God. I am well. I am happy. Great abundance is on its way because, as God's child, I am empowered to create miracles."

"Beyond the Entrance: Where We Live, Work, Play and Worship on The Other Side"

Look out any window of your home or office, or down from any airplane, or across the expanse of anywhere on earth you travel to, and imagine that exact same topography, but without strip malls, parking lots, high-rises, freeways, interstates, pollution, litter, and all the other debris of what we hilariously call "progress."

Now, with the clean slate of a thriving, flawless, unmolested landscape, you can begin to picture The Other Side.

But first, a word about physics. No, not "psychics." Physics.

Francine has tried to explain the physics of The Other Side's dimension to me over and over again. My eyes glaze just trying to understand the physics of *this* dimension, and I've still got the high school and college report cards to prove it. But I should acknowledge a reality of Home that fascinates me, even though I can't claim with a straight face that I comprehend it.

Just as our concept of time doesn't exist on The Other Side, neither does our concept of space. Hundreds, even thousands of us can live, work, and socialize together in a very small area without ever being crowded. Francine tells me it's because their matter is much denser than ours, and that vaguely rings some distant bell of truth with me—the older I get, the more my body demonstrates all too clearly that we're cursed with a ridiculously loose molecular structure here on earth, and frankly, I don't appreciate it one bit.

At any rate, an accurate sketch of The Other Side can't be drawn without stressing that our laws of physics here are antiquated by comparison. So as difficult as I know it is, please try not to limit your images of Home by confining them to the annoying, irrelevant spatial constraints we're stuck with here.

Housing

I still remember how relieved I was to hear from Francine that we actually have our own places to live at Home. Even in paradise, the thought of wandering around without a space to call mine seemed so sad and lost that I wasn't sure that arrangement could ever make me truly happy. And practically speaking, we could live without houses on The Other Side. In fact, some do, even though, as we'll discuss momentarily, they could easily create them if they wanted to. Our bodies at Home, real as they are, are much more low-maintenance than they are here. We can assimilate food for the taste and experience of it if we choose, and prepare food if it's something we happen to like doing, but we don't need to eat or cook. We can lie down and rest if it's something we enjoy, but we don't need sleep. We have hearts that pump blood and lungs that breathe, and we have all our other organs as well—interestingly, on the opposite side of our bodies from where they're located in our bodies on earth, an exact mirror image of the human anatomy. We aren't inconvenienced, though, by what we'll politely call the earthier bodily functions, so we don't need a handy bathroom to dash to on even an irregular basis. We create our looks and our clothing with the same projected thought with which we create our houses, so we don't need wardrobes and closets and makeup and grooming supplies. And we certainly don't need protection from the elements in an atmosphere of a constantly calm and clear 78 degrees. In other words, there's really no pragmatic purpose to having a residence on The Other Side at all.

And yet most of us do have houses at Home, even if we visit them infrequently, for the simple reason that most spirits are naturally soothed and comforted by a place that's ours, an environment, no matter how elaborate or modest, that uniquely represents our lifestyle, preferences, and tastes; a space of singular familiarity whose doors we step through and immediately feel, "There."

The Other Side itself offers its own sense of Home, but creating a home within a Home is an experience most of us deeply appreciate, just as we do on earth.

The facile answer to "Where do we live on The Other Side?" is, "Anywhere we want." It also happens to be the truth, because houses there are perfect reflections of the resident's wishes. If you've always wanted to live in a looming stone castle, or a Tudor mansion, or a penthouse, or a gingerbread chalet, or a contemporary split-level ranch, or a modest one-room log cabin, or a communal apartment, that dream is just a quick dimension away. It has nothing to do with what kind of housing you can afford, since there is no money at Home and certainly no concept of status, or lack of it. What it has everything to do with is the fact that most of the houses on The Other Side are built *by projected thought*.

Please don't misunderstand—houses built by projected thought are not imaginary. Our understanding of the power of projected thought is still in its infancy on earth, but if it helps bridge the credibility gap, remember that nothing human-made exists here that didn't start out as a projected thought. On The Other Side we're simply able to jump from the thought to the reality without all the muss and fuss in between. We project the kind of house we want and where we want it, and it's there. Houses at Home are as real as our houses here, but far better, because with that same projected thought we can make them smaller or larger, add a wing, open a roof, remove a wall, or move them to an entirely different area. It's not magic, it's the power of the mind—again, a concept that we on earth are only beginning to fathom.

Not all houses on The Other Side are the direct result of projected thought, though. Many builders, carpenters, architects, stonemasons, landscape designers, et. al., prefer the gratification of constructing homes and other structures in the traditional hands-on way, out of sheer love for their work and the opportunity to express their craftsmanship. They're encouraged and very much admired, and they're never at a loss for volunteer crews who are eager to learn a new range of skills. The one rule that applies to all construction, whether it's by projected thought or by hand, is that nothing is ever to be destroyed in the process, so that not a single flower, tree, stream, or hillside is touched, and all existing structures and natural beauty remain perpetually, flawlessly intact. That rule obviously extends to building supplies, which aren't a problem, since they come from the same projected thought from which entire houses are assembled.

The "whatever we want" answer settles the question of furnishings and household luxuries, too, by the way. If you have an affinity for jacuzzis, or recliners, or a house wouldn't be a home to you without a grand piano or an entertainment center, project it into place and it's yours. The options are as limitless as our ability to dream them.

Some of us create houses for ourselves that we'd always yearned for on earth. Others of us like to recreate houses that remind us of a cherished home in our most recent lifetime, or in a lifetime before that. I was especially touched by a talk I had with a client's deceased mother shortly before the client's father died—she was excitedly preparing a house for my client's father identical to the home they happily shared during their marriage, right down to the yucca plants that surrounded it, as a surprise for him when he came Home.

We'll discuss relationships and our choices of home-mates in the next chapter, but for now, don't let me give you the mistaken impression that living alone or with one significant other is the only option if neither of those ideas appeal to you. Apartment and condominium buildings are popular on The Other Side for their camaraderie, and communal living is many residents' idea of heaven. It's worth pointing out that communes are a perfectly acceptable option there. In fact, there is no such thing as "unacceptable," for the simple reason that where God's presence fills the very air we breathe, there is no judgment, no sin, no guilt, no right or wrong, only the joy of thriving in absolute, infinite love.

There are no cities, suburbs, or even large towns on The Other Side. The reasons for that are simple:

- We don't need to live near our work, since travel is a nonissue. For the most part, travel is accomplished through the same power by which so many houses are built—*projected thought*. We simply "think" ourselves somewhere, and we're there. The closest we come to this form of transportation on earth is astral travel, those trips our spirits take away from these heavy lumps called bodies with which we're weighted down here. We absolutely have bodies on The Other Side, as we've discussed, but at Home we are spirits who have bodies, while here we are designed by God to be bodies that have spirits for these learning challenges we choose to undertake. Free of earthly limitations, our spirits soar and flourish, and thought becomes reality at our discretion. As with building a house without all the strenuous labor and stress between the concept and the completion, travel by projected thought is like planning a trip on earth and arriving at our destination moments later, without having to deal with luggage, maps, airports, reservations, and traffic jams. So again, since we can live anywhere on the globe of

The Other Side we want and be at work in an instant by simply thinking ourselves there, why would cities and suburbs be remotely necessary?

- The second primary reason there are no cities, suburbs, or large towns at Home is that there is no commerce there, no money and therefore no need to earn it or spend it. This means there are no stores, no malls, no markets, and not a single shopping consideration to factor into our real estate preferences. When homes are clustered together at all, it's in the form of small villages, populated by a few hundred people at most and utterly charming in their infinite variety of size, architectural styles, landscaping, and luxuries.

As important as houses are on The Other Side, though, they only make up a small fraction of the structures that gorgeously dot the topography and act as bustling centers of constant, exhilarating activity. In a later chapter we'll address the specifics of those countless activities, by the way. For now, we'll simply continue to focus on the rest of the "skyline" we have to look forward to.

Mind Expansion

Among the busiest, most treasured, and most prolific structures of Home are the vast libraries, schools, and research centers. They're everywhere, and they're as vital to our joy on The Other Side as our beloved friends and animals.

The libraries are supplements of the sacred Hall Of Records, filled with every word ever published and every word being written on The Other Side that will one day be infused to writers on earth for the benefit of humankind, on every subject imaginable and many we have yet to fathom. These breathtaking collections of works offer infinite resources for literally anything that interests us, and there isn't a moment when every library throughout paradise isn't alive with eager activity.

Structurally, the libraries are as varied and stimulating as the subject matter they house. To list their architectural styles would be to list every architectural style in existence, from small, modest wooden spaces with one or two rooms to sprawling, contemporary glass monoliths with seeming miles of spiral marble staircases winding through floor after floor of shelves upon shelves toward symbolically wide-open ceilings.

As numerous as the libraries, as constantly populated, and as architecturally diverse are the schools and research centers where, as we'll explore later, studies and experiments are eternally ongoing for the good of humankind throughout the universe, as well as for our own enlightenment, because, thank God, we are all created with minds that are infinitely curious and crave stimulation. One of the endless things we could and are slowly learning by infusion from Home is that we do our best work and our most effective study in environments that combine beauty and serenity, where we look forward to going and are reluctant to leave. No matter how simple or complex the structures themselves are, cubicles, windowless walls, hard wooden seats, cold linoleum floors, and drab airless hallways are unheard of. Exposure to the magnificence of nature is integral to the design of every classroom and every research lab, and there is not a comfort of the most well-appointed home that isn't available to every student, professor, and researcher. No matter what the ambience, we would flock to the schools and research centers out of sheer passion. With their ambience at Home, we count them among our greatest joys.

"Downtime"

We don't need "time off" on The Other Side, because we love everything we do there and have no desire to take breaks from any of it. We simply engage in extracurricular activities and social lives because we love them as well, and the facilities that house them are yet another prominent, cherished part of the landscape of Home.

Concert and lecture halls, perpetually filled to capacity, offer nonstop appearances by the most brilliant performing artists and speakers humankind has known. Breathtakingly beautiful and acoustically impeccable, they have been infused and recreated throughout our world, from the great Coliseum of Rome to Athens' Parthenon to the modern-day Hollywood Bowl, all graceful, open-air marriages of The Other Side's reverence for nature and our own God-given excellence.

Noncontact sports are celebrated activities at Home as well, embracing everyone who loves to play and those who simply enjoy watching. The landscape would be unrecognizable without magnificent athletic stadiums, golf courses, tennis courts, ski slopes glistening with eternal artificial snow, perfect waves for surfing crashing onto pure, white shores, and accommodations for every other form of organized exercise, all of which make our finest "playgrounds" here look humble by comparison.

We are inexhaustibly, blissfully social on The Other Side, from small gatherings to huge, busy, laughter-filled ones. We create every possible opportunity for parties and dancing and picnics and festivals and quiet outings with a few of our closest loved ones. Because there isn't a structure, plaza, park, garden, meadow, hushed grotto, hidden reflecting pool, or brightly tented fairground that's restricted from the public or limited by closing times, the options for where and when to socialize are literally countless.

Also countless are the number of clients I've regressed to their lives on The Other Side who have described a sparse but continuous series of roads that wind unobtrusively through every quadrant of all nine continents. It struck me as perfectly natural for longer than I care to admit—until it finally hit me—if travel is accomplished by projected thought, what possible use could there be for roads? So I started asking the clients who mentioned roads how they got around at Home, and I kept getting the same answer every time, which Francine later confirmed. "Usually I just think myself wherever I want to be," client after client told me, "but sometimes my friends and I enjoy jumping in a little car and taking cross-country trips together." They each proceeded to describe the same vehicle, a kind of combination golf cart and hovercraft, atomic-powered and open-sided, that moves along several inches above the ground without ever touching or therefore molesting it. Francine has since explained that these roads and hovercrafts are not just there for enjoyment. They're also, like so many of the architectural and lifestyle options we've mentioned, another common thread between The Other Side and earth, so that there are tiny details in each dimension that are God's way of trying to make us feel the comforting familiarity of Home no matter where we are.

Worship

I often wondered, as you might be too, if going to church regularly would be redundant on The Other Side, where God's adoration and presence fill every breath we take, and our adoration of Him motivates our every moment. It turns out there is nowhere you can stand on The Other Side in which a house of worship isn't in view, and no structures are more cherished or more constantly filled with eager, joyful throngs. Magnificent temples, churches, and synagogues share the countryside with modest chapels and simple altars of every religion, all of which co-exist in peace and profound mutual respect. We here on earth could take a lesson—these houses of worship are also great learning centers, and the residents of Home find joy in educating themselves on the hundreds of rituals, customs, and theologies besides their own that share the same common goal, of feeling, expressing, and uniting in their reciprocal adoration of God. Methodists and Buddhists happily and knowledgeably pray side-by-side at Judaic services. Catholics and Muslims are utterly comfortable singing hymns of praise with the Shinto monks and the Bahai. Joining to glorify God hand-in-hand is natural, necessary, and nurturing, as essential to our survival as the beating of our hearts.

We respect and embrace the rituals of every faith, from the most modest to the most elaborate and formal, and we revere our own messiah and everyone else's for the highly advanced, divinely incarnate spirits they are. We welcome and are welcomed wherever prayers are prayed and voices are raised in songs of grace and thanks, because our souls are sublimely sure on The Other Side of something that we here on earth keep forgetting far too easily:

By whatever name we call Him, *we are all praying to the same God.*

Now that we have some idea of what The Other Side looks like, we can start filling in the magnificent landscape with the equally magnificent and varied population we're Homesick for from the moment we leave them until the moment we return.